**American Security
Policy and
Policy-Making**

American Security Policy and Policy-Making

The Dilemmas of Using and Controlling Military Force

Edited by
Robert Harkavy
Pennsylvania State University
Edward A. Kolodziej
University of Illinois

LexingtonBooks
D.C. Heath and Company
Lexington, Massachusetts
Toronto

Library of Congress Cataloging in Publication Data

Main entry under title:

American security policy and policy-making.

(Policy Studies Organization series)
1. United States—National security. 2. United States—Military policy. 3. Strategy. 4. Arms control. I. Harkavy, Robert E. II. Kolodziej, Edward A. III. Series: Policy Studies Organization. Policies Studies Organization series.
UA23.A6626   355.03'35'73   77-14868
ISBN 0-669-01998-4

Copyright © 1980 by D.C. Heath and Company

All rights reserved. No part of this publication may be reproduced or transmitted in any form or by any means, electronic or mechanical, including photocopy, recording, or any information storage or retrieval system, without permission in writing from the publisher.

Published simultaneously in Canada

Printed in the United States of America

International Standard Book Number: 0-669-01998-4

Library of Congress Catalog Card Number: 77-14868

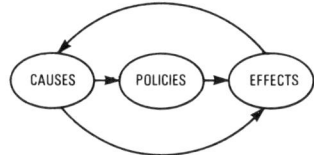

Policy Studies Organization Series

General Approaches to Policy Studies

Policy Studies in America and Elsewhere
   edited by Stuart S. Nagel
Policy Studies and the Social Sciences
   edited by Stuart S. Nagel
Methodology for Analyzing Public Policies
   edited by Frank P. Scioli, Jr., and Thomas J. Cook
Urban Problems and Public Policy
   edited by Robert L. Lineberry and Louis H. Masotti
Problems of Theory in Policy Analysis
   edited by Philip M. Gregg
Using Social Research for Public Policy-Making
   edited by Carol H. Weiss
Public Administration and Public Policy
   edited by H. George Frederickson and Charles Wise
Policy Analysis and Deductive Reasoning
   edited by Gordon Tullock and Richard Wagner
Legislative Reform
   edited by Leroy N. Rieselbach
Teaching Policy Studies
   edited by William D. Coplin
Paths to Political Reform
   edited by William J. Crotty
Determinants of Public Policy
   edited by Thomas Dye and Virginia Gray
Effective Policy Implementation
   edited by Daniel Mazmanian and Paul Sabatier

Specific Policy Problems

Analyzing Poverty Policy
   edited by Dorothy Buckton James
Crime and Criminal Justice
   edited by John A. Gardiner and Michael Mulkey
Civil Liberties
   edited by Stephen L. Wasby

Foreign Policy Analysis
    edited by Richard L. Merritt
Economic Regulatory Policies
    edited by James E. Anderson
Political Science and School Politics
    edited by Samuel K. Gove and Frederick M. Wirt
Science and Technology Policy
    edited by Joseph Haberer
Population Policy Analysis
    edited by Michael E. Kraft and Mark Schneider
The New Politics of Food
    edited by Don F. Hadwiger and William P. Browne
New Dimensions to Energy Policy
    edited by Robert Lawrence
Race, Sex, and Policy Problems
    edited by Marian Palley and Michael Preston
American Security Policy and Policy-Making
    edited by Robert Harkavy and Edward Kolodziej
Current Issues in Transportation Policy
    edited by Alan Altshuler
Security Policies of Emerging States
    edited by Edward Kolodziej and Robert Harkavy
Determinants of Law-Enforcement Policies
    edited by Fred Meyer and Ralph Baker
Evaluating Alternative Law-Enforcement Policies
    edited by Ralph Baker and Fred Meyer
International Energy Policy
    edited by Martin O. Heisler and Robert M. Lawrence
Employment and Labor-Relations Policy
    edited by Charles Bulmer and John L. Carmichael, Jr.
Environmental Policy Formation
    edited by Dean E. Mann
Environmental Policy Implementation
    edited by Dean E. Mann
Taxing and Spending Policy
    Warren J. Samuels and Larry L. Wade

Contents

	Preface	ix
Part I	*Historical and Contemporary Setting for the Use and Control of Force*	1
Chapter 1	**The Theory of Long Cycles and U.S. Strategic Policy** George Modelski	3
Chapter 2	**Living with the Long Cycle: New Assumptions to Guide the Use and Control of Military Force** Edward A. Kolodziej	21
Chapter 3	**Defining Strategic Value: Problems of Conceptual Clarity and Valid Threat Assessments** W. Harriet Critchley	45
Part II	*Selected Problems in American Security Policy and Policy-Making*	67
Chapter 4	**Arms, Arms Control, and Alliance Relationships: The Case of the Cruise Missile** Joseph I. Coffey	69
Chapter 5	**NATO Defense: The Problem Is Not More Money** Steven L. Canby	85
Chapter 6	**Population Defense Reconsidered: Is the ABM Really Inconsistent with Stability?** Jerome Slater	101
Chapter 7	**Arms Control through Communication and Information Regimes** Davis B. Bobrow	115
Chapter 8	**Harmonizing Policies across Arms Control Domains: Dilemmas and Contradictions** Robert Harkavy	129
Chapter 9	**The Arms Control Impact Statement: Program and Logic** Robert Lyle Butterworth	149

Chapter 10	**Military Research and Development: Institutions, Output, and Arms Control** *Judith Reppy*	165
Chapter 11	**The Process and Problems of Linking Policy and Force Structure through the Defense Budget Process** *Lawrence J. Korb*	181
Part III	*Approaches to the Use and Control of Force*	193
Chapter 12	**Defining Strategic Issues: How to Avoid Isometric Exercises** *George H. Quester*	195
Chapter 13	**Arms Control: A Theoretical Perspective** *Patrick M. Morgan*	209
Chapter 14	**American Approaches to Military Strategy, Arms Control, and Disarmament: A Critique of the Postwar Experience** *Lincoln P. Bloomfield*	225
Chapter 15	**The SALT I Negotiations: A Game Theory Paradigm** *Louis A. Picard*	239
	Index of Names	255
	Index of Subjects	259
	About the Author	267
	About the Contributors	269
	About the Editors	271

Preface

In preparing this book, we asked more than two hundred specialists in security policy for ideas. We received replies from more than one hundred researchers, who proposed a wide range of topics. From these we fashioned a group of contributions that met two general tests. First, we wanted contributions that approached the use and control of military force as different aspects of a single problem facing American policy-makers. There has been a tendency among researchers to treat these questions as separate problems. There are even some who view solutions to problems of use as obstacles to problems of control, and the reverse—a kind of zero-sum game. Many modern researchers have trouble seeing the two as parts of a larger whole, that is, the role that force and its control must play in assuring a nation's security, economic, and regime interests.

This conceptual compartmentalization has also been institutionalized in the security policy-making community. Within the government, the Pentagon is supposed to be concerned about the use or threat of force, while the Arms Control and Disarmament Agency is expected to deal with the problem of control. Academic centers for the study of strategic policy are accused of advocating the use of force because they focus, for example, on the strategic balance between the superpowers or regional warfare in Europe or the Middle East. On the other hand, arms control and especially disarmament questions have become the preserves of "peace researchers" and the research centers that are correspondingly named. So, while some researchers study the causes of war, others worry about the conditions of peace. This same inclination to divide into parts what should be viewed as a whole also characterizes the think tanks, research centers, and special-interest groups that make up the nonacademic research community. They, too, can be roughly categorized according to whether they concentrate on the use or the control aspects of the security dilemma.

This volume is a contribution to the lowering, if not the dismantling, of these conceptual and institutional barriers. Our initial optimism about engaging authors who could treat these two questions simultaneously in their chapters was partially frustrated by the difficulty of forcing contributors into a framework of analysis that, however attractive, was not congenial to the thinking habits of each participant. We decided to make our point through a blend of chapters rather than through a certainly fatal attempt to force knowledgeable, experienced, and tough-minded authors to follow a rigid line. Besides, some security issues necessarily require emphasis on one or the other of the elements of use or control.

Part II, dealing with specific policy and process issues, illustrates the mix that we were attempting to create. Joseph Coffey's discussion of the cruise missile and Jerome Slater's chapter on the antiballistic missile (ABM) address both use and control issues. Steven Canby's piece on NATO defense planning and Davis Bobrow's discussion of communication and information systems accent, respectively, the use and control dimensions of the symposium.

This same constructive tension is present in the chapters on the policy-making process. Robert Harkavy identifies the much-overlooked problem of coordinating arms-control domains and relating them to other strategic issues concerned with the use of force or its deterrence. Robert Butterworth similarly focuses on these problems through an analysis of the bureaucratic politics surrounding the arms-control impact statements mandated by Congress. These same themes are struck in Lawrence Korb's discussion of the defense budgetary process and in Judith Reppy's analysis of research and development on new weapons. This latter issue acutely poses the problem of use and control, since our futures as individuals and as members of the American polity are fundamentally linked to decisions on future weapons development.

In addition to the use and control of force, the editors were also concerned about another artificial division: the separation of practitioners and policy-makers from researchers and students of security policy and international relations. The authors are convinced that good policy depends on good theory and that these diverse segments of the security-policy community must work more closely together. Every governmental action or policy statement about the use or control of force implies that by doing or not doing something policy-makers can affect the exterior environment in ways that reflect American preferences. Thus, each act or nonact suggests a behavioral theory whose assumptions can be stated explicitly and tested. For example, George Kennan's celebrated Mr. X article in *Foreign Affairs*, written more than thirty years ago, argued that containment would eventually "mellow" Soviet expansionism.[1] Similarly, the Carter administration pressed the issue of human rights partly on the expectation that American leadership, in pursuing this goal, would actually help create an international environment that would reflect American notions of individual liberty. Whatever the virtues of these two attempts at marrying theory and practice, the effort of joining the two is eminently sound. In the absence of theory, no action can be justified except perhaps by the exigencies of the moment. That may be satisfying to the decision-maker, who is harrassed and hurried by circumstance and conscious of the limitations of his actions, but such a pragmatic stance ill serves a community over time. Policy direction then comes from the outside. Policy-making becomes more an exercise in registering what appears to have been foreordained than an enterprise that seeks to shape the environment in ways that reflect the needs and values of the American society.

With this latter perspective in mind, we have grouped in parts I and III chapters that attempt to go beyond the immediate policy and process problems of the day. They seek to define the conceptual and environmental determinants of those problems. In part I, George Modelski traces the historical cycles that appear to underlie the play of force and alternations of power in interstate relations since the emergence of the nation-state system. He finds that we are again in the upswing of such a cycle, in which, unlike what many analysts would have us believe, force will have increasing importance in our lives.[2] Moreover, the need of the United States to exercise a leadership role in international security for its own national interests has never been greater. The chapter by Edward Kolodziej tries to specify the assumptions on which American security policy will have to be built in the immediate future if it is to be consistent with profound changes in the internal and external environment within which force operates today. W. Harriet Critchley probes the meaning of *strategic value*. She identifies three significant components—territory, worth, and access. Of these, access is viewed as the most important in an increasingly interdependent world characterized by multiple centers of power and authority.

These theoretical concerns are pursued in part III. George Quester cautions against posing strategic problems in ways that fail to take the adversary's behavior into account and that, instead, mislead decision-makers into reacting to their own concerns rather than those of rivals abroad. Patrick Morgan and Lincoln Bloomfield look at arms control from two different, but complementary, perspectives. Morgan tries to stipulate the conditions for arms-control agreements, while Bloomfield examines our evolving ideas about arms control and links this historical process to progress in reaching accords. The final chapter by Louis Picard applies insights drawn from game theory, particularly the prisoner's dilemma, to identify and explain the essential elements of the strategic arms limitation talks (SALT).

These chapters obviously do not exhaust the subject of the use and control of military force. Not enough space is available, nor is there sufficient agreement among the contributors on what is important or should be included. In addition, we have left out a discussion of SALT II, because it would have repeated much of what can be found in the Senate debate on the treaty. Rather, we hope to stimulate new thinking along the two lines of thought sketched here. If we can do that, the symposium will have accomplished its announced purposes. In fairness to the contributors, however, each essay should be judged finally on its own terms, not solely by our symposium criteria.

The Policy Studies Organization gratefully thanks the International Division of the Ford Foundation for its aid to the symposium on which this book is based. However, no one other than the individual authors is responsible for the ideas expressed herein.

Notes

1. "Sources of Soviet Conduct," *Foreign Affairs* 25, no. 4 (July 1947):566-582.

2. Robert O. Keohane and Joseph S. Nye, *Power and Interdependence* (Boston: Little, Brown, 1977), pp. 27-29.

Part I
Historical and Contemporary Setting for the Use and Control of Force

1
The Theory of Long Cycles and U.S. Strategic Policy

George Modelski

It is difficult to quarrel with the notion that the strategic policy of the United States ought to be rooted in a systematic knowledge of international affairs, in short, in a theory of world politics, for we know now not only that there is no conflict between theory and practice but also that there is nothing as practical as a good theory.[1] But disagreements are likely to arise on whether a good theory of world politics is in fact at hand and whether it is usable as the basis for grand strategy. For decades students of international relations have labored in the vineyards of abstract thought; has their produce yet reached the degree of sweetness needed for the heady wine of theory? It is, in fact, widely believed today that the prospects for distilling such a theory are, on the whole, poor. This chapter records the author's dissent from that position and argues for the view that a promising basis for U.S. strategic policy is the theory of long cycles.[2]

The Theory of Long Cycles

The theory of long cycles is a set of propositions about the behavior of the global political system; it is a concise statement of the key patterns and regularities governing world politics. It is therefore, in fact, a theory of world politics (not, of course, the only theory). This theory highlights the crucial role and significance of the long cycle (or circular sequences of events).

This theory may serve as a basic science for students of international relations and for practitioners of international affairs. But it also revolves around the concept of world power, and for that reason it is quite pertinent to anyone interested in the role and the position of the United States. The theory of long cycles gives a coherent and meaningful account of the past role of the United States and helps define U.S. strategies for the future. Finally, the theory of long cycles of global politics also revolves critically around the concept of global wars and their role in the global political process, subjects of obvious interest to those concerned with grand strategy and those who follow shifts in the distribution of world power.

The author wishes to thank Dr. Kai Lee for his comments on one draft of this chapter.

Basic Propositions

The basic propositions of the theory of long cycles may be formulated in seven statements:

1. A global political system of determinate structure has been in existence since about 1500 A.D. This is the modern system of world politics of our experience. The theory explicates its behavior, and the patterns it identifies are attributes of the system.

2. At intervals of over one century the global political system has experienced global wars, each war finalizing a general and legitimizing peace settlement. Among the more recent of such conflagrations we might mention the French Revolutionary and Napoleonic wars at the turn of the nineteenth century, and the two world wars of the twentieth century. Global wars have been the critical turning points in the evolution of the global political system, and the time elapsed between two such wars has marked the period of the long cycle.

3. Each global war has led to the emergence of a preponderant world power as the system's principal provider of the public goods of security and world organization (including the framework of international economic relations). The world powers since 1500 have been Portugal, the Dutch Republic, Great Britain, and the United States.

4. Each world power is, at first, a preponderant (monopolistic) supplier of public goods, largely as the function of its sea (and later air and space) power and the related command over the sea (air, space). This gives the global political system a structure of unipolarity (high power concentration). But over the life-time of the long cycle this preponderance gradually erodes, and the system moves into multipolarity (low power concentration).

5. Each successive global order (as defined by its preponderant world power) has gradually decayed and deteriorated into another global war, thus completing the long cycle.

6. The global political system has bred the nation-state. All preponderant world powers have been successful nation-states, and through competitive emulation the nation-state has become the dominant political organization in the world system.

7. The global political system has been associated with a high-growth economy. All world powers have, in their time, been (in Francois Perroux' term) economically "active zones," known first as mercantile and more recently as industrial powers. Through competitive emulation their example has propelled the world onto a path of rapid growth and development and instigated the formation of economic organizations of global scope.

The Theory of Long Cycles

Empirical Basis

The theory of long cycles gains empirical support if we review, with its help, the principal events that characterize the evolution of the global political system in the past 5 centuries.[3]

The prototype, as well as the embryo, of modern world organization was the structure of Italian and Mediterranean politics in the fifteenth century. The core of it was Renaissance Italy, a thriving, prosperous, and advanced area organized into a number of independent states. The beginnings of modern statecraft, advanced military organization and technology, alliances coordinated by resident ambassadors, the evolving concept of a balance of power, all these standard features of modern international relations originated here. Of greatest interest among the states of Italy was Venice, a city-state of sophisticated political and commercial organization. Not only was Venice one of the major powers in the Italian system of states, but it also linked Italy with the world outside and organized long-distance trade in the Mediterranean Basin and as far as Northern Europe. By about 1400 Venice had become the predominant sea power of its world. She held colonies and trading posts in the Mediterranean and the Black Sea, she monopolized the lucrative Asian spice trade through Alexandria, she was herself a major industrial power, and she had lately also acquired significant possessions on the Italian mainland (known as *terra ferma*).

The splendor that was Venice is still admired today; but its power first began to erode under pressure from the Ottoman Turks who seized Constantinople in 1453, and it finally collapsed in the course of the prolonged series of "Italian wars," beginning with the French invasion of 1494, that shattered the regional system of states and brought the entire peninsula under the domination of Spain some three decades later. The Spanish Hapsburgs assumed the leadership of the struggle against the Turks in the Mediterranean, while the Austrians fought them in the Balkans.

The eclipse of Venice was in part the consequence, and in part the precondition, of the reorganization of world trade and the establishment of the modern world system. But the prime mover in these latter developments was the king of Portugal. At least since 1415 agents of his had been exploring and trading along the coasts of Africa, and this sustained investment in innovation paid off when the first of the king's fleets reached India in 1498 and laid the ground for cutting off the spices that flowed to Venice. The Portuguese gained command over the seas when they won the decisive sea battle off Diu against an Egyptian and Arab fleet in 1509, 3 months after Venice's land army was decisively routed in northern Italy.

"Ever since that time," wrote Leopold von Ranke quoting Ascanio Sforza, "Italy ceased to be the world's interior courtyard and Europe's traffic center."[4]

Thus Portugal became the first world power by pioneering global communications, destroying the Venetians' profitable monopoly, and gaining command over the oceans. Through a string of bases in the Atlantic and the Indian oceans she came close to establishing her own monopoly of global trade routes. Portugal did not "succeed" Venice because Venice was not a world power, but it did earn its position in conditions of global conflict, and it did proceed to lay down its own framework of world organization in cooperation with Spain. For by then Spain too had entered the global system, not (like Portugal) as the result of careful and sustained activity but rather through the largely fortuitous sponsorship of Columbus' expedition to the New World. With papal sanction Portugal soon negotiated a division of the world's oceanic spaces with Spain. While Portugal oversaw trade and fought the Ottomans in the East, Spain contained them in the Mediterranean, mined the New World for bullion, and was deeply embroiled in the politics of Europe. For an entire century after Columbus and Vasco da Gama, Portugal (in association with Spain, with whom dynastic links were especially close) dominated the world's oceans and therefore also access to the trade of Asia and the resources of the Americas.

Portugal's world system was a bold and daring conception. But its strength began to wane in the second half of the sixteenth century, and the disastrous scheme for the landing in Morocco (1578) brought about the death of the King and a swift take-over by Spain's Philip II (claiming dynastic rights). The loss of independence accelerated the decline of the Portuguese system; Philip II did not measure up to the responsibilities of the world role he was trying to assume, and the Dutch revolt he was attempting to crush exposed Portuguese trade and possessions, as well as Spanish dominions, to dangerous attacks by the disgruntled and aggressive Netherlanders.

Turmoil and civil strife in the rich Dutch provinces had been a problem for the Spanish Hapsburg for close to two decades. Portuguese and Spanish connections with the low countries and with Burgundy had been strong for centuries; Antwerp had served for over fifty years as the northern distribution and banking center. When the Northern Netherlands set up their own separate institutions (1579) and proceeded toward declaring their independence (1581) Philip II replied by embargoing all Dutch ships in Portuguese and Spanish ports (1585, 1595). These acts changed what so far had been a regional disorder (even while disrupting Europe's wealthiest and most urbanized area) into a conflict of worldwide proportions.

For the Dutch Republic had put its seapower to good use primarily by relying on the naval resources of Holland and Zeeland and helping to seize and hold islands despite the superiority of the Spanish forces on land. By 1590 Dutch merchant shipping already was the largest in the world. The Dutch also realized that a break in their trade with the Iberian peninsula threatened disaster, and so they reacted by sailing directly to the producing areas for the goods they needed—to the Caribbean, to Spanish America, and to the Portuguese East. The defeat of the Spanish Armada (1588) by the English navy in alliance with the Dutch fatally shook Spanish morale, and by 1607 a Dutch admiral scored a devastating victory against the Spanish fleet right on its doorstep near Gibraltar. The "Twelve Years' Truce" of 1609 broke the Iberian monopoly of access to the world's oceans, legitimized Dutch trade with the East, and confirmed the principal elements of the new global system: The United Provinces of the Netherlands had become the second world power. The succession had been fiercely contested, but it did not fall into utterly alien hands: the Dutch had after all been former subjects of the King of Spain who, at that time, also was the King of Portugal.

The seventeenth century is still known as the Dutch Republic's golden age. The United Provinces rose to world power in alliance with England and France when both these powerful countries were rent by internal dissension, religious conflict, and civil war. Their weakness was a condition of Dutch power. But in the second half of the century first France and then England recovered their strength and also launched their own global activities. Now the Dutch found themselves under increasing pressure. They fought three naval wars against the English and a hard land war against Louis XIV of France. Their investment in the spice trade with the East was not really paying off, and their effort to develop the resources of North America proved inadequate. The Dutch system was under severe strain.

In 1688 William III (the *Stadholder*, an executive officer of the Dutch Republic but also a sovereign Prince of Orange in his own right) assumed the British throne on dynastic grounds, and reestablished the Dutch-English alliance as the cornerstone of a new grand coalition against the aspirations of the Sun King. By itself, this "Glorious Revolution" of English politics was a largely bloodless transition of power, but in global terms it also initiated a gradual withering away of the Dutch position. Great Britain, as it soon came to be known, rose to be the successor world power by victoriously leading the Protestant and anti-French coalition through more than two decades of global warfare and by organizing the peace thereafter. Whereas in 1689 the French navy ranked first both in respect of size and of quality (the British second and the Dutch third) "in the twenty-five years from 1689 to 1714 . . . England became the dominating sea power of Europe. Throughout the half-century that followed, as the classic authority on the subject (A.T. Mahan) has remarked, 'on the few occasions in which [the navy] is called on to fight its superiority is so marked that the affairs can scarcely be called battles.'"[5]

This first global British order fulfilled two systemic functions: in Europe, it managed the balance of power by averting the danger of any one power attaining continental supremacy; worldwide, it provided the infrastructure of world trade. While maintaining a generally mercantilist system of regulated commerce with the colonies, it also coopted into its own global network important parts of earlier ones (those of Portugal, Spain, and the Netherlands), and it gave coherence to the whole. It suffered its first important setback in the American Revolution. Soon Britain experienced complete diplomatic and political isolation, and for a time she lost her command of the sea. With the advent of the French Revolution her global system was becoming unstuck, and the question of succession was open once again.

Great Britain regained her position as the dominant world power as leader of the coalition against the forces of the French Revolution and the imperial aspirations of Napoleon, as the keeper of the balance of power and the organizer of the Industrial Revolution. Despite Napoleon's brilliantly led campaigns on land, the French challenge was doggedly fought off in a major war lasting over two decades, with a successful strategy that can best be described as "Periclean." The political structure of Europe was firmed up with the evolution of the Concert of Europe, the decolonization of Latin America was successfully overseen, and China and Japan were opened to the world. While the Indian territorial commitment had been added to and was becoming increasingly burdensome, Britain also launched a reorganization of world commerce on the basis of the new principles of free trade.

The Pax Britannica was impressive while it lasted, but it began to deteriorate when Bismarck successfully overthrew the post-Napoleonic Vienna settlement in Central Europe and established the new German Empire as the strongest power on the continent. The rise of the United States and Japan as global powers altered the structure of world politics outside Europe. Industrial competition put into question Britain's vaunted technological leadership. In her bold naval construction program Germany set out deliberately to challenge Britain's command of the seas, long recognized as the secret of its success.

The question of succession once again appeared on the agenda of world politics, but the world system had not yet evolved regularized arrangements for displacing a declining world power in a nonviolent manner. The encroaching decay was signalled by the growth of nationalist sentiments and policies beginning with the Italian and German movements and then moving into the Balkans, the Near East, and the Far East. The rising global powers reached out for a world position, building navies, seeking bases and colonies, and, generally, imitating Britain. Difficult economic conditions in the third quarter of the nineteenth century set the stage for increasingly sharp competition, economic protectionism, and a scramble for colonial

The Theory of Long Cycles

markets. So marked was the deterioration in the quality of international life that the entire period became known as the age of imperialism.

Two obvious successors gradually emerged: Germany and the United States. In the age of Bismarck, Germany had established a military, diplomatic, and economic ascendancy over continental Europe. Prussia had been Britain's ally in the two previous global wars, and the British royal family had strong ties of long standing with German ruling houses. At the turn of the century a British-German alliance was in the air, but for a variety of reasons the relationship turned sour. The essence of it seems to have been that, faced with the necessity of succession, the British leaders decided to throw in their lot with the United States. Conciliating the United States became a guiding principle of British foreign policy; naval deployments were directed away from Caribbean, Atlantic, and Pacific stations and toward the North Sea, and while British possessions became preferred locations for American multinationals, Anglo-American relations flourished at the elite level also. The British signals were warmly received by such American leaders as Theodore Roosevelt and John Hay.

The stage was set for a change of principal characters, but the process of succession was neither easy nor short. Two world wars were fought before a new global order could crystallize around the United States. In 1918-1919 Woodrow Wilson took the lead in shaping a world order, but in the end he failed. So the weakly founded League of Nations was left to stand without its principal support, and the world system was allowed to drift into two decades of economic chaos, political disarray, and military adventures, finally culminating in another, yet more costly, replay of the German challenge.[6] But this time Winston Churchill effectively transferred world power to Franklin Roosevelt in 1940-1941, and throughout the war the President was already engaged in laying the foundations of a new world order. His sudden death (recalling Wilson's breakdown in 1919) once again threw a spanner into the process of transition. The thread of continuity was almost lost until Harry Truman and his associates refocussed America's energies once again with the Truman Doctrine and the Marshall Plan in 1947.

The Fifth Cycle of Global Order since 1945

Since 1945 the United States has held the role of world power in the fifth cycle of global politics.[7] That position is rooted, as was that of Britain, in the leadership of, and in the proven capacity to sustain, the coalition that fought successfully to maintain a system of independent states in Europe and in East Asia and defeated yet another challenger to the established order. By virtue of that position the United States took a leading part in negotiating the peace settlements and in creating the basic institutions of the new global order: a political leadership capable of responding to world responsibilities and backed by adequate organizational arrangements; a nuclear and conventional power distribution such as to assure stability at the global level, with particular emphasis on air, naval, and space power; a family of world organizations as focus for a myriad of global services and as a framework for international economic relations and an expanding world economy: and a system of alliances and security arrangements to distribute security into parts of the world that needed it.

Hence the American position in the world may be explained as the result of normal if rather eventful processes of "recruitment" to the role of world power that had been at work for something like half a millennium. Put into that perspective the gravity of the responsibilities attaching to that role becomes more apparent. To describe that role as one of world policeman is to misconceive it. To argue that it is now over because of the Vietnam war or because of the erosion of U.S. power is to misunderstand the workings of the global political system and the lessons of the past. For in each preceding cycle the process of erosion has been slow. The global political system does not change so abruptly as to negate the interest of the United States in maintaining the world system it has had such a large share in bringing about—a system that continues to work largely in accordance with those interests.

To justify or explain the United States' world role we need not resort at all to the concepts of cold war or containment (viewed as the necessity to resist the Soviet Union or to contain the expansion of communism). As should by now be clear that position owes everything to the global wars and nothing in particular to the cold war. Whereas the onset of the cold war did coincide with the last phase of the assumption of the world role, this might have been partly accidental and attributable chiefly to the break in political continuity caused by the sudden death of President Roosevelt.

It is clear nevertheless that certain characteristic post-1945 world policies, including the Truman Doctrine, the Marshall Plan, two series of security alliances, and the Korean and Vietnam wars were publicly defended and justified on the grounds of their usefulness in containing the Soviet Union and fighting communism. Hence public support for those elements of the world power role was in substantial part mobilized under the auspices of the cold war. Public understanding of that role (as distinct from the understandings of some practitioners and some students of these matters) has therefore been insufficient and has had little sense of continuity with the past. Unsurprisingly therefore, detente, seen as the end of the cold war, brings into question the public's support for the world power role; or else, its continuation is seen to be linked inextricably with perceptions of the Soviet threat. Yet creeping multipolarity does not reduce the need for world leadership; mostly it only circumscribes its freedom and makes its exercise

The Theory of Long Cycles

more difficult. Britain continued to fill the role right through 1945, albeit not always with the necessary vision.

Much has been written about military power and a strong economy as the foundations of world power. Without doubt, they are important, and without them such status is unsupportable. But despite relative declines in the past two decades the United States remains militarily strong and economically productive. Yet the world has known many strong and wealthy states that in a test proved incapable of reaching or supporting world power status—among them Hapsburg Spain, France, and Germany. For in addition to public will and support, the objective basis for such a role is the condition of "surplus security." Security is a public good that is produced and consumed by political communities at various levels, and we judge its abundance by the quantity and quality of public order within and around them. World powers have tended to be successful (that is, low cost) producers of security for two reasons. First, because of their insularity (Venice, Britain) or semiinsularity (the United States, Netherlands, peninsular Portugal), they have been free and secure from external attack or invasion or even ordinary cross-border raids by easily mobilized land forces; their enemies had to launch expensive and elaborate naval campaigns allowing long warning times, and none succeeded. What they save on border protection, land armies, and frontier fortifications and surveillance they can invest in sea and air power.

Second, world powers have emerged because of their stability, combining internal political continuity with considerable freedom. Their leaders have had less to worry about their own survival (as most governments do when susceptible to coups and internal and external threats, turmoil, and discontinuity) and have the time and leisure for raising larger questions. All world powers have had remarkably stable and relatively open, constitutional, mostly representative, competitive and multilevel type governments. None experienced a military coup, an unconstitutional change of government, a civil war or a metropolitan uprising while in the status of world power (the nearest exceptions being party strife in the Dutch Republic, and the Scottish uprisings in the first, and Irish nationalist movements in the second British system).[8]

Is the United States losing the advantages of surplus security? In particular, have long-range missiles and space developments diminished the inherent value of an insular or semiinsular position? Arguably not, provided that effective mutual deterrence is maintained between all states wielding those weapons (and provided good-neighbor relations continue with Canada and Mexico). As long as mutual deterrence continues, states without exposed, contested, or heavily defended land borders retain an absolute advantage over all others that face defense problems across land frontiers. Equally important is political stability, which in part is a function of external security and freedom from foreign occupation. Next to Britain, Sweden, and Switzerland, the United States still is the most continuously stable and predictable, and also the largest such political system in the world.

Surplus security provides that extra margin of activity and, in favorable circumstances, can be redistributed and exchanged for influence, status, and other values. It affords the sinews of world power.

Oceanic Theories As Antecedents of Long Cycles

The elements of the theory of long cycles may seem novel, but they do not come out of nowhere, although it may be said that they come out of the "blue." They can be traced to a tradition of writing on international affairs that might best be described as "oceanic," mostly because sea power, the implications of an island position, and the importance of international trade are its distinguishing characteristics.

The early writers on British statecraft (seventeenth and eighteenth centuries) must be mentioned first, the foremost names being Francis Bacon, Lord Bolingbroke, and David Hume. All three combined scholarship and writing with practical experience in international relations, and their prescriptions of strategic policies for Britain rested on a percipient appreciation of the importance of the sea, and its command, to all international engagements.[9]

The Federalist papers come next. While searching for strategic models for the United States, Alexander Hamilton argued that those states "whose situations have borne the nearest resemblance to our own" were the "commercial republics" of Athens, Carthage, Venice, Holland, and Britain.[10] He made use of their experience in arguing the case for the new constitution, and that is why he urged upon his readers the essential features of those states and their strategies: concern for external trade, a strong navy, a federal system, and a republican form of government.

The third important oceanic tradition is that centered on Alfred Thayer Mahan, a U.S. naval officer and historian writing at the turn of the twentieth century. Mahan's study of sea power was in fact a thorough analysis of the mechanisms of the two British systems of world order. His doctrines

> had a simple grandeur about them. . . . Sea power was the basis of world power. Throughout most of the nineteenth century, British naval superiority had been unchallenged and had enabled a small island kingdom to dominate an unprecedented world empire. By the beginning of the twentieth century, however, the power of the British fleet had begun to decline. . . . Mahan [concluded] . . . that the United States . . . should cooperate with Britain in establishing and maintaining Anglo-American sea power . . . as the basis of world peace and of a stable and just world order.[11]

The group of leaders who accepted and implemented Mahan's principles included Theodore Roosevelt, Henry Cabot Lodge, Elihu Root, Henry Adams, and Franklin D. Roosevelt.[12] They went beyond the technical and naval aspects of Mahan's work and saw in it a repertoire of strategic models for the management of a global order.

Finally, reference must be made to the classic prototype (and sometimes the direct source) of all ocean models, *"History of the Peloponnesian War"* by Thucydides or, more precisely, the Periclean strategy as reported by Thucydides. Pericles was the leader who took Athens into the Peloponnesian war, well aware of Sparta's power on land but also conscious of the uses and the value of the command of the sea. In less than two generations Athens had risen to power in the world of the Mediterranean; she was a brilliantly successful and cohesive democratic polity and a sea power that had repeatedly defeated the massed navies of Persia; she was commercially and financially active, and she was the leader of a league of maritime states. It was Pericles' overriding desire to preserve these assets by devising an effective strategy for a long war. "For Pericles had said that Athens would be victorious if she bided her time and took care of her navy, if she avoided trying to add to the empire during the course of the war and if she did nothing to risk the safety of the city itself."[13] But when he died, Athenians ignored his advice and abandoned his defensive strategy for a policy of expedition and land conquest in Sicily that soon brought disaster to the city and decay to her world.

The oceanic models share the following features: They adopt a global perspective derived from knowledge about and concern for maritime communications. They deal with major war and ways of fighting it effectively, especially by sea. They focus on the world power and understand the sources of its predominance as the command of the sea. Some recognize a law of decay, but they all stress trade and industry rather than large populations and territorial dominion.

Thus, the theory of long cycles has solid roots in the practice of statecraft and in the strategic thought of significant writers. What differentiates it from earlier statements beyond being up-dated and involving a broadened concept of seapower to encompass all global-level interactions, are the usual characteristics of social science theory: greater explicitness and formalization and concern for empirical grounding and verification. But to be fully appreciated the theory of long cycles needs to be set in contrast with two alternate sources of strategic insight, each of which has its own implied theory of world politics. One of these is the traditional model of the states-system, whose logic usually finds expression in a balance-of-power model, understood abstractly and schematically as a prescription for all members of the states-system. The other is the imperial model. If the classical age of European diplomacy (the eighteenth and nineteenth centuries) is the origin of the first; the history of Rome is the obvious source of the second model.

The States-System Model

The states-system model assumes a world that is composed of a large number of basically similar states. These states each have their own interests and may differ in their power resources and rank but are otherwise merely units in a complex game of strategy. Their position in time and space or their relation to the global system are not theoretically relevant. World politics combines these powers in a great many arrangements, including alliances and balances of power, and states-system theory elucidates the abstract logic of these relationships.

This timeless, ahistorical, and ageographical model is the core of traditional, mainstream international relations. It is also the model from which strategies for the United States have been derived. For instance, the view popular in the early 1970s—the emergence of a five-power system, or, somewhat later, of a triangular relationship among the United States, the Soviet Union, and China—drew on precisely this logic of the states system; since the withdrawal from Vietnam, moreover, it moved toward the assumption that the United States was becoming "an ordinary country," one state among several, if not many, that exercise influence over world affairs.[14]

The Imperial Model

The imperial model addresses this inadequacy of conventional international relations (which relegates the United States to the role of an ordinary power). It recognizes the central role of the United States in the contemporary international system.[15] It has much to say about the management of client states and the defense of frontiers threatened by barbarians but has some problems in developing theory and in establishing the precise relevance of its strategic formulas.[16]

Rome is the obvious source of such strategic analogies, but Rome as a political system lasted for about two millennia, and it is not immediately obvious what portions of that experience are relevant today. For instance, Edward Luttwak writes about the problems of the first through third centuries A.D., which was the time when the Empire, having absorbed some four-fifths of the population of its world, was able to concentrate on defending frontiers and arresting internal decay.[17] This hardly seems to be a fruitful analogy for the United States today. Theodore Geiger turns to Eastern Rome (Byzantium) in the fifth through thirteenth centuries A.D., when the strategic and diplomatic skills of the heirs to the glory that was Rome held on to an embattled citadel until they finally succumbed before the onslaught of barbarian and infidel forces.[18] That does not seem to yield a compelling

The Theory of Long Cycles

model either. Neither of these seems as irrelevant, though, as the period 250-150 B.C., when Rome, still a republic (accounting for maybe one-tenth of the population of its world) had risen in large part through the superior use of seapower by destroying the mercantile republic of Carthage in three hard-fought wars. This last variant of the imperial model is posited on an offensive policy of conquest and annexation, propelled and sustained by war. To say the least, the political premises of such a strategy appear entirely dubious today.

The states-system and the imperial models highlight certain aspects of the contemporary experience: the first begins to look applicable as the global system is moving into multipolarity; the second seemed more appropriate in the phase of unipolar or highly concentrated power distributions. Neither is tuned finely enough to the realities of the modern world system.

Implications for Strategic Policy

The theory of long cycles, a development of the oceanic models, offers a good basis for strategic analysis. Tentatively, the implications for U.S. strategic policy may be formulated in a number of directions. First, the United States is not an ordinary country; it is engaged in world affairs because it is a successor and heir to a line of world powers, most recently to Britain, and its accomplishments in organizing world order in the past generation have been substantial. The difficulties that have been encountered have stemmed from overplaying the role rather than from its very nature. The role must be recognized and understood if public support for it is not to evaporate. Collective memory has to make room for the experience of global statecraft. These are the lessons to be drawn from the experience of other world powers and for the definition of strategic options for the future.

Second, the U.S. world role calls for a fundamentally defensive strategy. The reason for this is the fact that the contemporary world order is substantially American in conception and execution and in important respects redounds to its benefit. The goal of U.S. strategic policy must therefore be to protect and to maintain that order rather than to overthrow it. The preferred strategy could therefore best be characterized as Periclean: an attitude of watchful waiting, no conquests or interventions; the protection of the security of the home base through invulnerable deterrents, and the cultivation of the "command" of sea, air, and space as the elements most strategic to a global position.

Third, a defensive strategy will necessarily avoid the imperial presumption. Such presumption can take the form of turning allies into client states subject to management or manipulation (this is the hegemonial trap characteristic of the Athenian experience). Or else it may take the form of aspirations for continental acquisitions or merely the urge to control events in distant nations (this is the territoriality trap exemplified in Athens' Sicilian expedition or in the Venetians' acquisitions of *terra ferma*, which cost them their leadership position in Italy). The imperial presumption is liable to call forth a grand countercoalition (such as Venice experienced in 1509, and Britain suddenly confronted in the war of American independence). This is the terrifying war of all against one; Rome was lucky never to have experienced such a countercoalition; it divided and ruled its world. That strategy is unlikely to be successful in today's well-organized and closely knit global system, underwritten by information and communications systems of unprecedented quality.

Fourth, the international environment of the defensive strategy can be broadly defined by the appropriate phase of the long cycle. According to the theory of long cycles, the global political system saw the end of its last global war in 1945 and might now have passed the next phase of the cycle. On past experience, another global war is not now imminent and even though accidental wars among some (although not all) global powers are not inconceivable (the Crimean War of 1853-1856 was one such war in the second British system), the theory does not predict another global war for at least another generation. Hence strategies that heavily prepare for such a war are likely to be wasteful.

Fifth, the major immediate problems (for the next decade or two) are the decline of the preponderance of the United States that has already taken place and the crystallization of a bipolar, if not a multipolar, structure of world politics. The process of deconcentration is one of challenge and rejection of the established structures of authority. Given the mechanisms of the long cycle it is in fact predictable, but it can take a variety of forms, all of which invoke the symbols and the strategies of nationalisms: movements for independence (as in the Basque country or in Quebec); populist revolts (as in Iran); terrorism; economic protectionism (as in the United States, or as directed against multinationals elsewhere); rising support for the European Community (in the formation of a European monetary system, or in direct elections). Nationalisms may disrupt existing states as constituents of the established order, or they may rouse national sentiment against the global system. These are symptoms of the deterioration of the quality of international life, and they put world order on the defensive. But the nationalist tide is difficult to stem. It must be seen, in the aggregate, not as a disease to be eradicated but rather as a sign of weakening of global institutions, to be remedied at the global level rather than through ad hoc local interventions.

Sixth, the long-term problem confronting the global system is the decay of its political structure. That decay has, in the past, been a necessary response of the system to the later phases of the long cycle. In periods of decay the principal item on the agendas of world politics has been the question of succession to world power, and it always has been resolved through global war. The nationalist phase of the long cycle foreshadows the processes of decay; these may also take the form of disruptions to the world monetary and financial systems, economic decline through the falling off in innovation and key investments; strategic deterioration (through imbalances, proliferation, and destabilizing policies), rise in world insecurity levels, and a general failure of political will.[19] That is why ultimately the greatest challenge facing the world will be the need to face up to the problem of the long cycle: Will the question of succession again dominate world politics (with another global war casting forward its ominous shadow), or will new modes of political organization be found that will push the world out of its customary but now deadly procedures?

It is now widely accepted that the aim of nuclear deterrence is to prevent wars, not to win them. In this sense deterrence becomes a form of strategic arms control, and if that concept is accepted, its logical extension also follows: if (global) war prevention is the goal of arms control then measures for adapting (or refashioning) the global political system so as to change its long-range cyclic proclivity and so avert another global war (that inevitably would be a nuclear war) become part of an expanded concept of arms control. This makes arms control not merely a technical and abstruse subject for weapons experts and verification specialists, or even for strategic arms negotiators, but a field of fundamental political innovation for leading world politics out of the compulsion to global war.

Conclusion

It is the conclusion of this analysis that U.S. strategic policy may best be designed on the foundations of that variant of oceanic political thought we have described as the theory of long cycles. Important prescriptions for strategic analysis emerge as the corollaries of that theory and find support in the experience of earlier world powers; they are the prescriptions for a short-term strategy that is conservative and minimalist.

But if the experience of the past five global cycles is to be taken seriously, a paradoxical result is reached. Those who are indeed serious about the defensive strategies just described will also be impelled to devise drastic measures of political innovation for the modern world system, measures that would ultimately make redundant the theory of long cycles. For if we want things to stay as they are, things will have to change. The aim of grand strategy for the long haul must become transformatory and maximalist: significant modifications of global political structures may be the ultimate expression of arms control.

Notes

1. The term is used in Liddell Hart's sense of "grand strategy," which, in a free adaptation, may be defined as the harmonious orchestration of all instruments of policy, including the military, toward the aim of achieving a "better" peace and a stable world order. See *Strategy*, 2d rev. ed. (London: Faber & Faber, 1954), especially chaps. 19, 22.

2. For definitions of concepts and an initial statement see George Modelski, "The Long Cycle of Global Politics and the Nation-state," *Comparative Studies in Society and History* 20, no. 2 (April 1978):214-235.

3. See also ibid., pp. 218-225.

4. Leopold von Ranke, *Saemmtliche Werke*, vol. 33 (Leipzig: Duncker and Humblot, 1874), p. 244.

5. John Ehrman, *The Navy in the War of William III, 1689-97* (Cambridge: University Press, 1953), p. xv.

6. Charles Kindleberger has argued that the absence of firm world leadership was a principal cause of the Great Depression of 1929-1933.

7. It seems preferable to avoid the term "Pax Americana" because of its imperial allusion.

8. These two conditions of "surplus security" have their problems too: insularity tends to induce ethnocentrism, and internal stability brings on complacency, and both dampen the sources of initiatives for world leadership.

9. Arnold Wolfers and Laurence W. Martin, *The Anglo-American Tradition in Foreign Affairs* (New Haven, Conn.: Yale University Press 1956).

10. *The Federalist* (New York: Everyman's Library, 1911), No. 6.

11. Joseph P. Lash, *Roosevelt and Churchill 1939-1941* (New York: W.W. Norton, 1976), p. 35, quoting T.B. Kittredge.

12. Ibid., p. 37; in F.D. Roosevelt the doctrines of Mahan had found "an eager apprentice."

13. Thucydides, *History of the Peloponnesian War*, trans. Rex Warner (New York: Penguin, 1954), Book II, para. 65; see also Book II, paras. 60-64; Book I, paras. 140-144.

14. Richard Rosecrance, ed. *America as an Ordinary Country: U.S. Foreign Policy and the Future* (Ithaca, N.Y.: Cornell University Press 1976).

15. George Liska, *Imperial America: The International Politics of Primacy* (Baltimore: Johns Hopkins Press, 1967); Raymond Aron, *The Imperial Republic* (Englewood Cliffs, N.J.: Prentice Hall, 1974).

16. It is not to be confused with the overseas experience of the European powers since 1500 and such colonial empires as those of Spain, Britain, or France.

17. *The Grand Strategy of the Roman Empire: From the First Century A.D. to the Third* (Baltimore: Johns Hopkins Press, 1976).

18. "Is the United States Renouncing Its Hegemonic Leadership?" *New International Realities* (National Planning Association, Washington, D.C.), 1 no. 2 (April 1976):8-17.

19. Cf. David C. Gompert, "Strategic Deterioration: Prospects, Dimensions and Responses," in *Nuclear Weapons in World Politics*, edited by Gompert (New York: McGraw-Hill, 1977), p. 215ff.

2

Living with the Long Cycle: New Assumptions to Guide the Use and Control of Military Force

Edward A. Kolodziej

Few would dispute that the rationale guiding American security policy, including arms control, since World War II is now a shambles, although there is considerable disagreement about what needs to be discarded or retained. Few doubt, moreover, the need for a new rationale, although, again, need does not inevitably yield a single, dominant perspective that commands the allegiance of strategists, political practitioners, or the concerned public.

As a contribution to the debate on a new design, this chapter attempts to stipulate the assumptions on which American security policy might well be founded in the next decade. The first section identifies the assumptions, now overtaken or undone by experience, on which successive administrations based American security policy since World War II. This sets the stage for the second section, which specifies four new assumptions on which American policy will have to be based if it is to be modestly effective.

The approach is synoptic. Within the short space of this analysis, no attempt is made to describe in detail the complex history, tergiversations, contradictions, or uncertainties of American security policy and behavior. The attempt rather is to specify the common elements underlying specific American security policy responses through most of the postwar period and to define, in as succinct a manner as possible, those assumptions that should animate American policy in the immediate future in light of fundamental changes in the exterior environment and in American domestic opinion regarding the use and control of military force.

In the absence of such a framework of analysis, security issues and the outcomes of interstate conflict risk being determined more by forces abroad and/or uninformed opinion at home than by the prudent exercise of American power. Defining those elements that are predicable of each particular security case or problem is a prerequisite for coherent decision-making. It permits the harmonization of specific, discrete initiatives and responses within a common framework of analysis sensitive to exterior and interior constraints yet alert to opportunities to shape the international security environment to suit American preferences. Lacking a guiding rationale, even one flawed by conflicting claims, policy-makers are forced to treat each issue separately and pragmatically. Such an approach invites drift, waste, gaps, and contradictions in making and executing security policy. The following discussion sketches the preliminary outline of a corrective. Defining the assumptions on which the different and often divergent aspects of American security policy will have to be made is a prerequisite for specifying the possibilities of the effective and legitimate use or threat of military force.

The Past Is Not Prologue

American postwar security policy rested on four key assumptions: (1) the division of the world between an American-led coalition of non-Communist states and an implacable, resourceful Soviet Union bent on organizing the world on security, economic, and political principles inimical to those of the American people; (2) the adequacy and applicability of American material strength, especially its military power, not only to meet the Communist challenge but also to organize a world compatible with American preferences; (3) the indivisibility of international and American security, economic, and political regime interests; and (4) the durability of domestic consensus that these assumptions were a timely and tolerable basis for the projection of American military power abroad.[1]

The Division of the World

The image of a world divided into two hostile camps formed a key pillar of American thinking. The capacity of other states to act independently of the superpowers was discounted as much as their wish to act beyond the protective shield provided by Moscow and Washington. The interests of allies and, later, of new states in the third world were viewed as polarized around one or the other of the superpowers. The Truman Doctrine provided ideological justification for a globe divided between the free and Communist worlds. This division was institutionalized through a series of treaties extending American security guarantees to countries in Latin America, Europe, and Asia. The Eisenhower administration solidified this alliance structure and extended it through additional commitments, such as those in the Middle East (the Eisenhower Doctrine and, indirectly, CENTO) and in Asia (the Formosa resolution, Vietnam, and SEATO). The Kennedy and Johnson regimes, if careful to use the rhetoric of interdependence, projected, nevertheless, the vision of America at the center of the global political universe. This was America's century. The race was with the Communist world directed from Moscow. Peking's rise as an adversary in the midst of the Cold War and as counterpoint to justify selected defense programs, like an ABM system, did not signal any recognition of the fundamental divergence between the Communist giants. Their mutual antagonism toward the United States was assumed to be greater than their mutual differences.

The Kennedy administration's articulation of a strategy of flexible response rationalized the global stuggle at several military levels. All were aimed at the Soviet Union and its proxies. At a nuclear level, sufficient material superiority was to be marshalled to implement a counterforce deterrent posture. While renouncing any first strike intention, American nuclear power was keyed to damage limiting objectives that were conceived as providing maximum incentive to the Soviet Union to avoid hitting American cities and, if war should erupt, to terminate hostilities on terms favorable to the United States. Allies could also be assured of the dependability of the American guarantee. The presumed nuclear superiority of the United States provided margin for maneuver vis-à-vis the Soviet Union in defense of allied interests at nuclear and subnuclear levels.

The expansion of American limited war and unconventional warfare fighting capabilities rounded out the strategic picture. Nuclear weapons, even under conditions of a fleeting American superiority, were so devastating that their use in support of allied security interests was not plausible except under the most dire circumstances. Nonnuclear capabilities were enlarged to increase the deterrent and defensive capabilities of a global security system directed by the United States. Allied and American interests were equated. Washington had difficulty understanding European criticisms of the nonnuclear role assigned to them, the cost of increased conventional forces, the weakening of the American deterrent in favor of European defense, and the American attack on independent European nuclear systems, that is, the French and to a lesser extent the British strike force. If strategists, like Henry Kissinger, recognized that the multilateral nuclear force (MLF) aggravated, rather than alleviated, these concerns, there was still general agreement on a manichean conception of America's strategic problems to be resolved eventually in favor of the United States (and allies) at the expense of the Soviet Union.[2]

Regional balances around the globe were cast in the image of the Soviet-American conflict. The Eisenhower administration was criticized less for its penchant to expand American strategic commitments than for its failure to implement them by enlarging American military capabilities, their forward deployment abroad, or their rapid despatch in crisis situations.[3] Deterrence theorists concentrated largely on a three-party scenario in which the United States was supposed to come to the aid of a beleaguered ally threatened by the Soviet Union or a Moscow surrogate.[4] Military assistance to Middle East states, like Jordan and Lebanon, or to Asian states, like Pakistan and

South Korea, was rationalized as means to fight the Cold War, the rival claims of client states engaged in regional disputes to the contrary notwithstanding. Whatever the complexities of the Congo episode, the underlying justification for intervention was the Cold War struggle. The Cuban invasion of April 1961 and the subsequent missile crisis a year and a half later reinforced the thesis of regional subordination. Increasing American involvement in Southeast Asia—first in Laos and later in South Vietnam, including the overthrow of the Diem regime in 1963, was defended as a response to the challenge posed by a unified Communist movement under the Kremlin's direction.

American interest in nuclear arms control was compatible with this vision of a global titanic struggle. Cooperation with the principal adversary was a prerequisite for the success of American military strategy. Preventing a nuclear war occasioned by inadvertence, accident, miscalculation, or misunderstanding was in the best interest of the United States. Arms control accords did not preclude American ascendancy. They assured it at levels that lowered the cost of the arms race and the risk of nuclear war, although not necessarily below nonnuclear levels, where a flexible response strategy, possessed of the means for its execution, promised an American-dominated security system.

The Adequacy of American Military Means and Their Suitability

If American leaders succumbed repeatedly to fears of growing Soviet ascendancy, they were no less certain that the United States possessed the means, if they could be mobilized and deployed efficiently, of meeting the varied nature of the Communist threat. Compromise or conciliation with a resourceful adversary was neither feasible, given an unswerving ideological commitment to expansion, nor necessary, since the means were at hand to contain it. Defining adequacy in specific military and economic terms was then more a technical problem for expert judgment than a political concern whether a compromise solution to the Soviet problem would eventually be found. Constraints were primarily internal, turning on posited levels of spending that successive administrations presented as an efficient allocation of resources at a tolerable political cost. As perceptions of the external threat enlarged from deterrence I to deterrence II and III situations, that is, from threats of military attacks on the American homeland (deterrence I) to military aggression against allies (deterrence II), to unconventional warfare and crisis management problems (deterrence III), the size and composition of American military capabilities likewise expanded.[5] Successive budget limits on military spending were raised to cope with the perceived increase in Soviet military capabilities and expansionist designs. The $15 billion ceiling set by the Truman administration before Korea rose to a level four times that amount during the war. The Eisenhower regime's allocations hovered between $35 and $40 billion. The Sputnik scare and the alleged missile gap prompted a national debate that led to the Kennedy election victory in 1960. Military spending was given priority, and the new budget ceiling was raised to approximately $60 billion annually. The deliberate ambiguity of the flexible response strategy in providing maximum choice of military means to the President to respond to a broad spectrum of crises from deterrence I through III situations assumed the development of a military budget that was similarly indeterminate.

The Kennedy administration's adoption of a Keynesian economic framework facilitated the rationalization and legitimation of defense expansion. Spending for arms was viewed as a positive economic stimulant, not as a drain on the treasury. The Truman and Eisenhower administrations, motivated largely by conservative economic doctrine of balanced budgets, considered military spending as a drag on the domestic economy. With Kennedy, defense expenditures assumed the character of public works reminiscent of New Deal efforts to prod a sluggish economy to increase productivity and growth. Modernization of the economy could also be promoted by defense and defense-related spending. The space program and moon shot were presented not only as an appropriate response to the Soviet Union's Sputnik success but also as a means of maintaining and extending American military superiority. The space program was a framework within which to develop and enlarge the American store of scientific and technological talent and expand its research, development, and industrial base. Defense spending and full employment were tied together. Within so optimistic a perspective, the traditional tension between guns and butter appeared misconceived. Each added, not detracted, from economic growth. An expanding economy, motored by increased spending for arms and the modernization of equipment, promised to produce both in abundance. The Cold War was thus less a burden than an opportunity to increase welfare and to meet simultaneously a pervasive exterior challenge.[6]

The productive capacity, monetary stability, dynamism, and competitiveness of the American economic system were considered decisive assets in the Cold War struggle, notwithstanding the fears repeatedly expressed in the 1950s and 1960s about the potentially adverse impact of increased military spending on the economy. Concern for ever larger trade deficits, balance-of-payments problems, and growing pressures on the dollar developed throughout this period, but they were never able to overshadow completely the basic optimism about American economic dominance abroad. From this perspective, the principal material response of the United States to perceived Soviet expansion after World War II was economic, not military. The threat posed by Moscow was perceived to be through internal subversion of the European non-communist states. They were confronted internally by Communist insurrection, as in Greece, or faced with wholesale economic and political dislocation, including important Communist electoral pressures, as in France and Italy.

The militarization of the Truman Doctrine largely awaited the shock of the Soviet nuclear explosion in September 1949 and, more pointedly, the North Korean attack of June 1950. Until then, the United States relied on its nuclear monopoly to deter Soviet aggression against itself and its allies. The Atlantic Alliance provided the political framework within which the American nuclear guarantee could be extended to Europe and within which European economic recovery could progress. American military spending was actually scheduled to decline in fiscal year 1950. The Marshall Plan was supposed to address the immediate threat of political subversion and economic upheaval in Europe. Until the Korean conflict, overt military aggression, especially a conventional attack against an ally, was deemed a lesser contingency. The rehabilitation of the European economies was advanced as a major American response to the Cold War and to traditional national rivalries in Europe that had led to two world wars in half a century. The possibility of gradually increasing economic competition from Europe was discounted, since the burden of maintaining the European economies was the immediate problem, and recovery would relieve that burden. Most agreed that the United States could afford these risks; in any event, there would be ample compensation in the strategic and political benefits anticipated to flow from European recovery. Intra-European cooperation, actively promoted as a condition for Marshall Plan aid, became an American strategem to fight the Cold War. There was little concern that the United States would lose its ascendant economic position. Its technological lead appeared to widen, partly as a result of its Cold War responsibilities. Its monopoly position seemed unassailable within the International Monetary Fund, where the gold standard was rapidly transformed into a dollar-convertible American system. American trade surpluses were more a problem than a blessing for global economic recovery. American investment was sought around the world. In the 1950s American capital became one of the most powerful forces in the development of the European Common Market.[7]

Even the American political system was judged to be an asset in the Cold War struggle. There were those who, in answer to deTocqueville's concerns about the capacity of democracies to conduct an effective foreign policy, argued that over time the pluralism of American politics not only met domestic political and economic needs but also was the best guarantee of effective strategic policy.[8] With the advent of the Kennedy administration, efforts focused on the reform of American political life to better fight the Cold War. The exterior struggle with the Soviet Union and security threats from abroad were seized on to mobilize support for domestic change. A subtle inversion of priorities crystallized. The objective of preserving the American political order as the object of strategy competed with the notion of using the political system as an instrument in the struggle with the Soviet Union. American social and economic reform was based partly on its salutary effect in strengthening the United States and in discharging its foreign responsibilities. The quality of American politics through improved race relations, greater political equality, and civil liberties was enlisted in the service of American strategic maneuvering. Responding to domestic ills of the United States was tantamount to addressing the Soviet and Communist challenge to American democracy.[9]

The political limits of American power were seen as imposed more by the nation itself—in part what Wilson meant by the higher virtue flowing from self-restraint—than by outside forces or adverse circumstance.[10] The implications of this widely held assumption were that American-preferred norms for the organization of the globe were held in check by its own lack of imagination and daring. American power was sufficient to implement American designs for global order. Under such assumptions material and psychological constraints were largely a function of American commitments and mobilized public support. For strategists and governmental leaders it was then quite logical to specify the conditions of effective national "commitment" strategies. Adversaries, allies, clients, and proxies were the objects of American manipulation. Strategists naturally concentrated on what Americans could do to others rather than on what others could do to America.[11] If American military, economic, and political power was adequate to meet the Communist threat and if these threats were global—expanding in breadth, depth, and complexity—it also followed that American interests were correspondingly worldwide in scope.

The view gradually took hold after World War II that unlimited American power essentially defined the nation's interests,[12] and not the reverse as had been the traditional relation of interest and power.[13] This principle of action emerged more as the result of a series of often hastily fashioned improvisations to exterior crises (for example, Point Four or the Truman Doctrine) than as the execution of a rational plan or of a conspiratorial design, as radical historians would prefer to believe.[14] The severest critics and proponents of American strategic and foreign policy were agreed ironically on this fundamental, if questionable, assumption in their common perception of the boundless possibilities of American power, whether viewed for good or ill. Radical critics pictured American expansionism as the cause of the Cold War and the primary explanation for world conflict.[15] Successive Washington administrations, on the other hand, viewed the enlargement of American military power and economic influence as a defensive response to Soviet and Communist aggression and a contribution to world peace built on liberal economic and political principles. Whatever the driving force for the expansion of American instruments of power, the results were the same: American capabilities became a crude measure of American interests, and not the reverse.

The Acheson-Kennan debate in the late 1950s rehearsed and elaborated on the Lippmann-Kennan exchange of a decade earlier, with Kennan placed in the awkward swing position of arguing the limits of power.[16] The Acheson wing of the Democratic party carried the argument and the United States accelerated the arms race under the Kennedy administration. The profound skepticism expressed by Walter Lippmann and the later Kennan about the utility of military force in meeting American security problems or about the capacity of the American nation to sustain a containment strategy of attrition built on the conscription of men under arms, was dismissed. So also was their implicit warning against identifying exaggerated claims of U.S. power with American core interests. America's power was not so great as proponents alleged nor were its interests so pervasive and global as they insisted. Advocates of moderation in defining the ends and means of foreign and security policy were, until recently, given little heed, nor were the assumptions on which their recommendations of restraint rested shared either by governing circles or by radical historians.[17] What mattered to both groups is that American interests be conceived in terms of the expansion of American power. If American power lacked material limits, so also did interests appear limitless. National and international security became different facets of a single problem.

Indivisibility of International and American Security, Economic, and Political Interests

The identification of unlimited power with universal interest crystallized around three specific principles of action. These might be termed the indivisibility of global and national security, welfare, and political regimes. The principle of indivisible security—American and international—was at once an objective and a measure of action. It reflected Wilsonian notions of world order. The Soviet challenge prompted the articulation of a counter ideology drawn from Wilsonian notions of an expanding American role and responsibility for a new international security system based on collective security, a process of free economic exchange (the "Open Door"), and a universe of democratic states.[18] The Truman Doctrine rationalized the security and political regime components of American security policy. The security of free peoples were presumably linked; security was everywhere or it was nowhere. The security of the United States thus extended around the globe. The Marshall Plan further insisted on the duty of the United States, in its own interest, to combat global economic deprivation. Secretary of State George C. Marshall cited these larger economic motives and the global strategy guiding American policy in his Harvard address:

> It is logical that the United States should do whatever it is able to assist the return of normal economic health in the world, without which there can be no political stability and no assured peace. Our policy is directed not against any country or doctrine but against hunger, poverty, desperation, and chaos. Its purpose should be the revival of a working economy in the world so as to permit the emergence of political and social conditions in which free institutions can exist.[19]

The global balance between the United States and the Soviet Union was assumed to structure local conflicts. Threats to non-Communist states in the Mediterranean (Greece, Turkey, and Iran), West Europe, and Asia (Japan, Korea, and later Vietnam) were cast in a Cold War mold. The loss of these states to one or the other of the superpowers was considered a blow to the strategic position of the losing state. In assuming that security was indivisible, American strategists and policy-makers transformed the Cold War into a zero-sum game.

After World War II, American intervention abroad was justified as support for democratic regimes. As a practical matter, qualification for support was based more on a government's anti-communist credentials than on its commitment to popular rule. This elastic standard was sufficient for domestic political purposes to join the American responsibility for global security to the creation of democratic regimes around the globe. Following Kantian notions inherited by Woodrow Wilson and passed into the postwar period through the Truman Doctrine, international security was identified with a world of democratic states. The Cold War would presumably be resolved in terms favorable to the United States. As added boon, there would be formed a world cast in the American image and dedicated to popular government.

Durability and Reliability of the Domestic Consensus

Policy-makers also assumed that national support for the assumptions of power and purpose, outlined previously, would be durable and that governmental policies could reliably be based on this expectation once public will and purpose were mobilized. The major task of political leadership was, as in the title of a book by one Kennedy appointee, *To Move a Nation*,[20] to see and to accept its international responsibilities, whose execution were in the nation's best interests. Few doubted that the nation would ultimately respond to an appeal to enlist the human and material resources at the disposition of the American people to surmount the perils of the Cold War. Public support came then to be considered as a kind of free, inexhaustible good that could be drawn on indefinitely.

Widely assumed, moreover, was the attractive, if dubious, proposition that the burdens of exercising American power abroad would be readily shouldered and equitably distributed. In President Kennedy's declamation, "Ask not what your country can do for you, but what you can do for your country," the psychological links between personal effort and commitment, on the one hand, and national interest and global security, on the other, were forged. American policy-makers assumed that most Americans were agreed on America's responsibility for world order and on their obligation to pledge their blood and treasure in support of that obligation.

These optimistic expectations rested on still another unarticulated assumption: the insularity of national decision-making. There was the expectation that divisions at home would be settled within a national framework, that is, that the public and competing elites would always prefer to support the administration in Washington versus other states, especially hostile powers, and that the formation of American opinion and the motivations underlying elite behavior were effectively protected from outside manipulation or machination. How else could the harmony of interests, real or potential, assumed by strategists and policy-makers with respect to public support of government security policies be maintained? It was not conceivable to governmental leaders that the public would stand against its own government in a crisis. The search for a bipartisan foreign policy and periodic campaigns to support the President in foreign policy were keyed, simultaneously and paradoxically, to a presumption of sustained public support and the need to create it. The ideological insularity of the American security debate, whatever differences might be manifested on secondary or tactical questions, was thus accompanied by an expectation that the process of institutional decision-making was also not subject to exterior influence. The contradictions in American political life were viewed as more apparent than real.[21] These could be moderated and ultimately enlisted in the service of foreign enterprise. Other states were penetrable and their peoples susceptible to influence, often hidden and insidious, but not the American people nor their governing processes. Containment was calculated to undermine the Stalinist argument of capitalist encirclement and expansion. By biding one's time a new generation of Soviet citizens would emerge to demand a liberalization that would lead to societal convergence between the United States and the Soviet Union.[22] Dissent at home was never fundamental, since interests were viewed as in essential harmony; division abroad, however, was real but finally reconcilable in imitation of the American example. The American experience was both morally superior to that of its detractors and competitors and eminently exportable.

Living with the Long Cycle

Alternative Assumptions for the Evolution of American Security Policy

These assumptions on which American security policy rested after World War II no longer hold. Since the Nixon administration, a redefinition of the new conditions under which strategic policy will have to be formed has gradually evolved. The distance that must still be travelled may become clearer by advancing an alternate set of four assumptions on which security policy will have to be based. These include (1) the multiplication of threats, allies, and adversaries, (2) the disparity between greater absolute military power at the disposal of the United States and greater relative impotence in wielding it to influence events abroad, (3) the globalization yet divisibility of American and international security, economic, and political regime interests, and (4) the persistence of divided domestic consensus as the shaky basis from which to project American military power to shape the international environment in ways congenial to often conflicting American preferences. These assumptions contrast sharply with those that largely prevailed from World War II through the Johnson administration in policy-making circles.

The Multiplication of Threats, Allies, and Adversaries

The division of the world into two military groupings no longer conforms to the patterns of alignment and divergence that dominated American strategic analysis for a generation. The split between Communist China and the Soviet Union is deep, perhaps deeper than between the United States and each of them. China's acceptance of American conditions for the establishment of normal diplomatic relations suggests as much. Chinese troops meanwhile tie down Russian divisions in the east and ease the pressures on NATO's central front. But in the turnabout with Peking, the security treaty with Taiwan was abrogated, prompting objections from the Nationalist government linked to conservative opinion in the United States opposed to the Carter administration and its policies.

Soviet-American alignment on nuclear arms control pits them potentially against China and other nuclear and nonnuclear powers to the degree that, through limited cooperation, they are tempted to define the terms of international security in their favor. To the extent that European and American security interests are decoupled, a wedge is driven into NATO relations. However much the European states favored the opening to China, the shift is not without its psychic costs regarding estimates of American reliability as an ally. European states are encouraged either to reinforce their military capabilities, whether as a hedge against or as leverage on the American nuclear guarantee, or to move toward a more neutral posture toward the superpowers (especially the Soviet Union) or following the Swedish example, to do both. The vulnerability of NATO conventional forces in Europe and the resistance of the United States and the European states to sizeable increases in spending or speedy modernization of these forces lends weight to a neutralist stance. Moves to increase European influence or control over American strategic decision-making heightens interallied bargaining and creates frictions. The outcomes sought by the NATO partners from detente are also differentially defined, and the benefits enjoyed from a diminution of East-West tensions are unequally distributed in terms of the national security interests of each of the states. The ambiguity surrounding the role of tactical nuclear weapons, whether as battlefield weapons, as a buttress for deterrence, or as a warning "flare" to stop a Soviet grab, is an additional source of tension among NATO allies.

These contradictions and lacunae within NATO's defense thinking and planning are aggravated by the increasing competition between the European states and the United States in domestic arms production and sales. The western alliance is weakened, therefore, not only by the competing responses of its members to the strategic problems posed by the Warsaw Pact but also—and increasingly—by the internal struggle between the economies of the Western nations. This mounting competition, characteristic of the defense industries, is reflected in the divergencies of interests on monetary, trade, and energy policy—fissures that have become more prominent since the first oil crisis in 1973.

The need to shift alignments and to reassess the weights to be attached to allied commitments may also be seen in U.S. relations with states other than the Soviet Union and western Europe. In Latin America, Brazil no longer follows the American lead and embarks on its own economic and military development program, featuring the construction of a nuclear reprocessing plant with West German assistance and the enlargement of its indigenous weapons production capability. Argentina, like Brazil, refuses to sign the nonproliferation treaty.

Regional realignment in the Middle East has also produced the most dramatic turnabout in American exterior alignments. These have been only partially motivated by the East-West struggle. Egypt and Saudi Arabia hold important keys to a viable Middle East settlement; without them the possibility of Soviet penetration is enhanced, and American influence and accessibility to the region's critical geographical position and oil resources are diminished. The sale of F-15s to Saudi Arabia signaled a reevaluation of the Israeli commitment. The American guarantor role of Israel's independence may not have changed, but the modalities of defining independence in terms or territorial, military, and diplomatic support inevitably depreciated Israeli interpretation and control of these issues.

A comprehensive and coherent matrix of threats and corresponding allies and adversaries within each cell is increasingly difficult to construct. Coalitions in one domain, say, the conventional and nuclear defense of Europe, do not neatly fit another issue, like security in the Indian Ocean, where the cast of characters, stakes, and weapon system deployments are different. As one moves beyond pure security issues to associated economic and regime support questions, the alignment of forces and the means of influence become progressively more complex and diffuse. Ties with Algeria are illustrative. Its economic development depends on long-term oil and gas contracts with the United States, while its opposition to a Middle East settlement hampers an accord. Yet its military establishment is principally equipped with Russian weapons. The Cuban case is also instructive and gives pause for reflection about the problem of choosing between rival groups in a revolutionary situation and the implications of choosing either unwisely or too well in being identified with a particular faction. Support for an unpopular regime, like that of the Shah of Iran, may be a useful temporary instrument of American policy, but should such commitments foreclose influence with a waiting opposition? Or, what are American security stakes in the rivalry between the Soviet Union and China and their respective clients in Vietnam and Cambodia over the control of Southeast Asia?

The cells comprising the matrix of security and security-related issues confronting the United States are by no means of equal strategic value at any point. They also vary in significance over time. Alignments of internal and external actors on each issue shift in composition as do the weights that each attaches to successive issues and the elements that comprise them. Nor are these issues all linked. An outcome in one domain or at one level within a cell does not necessarily register gains in another. Discontinuities are no less real than real linkages, whatever the merit of the tendency in American strategic thinking to link what is often unconnected or tenuously related. In this instance linkage may be more the product of a subjective fusing of the dissimilar than the objective recognition of a true joining. The dire predictions of falling dominoes in Asia, if South Vietnam should fall, suggests that linkages are not all what they appear in logic or imagination as they are in political experience. Lending support to Pakistan in its war with India over Bangladesh did not make Pakistan an unswerving ally. Doing little rather than much had more to do with improved American-Indian relations after the fall of Indira Ghandi than with shows of naval force in the Indian Ocean.

The bipolar threat system of the Cold War has given way to a multipolar threat structure. Viewed from the North American continent, threats posed to American security assume different forms, arise from divergent national and subnational sources, and impact with varying degrees of strategic significance on proxies, clients, allies, and antagonists. Alignments and mutual commitments between superpowers and local forces and between local elements become increasingly unpredictable, volatile, and susceptible to rapid restructuring. The turnabouts in Lebanon, the African Horn, or the Indian Ocean, as already suggested, appear to be more the pattern of the 1980s than the rigidities of the Cold War model of the 1960s or the mixed pattern of change and stability of the 1970s.

Living with Greater Absolute Military Power and Greater Relative Impotence

Absolute military capabilities, measured by quantitative standards, are no longer, if they ever were, an adequate predictor of conflict outcomes. Domestic proponents of the use of American military power, like Dean Acheson, tended to equate the rising military strength of the United States with international security; alternatively, domestic critics attributed the lack of international peace to the use of American military power for narrow national purposes, usually associated with the preservation of a capitalistic economic system. Both exaggerated the amount of force available to the United States relative to all states and its utility in creating the conditions needed for American and international security.[23]

The military power of other states is also growing, and they are able to present various stand-off capabilities to check American military power. There is little quarrel with the proposition that American military power has never been greater in American history, yet its relative influence in regard to other states has declined since World War II. Nuclear parity with the Soviet Union is now accepted where superiority had been the previous standard. The development and growth of modern military establishments around the world (and the diffusion of military technology and weapons) afford many countries a greater measure of independent maneuver than before. States, like Cuba, which had been dismissed as important international actors create new and serious problems for European and American security interests in Africa. Vietnam similarly poses problems for Cambodia and for China. North Korean pressure on South Korea raises questions about Japanese security and spurs rearmament efforts.

India affords a particularly interesting case. As part of its purchase of Jaguar aircraft, it will supply spare parts to the United Kingdom for the British-French ground-support fighter and, under license, will produce the aircraft domestically. Its explosion of a nuclear device in 1974 also ended hopes that even American-Soviet accord would be sufficient to control the diffusion of nuclear technology and check proliferation. Threatened South African nuclear tests and repeated reports of Israeli possession of nuclear devices provide additional evidence of the erosion of barriers to go nuclear. Technical know-how and industrial capacity have spread around the globe. One can metaphorically speak of a Belgium emerging from India or a Norway from Pakistan or a Netherlands from China. These states no longer can be considered simply as the objects of superpower manipulations. Often the latter are subjects of their strategic moves. The absolute military power of the United States may well be said to have grown since World War II, but its relative power and diplomatic influence in directly determining outcomes would appear to have declined.

If military force has never been so pervasive, its utility has never been more questionable, given the mutual capacity of states and peoples to neutralize each other's capabilities.[24] For any one state, controlling a foreign population, the norm under colonialism, is not easy, and, where feasible, costs usually outrun benefits. There is no ready substitute in the immediate future for the nation-state as the basic political unit of organization around which military establishments will be built. Assertions of national self-determination have contained, if not always deterred, the imperial pretensions of the superpowers. The progressive decentralization and diffusion of military power, catalyzed by increased arms transfers and technological know-how from an enlarging pool of suppliers, materially bolster claims of national independence. International security can hardly be conceived apart from a system of nation-state alignment. The security role of the United Nations or any other international body is defined by the limits imposed by nation-state accord and discord and the variable distribution of military power that these changing alignments imply.

What is also apparent—more apparent today than ever before and very likely more so in the 1980s—is that military force is a necessary but not a sufficient condition for determining outcomes of interstate conflict in most significant areas of state interest. The concept of security is larger than military capabilities. It extends to all those factors of national power that maintain the economic and political institutions of a people. In such a world, security signifies access to world markets, monetary order, balance-of-payments equilibrium, economic growth, full employment, and the domestic political stability and continuity of regimes. Military force alone is not able to assure these critical state objectives that hitherto were dismissed as low politics, not critical instruments or ends of policy.

Recent superpower behavior suggests the play of this larger conception of security. However important military power is in defining superpower predominant positions, it cannot guarantee their socioeconomic well-being. Accent on common interests and on nonmilitary means of influence are parts of each state's global security strategies in an increasingly interdependent world. Thus decreased tensions and detente, marked by arms control accords, have created the conditions for Soviet access to western markets and technology. The Soviet Union works within a complicated calculus of conflicting values, strategies, and alignments to optimize regime aims. Soviet food consumption requirements are partly a function of long-term grain contracts with politically conservative Midwest farmers; modernization also depends in part on continued access to advanced technology, including computers, drilling equipment, and machine tools produced by American business. Similarly, the United States sees advantages in increased economic ties with the Soviet Union and in reducing the costs and risks of the nuclear arms race.

The Divisibility yet Globalization of American and International Security, Economic, and Political Regime Interests

The multiplication of threats, allies, and adversaries and the limitations of American military and nonmilitary power prompt reexamination of the assumption of the indivisibility of American and international security, economic, and political regime interests. The stiff requirements of meeting a test of indivisibility cannot, nor need not, be met by the direct application of American military power. The experience of the 1960s suggests that all armed conflicts, however lamentable, do not necessarily threaten the security interests of the United States; and when such proves to be the case, the impact is neither uniform nor always grave. American withdrawal from Southeast Asia and the abandonment of its self-assumed international security functions did not leave a vacuum to be filled by the Soviet Union. Rather, three contending forces, including Vietnam, Communist China, and the Soviet Union, are at loggerheads to establish their rule on the subcontinent. These conflicts, if contained, need not be viewed as a threat to American security interests. That hostilities in Southeast Asia disturb international security is unquestionable; that they will have an adverse impact on American security is less clear.

Regional balances neither accurately reflect the superpower competition nor are easily manipulable by one or the other—or even both—of the superpowers. The balance of military power in South and East Asia owes much to the independent weight of India, Pakistan, China, and Japan. By the same token, the Arab states and Israel in the Middle East and the Latin American states are increasingly capable of frustrating superpower intrusions or designs. Expectations of the Nixon and Carter administrations based on the hope of using Iran and Saudi Arabia for American purposes have outrun realization. The need for oil and good offices in dealing with Arab states has made the United States hostage to the demands of these regional states for military equipment and political concessions. The benefits of easy access to American weapons are not clear either for them or for the United States. The Shah was forced to abdicate partly because of the burden that his military purchases imposed on the Iranian nation. Nor has Saudi moderation either to ease an Egyptian-Israeli settlement or to hold down oil prices been as demonstrable as supporters of arms to Riyadh might have wished.

Superpower assistance may, of course, aid the realization of a regime's objectives and facilitate big power access to a region. Without Cuban troops, East German advisors, and Russian weapons, the aims of revolutionary regimes in Angola and Ethiopia would have very likely been frustrated. On the other hand, to assert that Soviet influence in these areas is permanent and irreversible is more problematic. The Egyptian and Indonesian experiences are not encouraging for Russian interests.

Efforts to extend American military power abroad, even in the name of international security, have often been more mischievous than helpful. So long as the United States appeared to be in the ascendancy, bent on imposing its will on the world, it united otherwise rival states that were uneasily bound together by their resistance to American expansionism, not by shared political values. Included in this loose coalition were Gaullist France, Communist China, the Soviet Union and a mixed assortment of developed and developing states. The pursuit of international security under American aegis, such as in Vietnam, had the ironic effect of weakening American security interests. The converse, of course, is not necessarily true: that international security can be achieved without American participation or that the United States, acting alone and solely with the means at its disposal, can assure it.

The hierarchies of power that may be identified in security affairs, based on capabilities, geographic position, population, political circumstances, and a host of other strategic factors, do not correspond to the sets of hierarchically arranged states in the sphere of global economic relations. Whereas Switzerland, Japan, or many of the OPEC nations would not be rated highly as military powers, they nevertheless exercise considerable economic influence. The United States no longer dominates or determines global monetary, energy, investment, or trade policy. As in the realm of military security, it can bargain and negotiate, but it cannot dictate the international regimes that will guide global economic activity. American economic aims are increasingly a function of the decisions of other states and people. The announcement from Abu Dhabi by OPEC states, in December 1978, to raise oil prices by approximately 15 percent had an impact on the rate of inflation in the United States comparable to the raising or lowering of interest rates by the Federal Reserve Board. It had greater force than that of President Carter's successive antiinflation directors, who have had to rely principally on persuasion, cajolery, and voluntary compliance with their guidelines.

The cross-cutting security and economic alignments implied by a progressively multipolar world cast doubt, finally, on alignments based solely on democratic regimes. While these might well be favored, singular combinations of free states still do not assure by themselves American security and socioeconomic aims. Security and economic interests of democratic states, relative to each other and to the outside world, are not so compatible nor are those of nondemocratic states and peoples so competing that a simple division of the world can be made on internal regime grounds or on their internal handling of human rights. The attractive, if ill-founded, matrix of the postwar period that equated American and international security, economic, and democratic regime interests obscured the real choices that had to be faced and those that still remain to be made, in optimizing American interests. The issue is not one of abandoning democratic values or of ransoming commitments to other peoples to narrow security and economic opportunities. It is more a problem of recognizing that democracy cannot be easily imposed from outside. It is not likely to take root, as in West Germany and Japan, unless there is a large enough body of people capable and committed to make self-government work. The assumption made by Wilson that democracy must be everywhere or it cannot be preserved anywhere exaggerates the attraction of the democratic ideal and its applicability and depreciates the importance of the cultural and socioeconomic predeterminants on which its survival depends.

Choices today concern as much the prevention of coalitions dominated by states opposed to American interests as the creation of groupings that actively promote them. American interests remain global, but power to support those interests is inherently limited and insufficient by itself for the task, however ardent or unified the will of the American people may be. Like other states before it, the United States must align with other states and bargain for the best deal it can get in the many domains where its interests are at stake. The pursuit of security under conditions of widening potential hostility and threat is, for the foreseeable future, without respite or end. It will continue to involve simultaneous and incessant initiative and reaction at different levels within each security domain, for changing stakes, over varying and overlapping time frames in which the United States will often be aligned uncomfortably with divergent states whose varied interests will be at once compatible, conflictual, and competitive with its own.

Divided Consensus and Effective Security Policy

Perhaps the most intractable of the assumptions on which American security policy must be based is internal. For with the end of the postwar rationale, policy-makers—and the American public—must make their decisions and fashion their security policies on the assumption of chronic and sustained domestic division. Cleavage is of course not new. The Madisonian model encourages it. More, not less, conflict of interests was sought in extending the boundaries of the nation to touch two oceans. What better way to protect minority and property rights against a dangerous majority than to flaw the majority by its own inner contradictions, split by religion, ideology, socioeconomic interests, and sectional differences. Federalism and a system of checks and balances reinforced these cleavages. Ruling majorities were separated over time with a House elected every 2 years; a president every 4; a Senate every 6 with one-third retiring every 2 years; and a federal bench appointed for life. To act legitimately a majority consensus had to be formed from a divided population by a majority capable of overcoming the obstacles of space (different geographic bases for elected officials) and time (differing lengths of elected governmental service).

The potential tension between pluralistic politics in a democratic setting and the pursuit of an effective foreign policy, a problem much lamented by deTocqueville, was avoided not only by the usually cited factors of geographic isolation, the balance of power in Europe, and the protection of the British Navy, but also by the wide acceptance of Washington's neutrality policy and his caution against domestic faction occasioned by alignments with foreign powers. After the War of 1812 and the removal of British forces from the frontier, consensus-building in the United States could proceed almost independent of concern for external security imperatives and the choices that they posed. The process of forging a consensus on domestic issues—slavery, the national bank, internal improvements, settlement of the West—was largely insulated from foreign influence and manipulation.

The pressure of a clear and present danger—Imperial and Nazi Germany and Soviet Russia after World War II—provided, respectively, the Wilson, Roosevelt, and Truman administrations the occasion to rationalize the projection of American military power abroad. These rationales were sufficiently compelling to overcome the socioeconomic, ideological, and institutional divisions of American politics and government. They provided an ideological buffer for the domestic political process. Consensus building could go on without squarely facing choices between alternative futures based on different and conflicting images of the world to be promoted by American power and the impacts of these worlds on the particular interests and perspectives of groups and individuals in the United States.

Outside influence now penetrates American pluralism. These multiply and deepen cleavages in a political system already divided against itself. Alignments on specific issues are not simply formed between loose coalitions of domestic players but are mixed groupings cutting across state frontiers either in support of or in opposition to governmental policies or responsible officials. Coalitions are variously composed and internally contradictory as interests that cluster around some issues may well be divided on others. In such a fluid and uncertain setting the formation of a ruling coalition capable of developing a coherent and consistent national security policy is increasingly difficult either conceptually (how can all the mismatched pieces be put together) or politically (how to govern groups pulling in different directions simultaneously). If the United States, conceived as a unitary nation, confronts a multiplicity of threats and an embarrassment of allies and adversaries abroad, the United States, viewed as a pluralistic and penetrated polity, presents a picture of uncertainty about its objectives and inconsistency and contradictions in implementing announced aims. The hesitancies attributed to President Carter are partly rooted in the pluralistic and penetrated politics of the American system. The divisions envisioned by the Madisonian model become entangled in the more complex and hazardous webbing of global politics. An issue, like the revision of the Panama Canal treaty, can be delayed and modified to suit the demands of a single Senator, motivated by interests that are only indirectly related to the merits of the issue at hand. The president's right to recognize Communist China and abrogate a security treaty with Taiwan can also be challenged in the courts by groups that heretofore had supported a strong presidency in foreign and security affairs and American involvement in Vietnam.

The immediate objective of these specialized interest groups is to capture a part of the institutional terrain on which the government battles will be fought. Much of this process is hidden from public view; some, as in Koreagate, is corrupting and insidious. Not only is the society then pitted against itself but the government as well. It is not simply a flaw in character that prompted Richard Nixon and his advisor for national security to be secretive in making their foreign policy moves. Secrecy no less marked President Carter's handling of the China question. Information and its manipulation, controlled, created, or dispensed by governmental agencies variously aligned with or opposed to presidential preferences, are indispensable arms in the internal struggle to control governmental policy. Overlaying the inherent congressional-presidential conflict over foreign and security policy, encouraged by the Constitution, is the ceaseless tug-of-war between the president and his own advisors and the established civilian bureaucracies, linked to their own domestic and foreign support structures. Congress and the president are then as much the objects as subjects of the ceaseless struggle. Governmental institutions and the behavior of elected and appointed officials and the policies they pursue risk being made prisoners of the pressures and constraints imposed upon them. It may not be correct, as it is often charged, that the government merely reacts to events abroad, which are seemingly beyond its will or capacity to influence. Even its responses may be programmed beforehand.

Conclusions

New international and domestic conditions pose a series of related dilemmas for the use and control of military force. These specifically include the multiplicity of threats to American security, a growing diffusion of military power, and a continuing need for a global security posture in the face of the growing relative military strength of other powers. These exterior conditions are superimposed on a divided domestic consensus over the means and ends of military power. Together these external and internal conditions must form the elemental assumptions of a new and evolving rationale to cope with the nation's security problems. Recognizing these new realities gives little comfort. It is hardly reassuring to recognize that security policy will have to be based on these conflicting and competing exterior and internal imperatives. The problem of choice in responding to outside threats is made more difficult, and the political divisions at home promise to be deepened, not relieved.

Notes

1. Academic and practicing strategists have been consistent in their concern for the problem raised by de Tocqueville about the inclination of democracies to sustain great enterprises abroad for long periods. See, for example, Walter Lippmann, *The Cold War* (New York: Harpers, 1947) and Robert E. Osgood, *Ideals and Self-Interest in America's Foreign Relations* (Chicago: University of Chicago, 1953). Presidents from Roosevelt on have adopted the view that the American people can be spurred to accept major foreign responsibilities, largely in opposition to Communist expansion.

2. Henry A. Kissinger, *The Troubled Partnership* (Garden City, N.Y.: Anchor, 1965). However subtle was Kissinger's analysis of western division, he accepted then prevailing notions of the implacable, ideological nature of the struggle with the Soviet Union; see ibid., pp. 187-222.

3. See, for example, Robert E. Osgood, *Limited War* (Chicago: University of Chicago, 1956), especially pp. 195-233. Also see Maxwell Taylor, *The Uncertain Trumpet* (New York: Harper, 1959).

4. These strategic relations are treated extensively in Alexander George and Richard Smoke, *Deterrence in American Foreign Policy* (New York: Columbia, 1974), especially pp. 503ff.

5. The rapid expansion of American military capabilities under the Kennedy administration is detailed in William W. Kaufmann, *The McNamara Strategy* (New York: Harper, 1964).

6. This optimistic theme of American ability to produce guns and butter is sounded repeatedly by President Kennedy. See U.S. Senate, Com-

mittee on Commerce, *The Speeches of Senator John F. Kennedy: Presidential Campaign of 1960*, passim.

7. American penetration became so great that many Europeans felt threatened by American economic imperialism. See Robert Gilpin, *France in the Age of the Scientific State* (Princeton, N.J.: Princeton University Press, 1968), especially pp. 39-76. See also Jean-Jacques Servan Schreiber, *The American Challenge*, trans. Ronald Steel (New York: Atheneum, 1967).

8. This is the burden of Huntington's argument, Samuel P. Huntington, *The Common Defense* (New York: Columbia, 1961). Huntington is less optimistic about American pluralistic politics in his *Soldier and the State* (Cambridge, Mass.: Belknap, 1957).

9. This is part of the message of President Lyndon Johnson's *The Vantage Point* (New York: Holt, Rinehart, and Winston, 1971).

10. For useful commentary on Wilson, see Osgood, *Ideals and Self-Interest* and Arthur Link, *Wilson the Diplomatist* (Chicago: Quadrangle Books, 1957).

11. See George and Smoke, *Deterrence in American Foreign Policy*.

12. For this insight, see Robert W. Tucker, *The Radical Left and American Foreign Policy* (Baltimore: John Hopkins, 1971).

13. The writings of Walter Lippmann stressed the need to balance power with guiding interest. See, *United States Foreign Policy: Shield of the Republic* (Boston: Little, Brown, 1943).

14. See Tucker, *Radical Left*, for a critique of the radical left position; also see Jerome Slater, "Is United States Foreign Policy 'Imperialist' or 'Imperial'?" *Political Science Quarterly* 91, no. 1 (Spring 1976):63-87. Joyce and Gabriel Kolko, *The Limits of Power* (New York: Harper and Row, 1972) and Harry Magdoff, *The Age of Imperialism: The Economics of U.S. Foreign Policy* (New York: Monthly Review Press, 1969) are representative of the radical left position.

15. The dean of this school of thought is William A. Williams. See, for example, *The Tragedy of American Diplomacy* rev. ed. (New York: Delta Books, 1962).

16. Contrast Kennan's views in the following: "X," "Sources of Soviet Conduct," *Foreign Affairs* 25, no. 4 (July 1947):566-582; *Realities of American Foreign Policy* (Princeton, N.J.: Princeton University Press, 1954); and *Russia, the Atom, and the West* (New York: Harper, 1958). A very useful overview of the conception of American power since World War II is Seyom Brown's *The Faces of Power* (New York: Columbia, 1968).

17. David Halberstam, *The Best and the Brightest* (New York: Random House, 1972) captures the spirit of almost boundless optimism about the possibilities of American power—if resolve is maintained.

18. Wilson's view is discussed at length in N. Gordon Levin, *Woodrow Wilson and World Politics: America's Response to War and Revolution* (New York: Oxford University Press, 1968).

19. Quoted in Norman A. Graebner, *Ideas and Diplomacy* (New York: Oxford, 1964), p. 733.

20. Roger Hilsman, *To Move a Nation* (Garden City, N.Y.: Doubleday, 1967).

21. Louis Hartz, *The Liberal Tradition in America* (New York: Harcourt, Brace, 1955).

22. This is the hope of Kennan's Mr. "X" article, "Sources of Soviet Conduct."

23. See notes 12, 14, and 16.

24. The distinction between the pervasiveness of military power and its utility is curiously absent in much of the expanding discussion about interdependence. This myopia leads to claims that because military force is allegedly less useful it is also less present in interstate bargaining. This initial confusion leads to still another, to the identification of the utility of military force with its physical employment. Following Hobbes on the causes of war, so narrow a conception of military force and its impact on international politics is tantamount to identifying the conditions that create rain with actual rain. See Joseph Nye and Robert Keohane, *Power and Interdependence* (Boston: Little, Brown, 1977) for a representative discussion of the prevailing optimism about the declining importance of military force in international relations.

3

Defining Strategic Value: Problems of Conceptual Clarity and Valid Threat Assessments

W. Harriet Critchley

Introduction

The changing international environment for U.S. strategic policy formation is causing progressive uncertainty about the adequacy of threat assessment concepts and procedures. The clear-cut distinctions and certitudes of the 1950s and early 1960s—when there was substantial consensus in the West as to who the enemy was, what the enemy wanted, and how the enemy would try to get it—have been blurred. Now the who, what, or how can vary from policy issue to policy issue. Growing interdependence across the conventional boundaries of first, second, and third world groupings of states in certain areas of international economic and political relations has contributed to the problem, as have the heightened sense of vulnerability arising from the recognition of interdependence and the reaction of seeking out means to provide some independence from, or at least insurance against, the restrictive effects of interdependence.[1]

The confusion that continues to attend the concept of détente—and, more importantly, the boundaries of detente—has added to the problem. The intrusion of an increasing range of domestic political considerations has caused further complexity for threat assessment procedures in the United States: in the 1970s, the analysis of options has to consider environmental impact, women's rights, and energy policy, for example, along with the more familiar effects of policy options on the balance of payments and the economies of certain localities. Meanwhile, the apparently relentless momentum of technological change raises such a myriad of further problems and potential solutions that it threatens to outstrip our ability to comprehend or forecast its effects.

As a consequence of these trends, which are likely to continue into the 1980s and 1990s, the consensus concerning the nature of strategic threats and the appropriate responses is weakening in the United States, not to mention the West. And, as a corollary, there have been deficiencies in even short-term predictions and evaluations of events that can present threats to vital interests or values. One thinks, for example, of the recent uncertainty within the U.S. government over the meaning of events in Angola and what

45

should constitute the appropriate U.S. reaction, or of the apparent inattention to growing political instability in Iran and what strategic problems might arise as a result of that specific kind of instability.

While these trends have caused uncertainty they have also exposed as delusions two elements of strategic thinking that are at the foundation of post-World War II U.S. strategic policy. The first misconception consists in the view that we in the United States are *maîtres chez nous*—masters of our own house—in the sense of making policy and acting on it, unhampered in any significant way by events in and policies of other states, especially the third world states. The second involves viewing the strategic world as an exclusively zero-sum game wherein any gain by "us" (the western industrialized states) is automatically a loss of equivalent magnitude for "them" (the Communist states) and vice versa. These precepts have been questionable from the beginning of the postwar era, and evidence of their inaccuracy has accrued over the past 30 years. For example, a tripolar relationship amongst the United States, the Soviet Union, and China has been emerging for over a decade. Due to a resurgence of conservative Moslem values in the Middle East, we are now witnessing the potential rise of a bloc of Islamic theocratic states—with quite a different set of interests than those of the United States, the Soviet Union, or China—in a crucially important oil supply region. In spite of the fundamental reordering of most U.S. strategic threat assessments that should be occurring as a result of the change from a bipolar to at least a tripolar strategic setting, *maîtres chez nous* and zero-sum-game thinking still influences current threat assessments.

Another set of circumstances has exposed a third delusion: until recently, strategic threat assessments were based largely on those human, material, and financial resources at the immediate disposal of a state or group of states. The foremost problem has been preventing the outbreak of a nuclear war. Major elements in the worst-case scenario of the problem include little or no advance warning of an impending attack and, if the conflict begins on the level of conventional (nonnuclear) weapons, the probability of rapid escalation to a tactical, then strategic, nuclear conflict. The problem and its context have exerted such a compelling influence on the thinking of policy-makers and planners that "strategic" and "nuclear" are often regarded as synonymous adjectives, whereas deterrence is thought to depend on those military forces and weapons that can be used immediately or transported to the battlefield within a matter of days. Little attention has been focused on potential levels of military and industrial mobilization that could be developed over a period of months under wartime conditions. It seems that the terrible novelty of nuclear weapons has caused a hiatus in the established practice of including in threat assessment the panoply of short-, medium-, and long-term elements of military power and potential. The hiatus seems to be ending as substantial evidence accumulates to down-grade

Defining Strategic Value

the likelihood that a spasm-type nuclear war is the prime threat to what are perceived as vital values and national interests. With a post-1945 world history of some 133 wars[2]—killing approximately 25 million people—in which not one nuclear weapon was used by accident or design and with the U.S. experience of active involvement in two of these wars—Korea and Vietnam—the balance is being restored to the meaning of strategic.[3] It can no longer be equated only with nuclear weapons of intercontinental range. The production and deployment of intermediate range SS-20 missiles by the Soviet Union have even caused some West European analysts to make a distinction between global strategic and Eurostrategic nuclear weapons and threats. The possibility that NATO may be involved in a conventional war lasting for at least several months encourages, once again, consideration of long-term factors such as mobilization potential and resupply capabilities of domestic industries. The OPEC oil embargo of 1973 and the effects of rising world petroleum prices have been a significant impetus for examining types of strategic threats that are not directly connected to preventing the outbreak of a nuclear war.

The delusions are ending, but if consideration of the broad range of factors is to be reintegrated successfully with the several trends already mentioned, some concepts central to strategic thinking will require adjustment. If the use and the control of military force are to match current and future real conditions, concepts governing the prediction and evaluation of events that may present threats to vital interests or values must be modified.

Strategic Value

Several of the events and trends mentioned have caused a resurgence of attention to the idea of strategic value. The press, the defense, and foreign policy literature are replete with references to the "strategic value," "strategic significance," and "changing strategic value" of nonrenewable natural resources, regions, and transportation links. Current examples are oil, the Persian Gulf, and NATO's sea lines of communication across the Atlantic. In the past, political leaders and defense planners have often regarded possession of, or control over, such particular things as affecting their own state's security and their security relations with allies and potential adversaries. Hence the idea of strategic value and its fundamental role in decisions to use and control military force.

With some modification, the concept of strategic value can, once again, serve to clarify and inform threat assessment. Conceptual modification can also allow for coherent analysis of the nature of strategic threat in a changing international environment that is characterized by issue-to-issue variability of allies and adversaries, cross-cutting interdependence, intrusion of an increasing range of domestic political considerations, rapid technological change, the existence of non-zero-sum-game situations, and longer term nonnuclear types of military, economic, and political conflicts.

The concept of strategic value presented here is based on three key elements: territory, worth, and access. Each element will be examined in turn before combining them into a new definition of the concept.

A wide range of things can have a strategic value. In addition to nonrenewable natural resources, regions, transportation and communications links, the range can be illustrated by the following list: renewable natural resources, various features of a state's economy, level of scientific and technological development, population size and skills, geographical features and relationships, stability and efficiency of the governing regime, as well as the size, equipment, organization, deployment, and training of armed forces. The one element common to all these examples and to their strategic value is that they are locational. More specifically, they are closely related to the idea of territory. Thus, territory—what is on it, in it, near it, or what has to traverse it—is posited as the first key element in assigning or assessing strategic value. In many cases, the boundaries of the piece of territory analyzed will coincide with some state's boundaries, but in other instances the piece of territory will be a smaller or larger region such as Sinkiang or the Middle East. Nor is the idea of territory necessarily confined to land masses. It can describe all or parts of bodies of water such as the North Atlantic or the Strait of Malacca.

If one thinks of what is on a piece of territory in a broad sense, one can encompass population, economic structure, level of scientific and technical development, degrees of social cohesiveness and political stability, and military forces. Those strategic value examples in a piece of territory include natural resources and such geographical features as topography, frontiers, waterways, and coastlines. Relational geographical features—particularly the proximity of allies, neutrals, and adversaries—come under the heading of what is near a piece of territory, whereas lines of communication and transportation constitute the kind of considerations involved in what has to traverse a piece of territory.

The second key element in strategic value concerns the assessment of the worth of what is in, on, near, or going through that piece of territory. The word *value* itself has obvious connotations of material or monetary worth. Indeed, some examples, such as the financial strength of a regime or natural resources, are predominantly and objectively economic in their worth. But value has other meanings that allow for the introduction of social, political, and ethical considerations. The latter affect perceptions of worth that are not necessarily economic or objective. The terms *vital values* and *value judgement* indicate these other perspectives, and, as an individual's or group's values can be positive or negative and are held with varying degrees of intensity, these considerations can have a significant effect on assessing even monetary or material worth. Changes in the worth or importance of a piece of territory—broadly construed to include economic, social, political, and ethical connotations of worth—can, in turn, affect assessments of strategic value.

The third key element is the degree to which access to those things that have a strategic value can affect a state's own security and its relations with allies and potential adversaries. In the past, political leaders sought possession of or at least substantial control over the various things regarded as the most valuable in a strategic sense. Although this is still a practicable goal in some instances—leadership control over their own state's military forces, for example—the images conjured up by possession and control are too narrow to allow for acknowledgement of those instances where there is increasing interdependence among states or groups of states.

Access—the ability to enter, to acquire, to influence or as a description of a means of entering, acquiring, or influencing—allows for a more appropriate continuum of describing the international strategic environment. Access can be linked to the idea of territory and the strategic value of things by thinking of it in terms of the ability to enter a piece of (some other state's) territory, to acquire strategically valuable things from that territory, or to influence the disposition and use of strategically valuable things from that territory. Three types of access can be distinguished: exclusive, or unilateral, access signifies virtual possession of the piece of territory; bilateral access introduces the consideration of how the identity of those with access—ally, neutral, potential adversary— can affect a state's own security and the security relations with other states; multilateral access highlights both the fact that degrees of shared access indicate varying degrees of control or lack of control and encourages a focus on the mix of allies, neutrals, and potential adversaries who have access to the piece of territory. This method of distinguishing types of access provides the analytical continuum for an assessment of strategic value in all its current and future manifestations. Types of access and degrees of shared access are independent of worth, and thus access itself is a distinct element in the concept of strategic value. Changes in type and degree of access as well as changes in worth can affect strategic value in complementary or conflicting ways.

The three key elements of territory, worth, and access can be combined to yield the following definition:

> The strategic value of a piece of territory is a function of its worth and the effect that access to it has both on a potential adversary's capability to make various future moves and on our capacity to deter or resist those adversarial moves regarded as threatening to state security or vital interests.

Although this formulation of the concept owes much to Glenn Snyder's definition, it has been modified to reflect the influence of interdependence, the existence of non-zero-sum-game situations, medium- and long-term calculations, and the variable identity of allies and adversaries depending on the policy issue at hand.[4]

If the concept is to have analytical utility, dimensions for ascertaining worth and access must be chosen to allow for a discussion of the strategic value of any discrete item and make comparisons across time, between territories, or among items. The dimensions of access have been suggested in the discussion of that element in strategic value: the types of access and the identities of those with access. The former includes three degrees of shared access—unilateral, bilateral, and multilateral, and the latter includes at least four distinct identities: one's own state (self), an ally, a neutral or nonaligned state, an adversary. For the bilateral and multilateral types, where the identities are plural, self identity is collapsed into allies or some mixture that is designated as multiform. When, for the sake of concise illustration, analysis is confined to only two types of access, the combination of dimensions yields the matrix of access shown in figure 3-1. In figure 3-1 there are eight forms of access.[5] All possible access situations have been distinguished for an assessment of strategic value. At the same time all possible changes in access can be differentiated for the purposes of comparison of the strategic value of an item across time, of the strategic value of the same item across different territories, or of the strategic value of different items in the same territory.

As defined, access is related to strategic value in its effect on a potential adversary's capability and on our capacity. Therefore two views of any form of access or change in access must be considered.[6] In keeping with the possibility of non-zero-sum-game situations, it should be noted that the two views can be diametrically opposed, differentially opposed, or complementary. That is, a given access situation or a change in access may have a large positive effect on a potential adversary's capability and an equally large negative effect on our capacity (or vice versa) as indicated by the classic zero-sum game. But the definition of the concept also allows for the possibility of net positive or negative effect—when positive and negative are of different orders—negligible effect, and even the same positive or negative effect in both views. As strategic value is also a function of worth, concrete examples of the analytical utility of the distinctions in forms of access can be discussed only after the dimensions of worth have been isolated, examined, and then combined with the dimensions of access.

Two dimensions seem most useful for ascertaining worth: the scarcity of the item and the degree of dependence on the item. Something that is plentiful—low scarcity—and contributes little or nothing to defense capability in the short, medium, and long term—low degree of dependence—will obviously have a much lower strategic value than will something that is very scarce and on which there is a high degree of dependence. These are limiting cases, however, and much of the analyst's

Defining Strategic Value

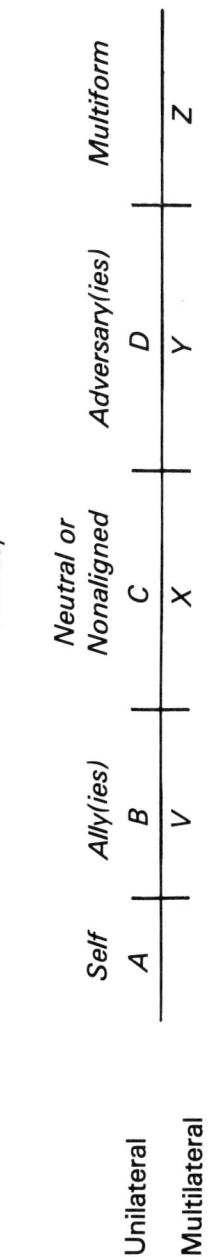

Figure 3-1. Forms of Access.

attention will focus on the intermediate range. Thus, given the characteristics of the discrete item, the analyst may wish to distinguish a different number of degrees of scarcity and of degrees of dependence. In assigning a particular degree of scarcity and dependence to an item, one would include such considerations as its type and quality, current and future levels of demand for it, the availability of substitutes and other sources of supply.[7] In this manner, a matrix of worth can be constructed and used to assess strategic value even in cases where quantification is not possible or advisable, as the following example shows.

The example involves a nonrenewable natural resource—a fossil fuel. The explanation will be simplified by assuming only two degrees of scarcity (low, high) and the following four degrees of dependence:

D_1 = Geological formations, or other physical evidence, suggest the probable presence of the fossil fuel in a specific piece of territory.

D_2 = Significant amounts of the fossil fuel have been discovered in the territory.

D_3 = All technical, economic, and ecological obstacles to extraction of the fossil fuel have been overcome, and fuel from that territory is available for delivery to domestic markets. Minor amounts of fuel may already be reaching domestic markets.

D_4 = Significant amounts of the fuel are being delivered, and sectors of the domestic economy depend heavily on that source of supply.

These degrees of scarcity and dependence yield the matrix of worth shown in figure 3-2. Figure 3-2 contains eight designations of worth. There is a sequence of increasing worth along the rows of the matrix but not necessarily

	Degree of Dependence			
Scarcity	D_1	D_2	D_3	D_4
Low	W_e	W_f	W_g	W_h
High	W_m	W_n	W_o	W_p

Figure 3-2. Designations of Worth (W).

Defining Strategic Value

along columns. Nor is W_h lower than W_m. The discontinuity between the two sequences of subscript letters emphasizes these features of the matrix. The evaluation of changes in worth along or across columns depends on the characteristics of the item, the form of access to the territory, the effect of access on a potential adversary's capability and on our capacity.

However, this matrix can be used to assess the worth of the fossil fuel in that territory to a particular state in terms of the state's fuel scarcity and its dependence on that source of supply. Given a knowledge of trends in scarcity and dependence on that fuel, a time factor can be added to allow for prediction of changes over time. The matrix can also be used for comparing the worth of the territory containing the fuel to other states in which there are differing degrees of fuel scarcity or of dependence on that type of fuel. This allows for a comparison of worth across states. When considering worth as a component of strategic value, two views must be considered: our view of the worth of the item and the potential adversary's view of its worth. As with the case of access, the matrix makes no advance assumptions on the relationship between the two views. They can be diametrically opposed, differentially opposed, or complementary.

Now that the three key elements of strategic value and the dimensions of access and worth have been explored, the findings can be combined to illustrate the analytical utility of the concept. If the simplified examples of the forms of access (figure 3-1) and designations of worth for fossil fuel (figure 3-2) are retained, a matrix of strategic value can be constructed as an aid to thought and explanation. The combination of eight forms of access and eight designations of worth yields a 64-cell matrix of strategic value. A part of the matrix is produced in figure 3-3.

Several features of this matrix have been schematically or symbolically expressed to emphasize the limitations of sequence and the types of discontinuity.[8] This matrix for the strategic value of fossil fuel can be used as an analytical framework to examine a set of cases concerning the strategic value of oil. The set includes an analysis of the value to the United States of Iranian, Saudi Arabian, and Chinese oil. In each case, as the oil is located on the territory of a specific state, the strategic value of oil in Iran, Saudi Arabia, and China is the focus of the analysis. Since the United States imports approximately 46 percent of its oil supply, we can safely assume that imported oil is in the high-scarcity category.[9] There is variation in the other dimension of worth—degree of dependence. Iranian oil accounts for approximately 6 percent of U.S. oil imports, while Saudi Arabia accounts for 16 percent.[10] There is no import of Chinese oil, and most of China's potentially huge oil reserves are indicated only by geological formations. In terms of the U.S. dependence on oil from these territories, Iran is D_3, Saudi Arabia is D_4, and China is D_1. When scarcity and dependence are combined, figure 3-2 indicates the following designations of worth: Iran is Wo, Saudi Arabia is Wp, and China is Wm.

	W_e	W_f	W_g	W_h		W_m	W_n	W_o	W_p
A	SV_{r_1}	SV_{r_2}	SV_{r_3}	SV_{r_4}		SV_{k_1}	SV_{k_2}	SV_{k_3}	SV_{k_4}
B	SV_{t_1}	SV_{t_2}	SV_{t_4}	SV_{t_4}		SV_{s_1}	SV_{s_2}	SV_{s_3}	SV_{s_4}
C	SV_{i_1}	SV_{i_2}	SV_{i_3}	SV_{i_4}		SV_{u_1}	SV_{u_2}	SV_{u_3}	SV_{u_4}
D	SV_{q_1}	SV_{q_2}	SV_{q_3}	SV_{q_4}		SV_{i_1}	SV_{i_2}	SV_{i_3}	SV_{i_4}
V	SV_{ϑ_1}	SV_{ϑ_2}	SV_{ϑ_3}	SV_{ϑ_4}		SV_{π_1}	SV_{π_2}	SV_{π_3}	SV_{π_4}
X	SV_{ϕ_1}	SV_{ϕ_2}	SV_{ϕ_3}	SV_{ϕ_4}		SV_{β_1}	SV_{β_2}	SV_{β_3}	SV_{β_4}
Y	SV_{α_1}	SV_{α_2}	SV_{α_3}	SV_{α_4}		SV_{λ_1}	SV_{λ_2}	SV_{λ_3}	SV_{λ_4}
Z	SV_{μ_1}	SV_{μ_2}	SV_{μ_3}	SV_{μ_4}		SV_{δ_1}	SV_{δ_2}	SV_{δ_3}	SV_{δ_4}

Worth

Figure 3-3. Strategic Value (SV).

Defining Strategic Value

The first dimension of access is type. Access to Iranian and Saudi Arabian oil is multilateral, while access to Chinese oil is unilateral. In terms of the identity of those with access to the oil in these territories, both Iran and Saudi Arabia are in the multiform category, since allies (including the United States), nonaligned states, and, in the case of Iran, an adversary (the Soviet Union) have access. Only China, a potential adversary, has access to Chinese oil.[11] When type and identity are combined, figure 3-1 indicates the following forms of access: Iran is Z, Saudi Arabia is Z, China is D.

When access and worth are combined, with reference to figure 3-3, the oil in each territory has a different strategic value for the United States—namely SV_{δ_3} for Iran, SV_{δ_4} for Saudi Arabia and SV_{j_1} for China. The meaning of these designations and an assessment of their comparative strategic value to the United States is deduced from, to use the strategic value definition, the effect that access to the territory has both on a potential adversary's capability to make various future moves and on our capacity to deter or resist those adversarial moves that are regarded as threatening to state security or vital interests.

If the Soviet Union is chosen as the potential adversary, the effect of access to Iranian oil on the USSR's capability to make various future moves is slight or negligible—since the volume of imported Iranian oil is so small in comparison to the Soviet Union's domestic production. The effect of access on U.S. capacity to deter or resist adversarial moves is slight. Thus SV_{δ_3} represents the slight or marginal value of Iran, in terms of oil, to the United States. The effect of access to Saudi Arabian oil on the USSR's capability to make various future moves is also negligible—the USSR imports none—but the effect of access on U.S. capacity to resist adversarial moves is very large. Thus SV_{δ_4} represents the very high strategic value of Saudi Arabia, in terms of its oil, to the United States. The effect of access to Chinese oil on both Soviet capability and U.S. capacity is negligible: SV_{j_1} represents the quite negligible strategic value of China, in terms of its oil, to the United States.

A comparative assessment of strategic value to the United States yields the result that SV_{δ_4} is much higher than SV_{δ_3} which, in turn is higher than SV_{j_1}. In terms of oil, Saudi Arabia is much more important to the United States than Iran or China.[12] This conclusion may be counterbalanced, overridden, or reinforced by the strategic value of other things in each of those territories—military forces, or proximity to allies and adversaries, for example. Separate evaluations of worth and access of each item are required before the overall strategic value of each territory can be assessed.

Changing Strategic Value

The foregoing analysis automatically raises several questions. How would a regime change or a change in foreign policy alignment in Iran or Saudi Arabia affect the strategic value of their oil to the United States? If large quantities of oil are discovered and developed in China (onshore and offshore) is export likely, what are the likely export markets, and how will the various possibilities affect the strategic value of their oil to the United States? These kinds of questions are specific examples of two central considerations of strategic analysis and threat assessment that can be couched in the terms of the strategic value definition. What effect will a change in access and/or worth have on current strategic value? What is the likelihood of such changes? In a fundamental way, the answers to these questions provide the context for decisions to use, threaten to use, or control military force.

Changes in worth can occur in the scarcity of dimension, the degree of dependence dimension, or some combination of both. That is, an item may become more or less scarce, and the degree of dependence on it may increase or decrease. One can also distinguish changes of magnitude and rate of change. When thinking of worth as a component of strategic value, however, several general observations seem to apply in all cases—regardless of which specific item is the focus of analysis. As noted earlier, items that are plentiful—low scarcity—and that contribute little or nothing to military power and potential (broadly construed)—low degree of dependence—have a minimal strategic value. Similarly, items that have a high scarcity and contribute significantly to military power and potential—high degree of dependence—have a high strategic value. The example of the strategic value of oil in China, however, suggests that the strategic value is minimal for items that have a high scarcity and a low degree of dependence. Finally, the strategic value is also minimal even for items for which there is a low scarcity and a high degree of dependence.

When the two dimensions of worth are combined, the figure 3-4 represents the four limiting cases. Items that can be categorized in quadrants 1, 2, or 3 have a minimal strategic value, whereas items in quadrant 4 have a high strategic value.[13] Changes in the worth of an item that move it within each of the first three quadrants or between them have little or no effect on assessment of strategic value. On the other hand, changes in the worth of an item that cause it to be recategorized into quadrant 4 or out of that quadrant would seem to represent a major increase or decrease in strategic value of the item. It is this kind of change in worth—particularly in the case of a major increase, or a recategorization into quadrant 4—that is the impetus for legitimate questions about using, threatening to use, or controlling military force. Depending on the number of degrees of scarcity and of dependence used for assessing the worth of items, there will be smaller or larger groups of intermediate cases where statements on strategic value are tied to the nature of the specific item. Generally, as the worth of items in intermediate categories increases both in

Defining Strategic Value   57

```
                      Degree of Dependence
                      Low              High

S
c                      1                2
a      Low
r
c
i      High
t                      3                4
y
```

Figure 3-4. Limiting Case of Worth as a Component of Strategic Value.

scarcity and degree of dependence, their strategic value increases. In terms of the example used earlier, changes in worth to a level of Wp (figure 3-2) and potential changes to this level over time should, therefore, be the focus of analysis and policy-making.[14] Further exploration of aspects of changing strategic value will focus on changes to this worth level.

Changes in access can occur in the type dimension, the identity dimension, or a combination of both. In theory, any change in access is possible, and the effects of all such changes in access to an item leads to a formidably large number of possible changes in strategic value. If attention is focused on changes in access that concern items already in, or moving toward, a worth of Wp, and if analysis is confined to the eight forms of access presented earlier (figure 3-1), there are 59 possible changes in strategic value. This number of changes is sufficiently manageable for discussing certain general patterns in the relationship between changes in access and changing strategic value.

When worth is held constant, a change in strategic value (CSV) is the effect of change in access (to a piece of territory) on a potential adversary's capability to make various future moves (SV_i) and on our capacity to deter or resist those adversarial moves (SV_{ii}). In other words, the effect is cumulative and can be thought of symbolically as

$$CSV = SV_i \text{ and } SV_{ii}.$$

If we think of change as being large, medium, slight, or negligible, the change in strategic value will be largest when a change in access confers a large advantage, or increase, in one of the SVs and a large disadvantage, or decrease, in the other. In the case where SV_i increases and SV_{ii} decreases, the change in strategic value is large and in the potential adversary's favor. In the opposite case, the change is of the same order, but in our favor. Using the restricted set of possible changes in access, a *CSV* of the largest order occurs in the adversary's favor when access to an item of the highest worth changes from unilateral self (*A*) or unilateral ally (*B*) to unilateral adversary (*D*).[15] A *CSV* of similar magnitude occurs in our favor when access changes from *D* to *A*. Large *CSV*s of a slightly lesser magnitude occur in the adversary's favor when access changes from several multilateral types to unilateral adversary (*V,X,Z* to *D*), from several unilateral and multilateral types to multilateral adversaries (*A,B,C,V,X* to *Y*), or from unilateral neutral (*C*) to *D*. Large *CSV*s of similar magnitudes occur in our favor when access changes from various mixtures of unilateral and multilateral types to unilateral self (*C,X,Y,Z* to *A*) or to unilateral ally (*D,Y,Z* to *B*) or to multilateral allies (*C,D,Y* to *V*).[16] These assessments are fairly straightforward and, although couched in different terminology, may be familiar to readers who are concerned with threat assessment.

What is far more interesting, however, and stems from the concepts and dimensions introduced in this chapter, are the changes in access that result in slight or negligible *CSV*s even though the worth of the item is at, or about to change to, the highest level. This includes at least 17 of the 59 cases, or some 29 percent. General examples of slight *CSV*s include: changes in access from unilateral self to unilateral ally or multilateral allies (adversary's favor); unilateral ally to unilateral self and unilateral adversary to multilateral adversaries (our favor). Examples of negligible *CSV*s include: changes in access within identity categories (*C* to *C*, *B* to *B*, *D* to *D*); certain changes to or from the multiform category (*C,X* to *Z*, and the reverse); and any change from unilateral neutral to multilateral neutral, or the reverse.

There still remain some 71 percent of the cases where possible changes in access to a high-worth item yield high or medium *CSV*s. It should be noted, however, that when all possible combinations of changes in worth and access are considered, the proportion that results in minimal changes in strategic value has increased. In addition to changes within or between quadrants 1, 2, and 3 (figure 3-4), further analysis has shown that some changes into or out of quadrant 4 have little or no effect on assessments of strategic value. This conclusion grows in significance when we turn to a consideration of what changes in access are most likely in the international strategic environment of the 1970s and 1980s.

Items that are increasing in scarcity and degree of dependence in the present and near future, and are thereby the focus of greatest concern in terms of the threats that they may present to vital values and interests, include some renewable and nonrenewable natural resources as well as certain transportation and communication links. Many of these items are located in

Defining Strategic Value

or near the territories of neutral and nonaligned states. In some instances they are on the periphery—offshore, or near frontiers—of states that are allies and potential adversaries. The combination of high worth and vulnerable location result in the addition of other items to the list of strategic concerns, such as the financial strength, the political stability, and the administrative efficiency of the governing regimes in these states. Regardless of whether we focus on food, energy supplies, the tanker route around the Cape of Good Hope, the financial strength of Mexico or Great Britain, or the political stability of Saudi Arabia, there has been a clear trend toward multilateral access. It is equally clear that the changes have been in the direction of growing multiform access, which includes a large neutral or nonaligned component. In general, as these trends continue, they represent the most likely changes in access in the future. The combination of the two trends causes concern—in the United States and elsewhere—about the security of supply of high worth items. But the latter phrase is quite misleading. The real concern is security of access, and lingering behind the concern is the idea that a reversion to increased unilateral control will provide more security or at least be less dangerous.

Both the concern and the idea behind it should be questioned seriously. Strategic value, the concepts and dimensions put forward in this chapter, can provide the key for such an examination. Large changes in strategic value are the most dangerous in the sense that we will feel the greatest pressure to prevent the occurrence of large *CSV*s in the adversary's favor, while the potential adversary will feel the greatest pressure to prevent the occurrence of large *CSV*s in our favor. As noted earlier, many of the large *CSV*s occur when the change in access is from several multilateral types to unilateral self, ally, or adversary.[17] On the other hand, slight or negligible changes in strategic value are the least dangerous. Many of these occur when the change of access is within identity categories, when the change is from unilateral to multilateral in the same identity category, or in some changes to multiform access.[18] In short, at the theoretical level of abstraction pursued here, many of the most likely changes in access are less dangerous than the proposed cure of reversion to increased unilateral control.[19]

Impact on Security Relations

Two authorities writing on the topic of energy problems have suggested that "access to raw material generally, and to energy in particular, is certain to be a major preoccupation in international political relations."[20] This essay makes a stronger suggestion: the preoccupation with access is applicable to a much broader range of things and therefore will be of central concern when evaluating events and trends in the international strategic environment.

Further, the quest for security of access, to decrease vulnerability, will remain the primary focus of threat assessment and security policy.

Since absolute security of access is a fallacy, the cause for anxiety is the problem of ascertaining sufficient relative security of access. As the scarcity of an item increases, for example, and the degree of dependence on it is high, there will be a consequent pressure to increased competition for access to that item. In this context, changes in access to items that have a high strategic value may be regarded as strategic threats and can thereby exacerbate current conflicts or lead to new conflicts. Such changes in access—impending or actual—tend to stampede the leaders of states into taking or threatening military action as a means of preventing or promoting the change. An assessment of whether or not the change in access is really a strategic threat can be derived from a careful analysis of the magnitude and rate of the changing strategic value of the item in question. The analysis will clarify exactly what or how much is at stake for the CSV of the item. On a theoretical level, we have seen that many of the most likely changes in access to items of high strategic worth result in slight or negligible CSVs. Taking or threatening military action in such situations are overreactions in relation to how much is at stake. Furthermore, neither response is necessarily the most effective means of preventing or promoting the change. Although changes in access to high worth items may lead to competition and conflict, they may also encourage new areas and forms of cooperation. We should not overlook the possibility that relative security of access can be achieved or maintained by encouraging cooperation as well as by winning a competition.

The large variety of possible means by which changes in access are prevented or effected can be grouped into several general alternatives if we think about what is at issue in access terms. Any effort to prevent such a change from occurring is, more accurately, an effort to deny access to some other state or group of states—regardless of whether or not we have access to begin with. In addition to denial, there are four other ways of preventing or promoting changes in access: it can be acquired, increased, maintained, or decreased. Together, these alternatives represent the five basic policy options that are applicable as methods of initiating or responding to changes in access. Although the entire range may not be available in all situations, at least two will be, and each option can be implemented by a variety of means.

As strategic threats on the part of the USSR are foremost in U.S. threat assessment and security policy considerations, two simplified examples of such threats will be used to illustrate this further development of the concept of strategic value.

In the first case, a piece of territory—an ally's colony—is regarded by the United States as having a worth of Wp due to the territory's proximity to both an adversary (I) and a major sea transportation route. As decolonization occurs, the United States fears that the postcolonial governing regime

Defining Strategic Value

will be an adversary (*II*): the change in access is perceived as unilateral ally (*B*) to unilateral adversary (*D*); the *CSV* is high and in adversary *I*'s favor.[21] The U.S. attempts to prevent the *B* ⟶ *D* change by using military force to install an allied postcolonial regime and thereby effect a *B* ⟶ *B* change (negligible *CSV*). The means of implementing the denial policy is a costly failure, and the feared *B* ⟶ *D* change occurs. At the outset, there was an alternate policy available: by maintaining, or increasing, access to the postcolonial regime and supporting the regime's nationalism, the U.S. could have effected a change from unilateral ally (*B*) to unilateral-nonaligned (*C*). The *CSV* for this alternative is slight and in adversary *I*'s favor, but the means of implementing the alternative policy (foreign aid or military aid, for example) is much less costly and far more likely to be a success from the U.S. standpoint. This case is not hypothetical: the territory is Vietnam, the ally is France, and the alternative policy has been used, with great success, with respect to Yugoslavia and its nationalist communist regime.

In the second case, a piece of territory is regarded as having a moderately high worth due to its proximity to the Soviet Union. With little advance warning, the internal governing regime changes from unilateral neutral (*C*) to unilateral adversary (*D*) and becomes an ally of the Soviet Union. Thus, there has been a further change in access to multilateral adversaries (*Y*). When these changes in access occur, the worth of the territory increases to *Wp* in both the U.S. and USSR views. The *CSV* is therefore high and in the Soviet Union's favor. In this case the United States does not have a denial option available—the change has already taken place. Other alternatives are possible. By encouraging other states—especially the nonaligned and U.S. allies—to acquire access, a change from multilateral adversaries (*Y*) to multiform (*Z*) can be promoted. Such a change has a differential effect that yields a high advantage in the favor of the United States.[22] The second case also is not hypothetical—the territory is Afghanistan.

The two examples chosen involve changes in worth within or into quadrant 4 (figure 3-4) and changes in access that result in high *CSV*s in the adversary's favor. Both examples are regarded as strategic threats of the kind that often involve the use of military force. In one case military force was used to no effect, in the other case even the threat to use military force is not an option available to the United States. These examples were not chosen to argue against the advisability of using or threatening to use military force in all situations where a strategic threat of high order is perceived. The purpose is to illustrate the analytical utility of the concept of strategic value, the way in which the concept helps to clarify threat assessment, and the way in which the concept helps to inform the choice among available security policy options.

Strategic value and changing strategic value can be used to analyze other aspects of security relations as well. The following questions give some indication of the range of issues that can be examined with respect to one item—a natural resource. How does access, or a change in access, to a natural resource in a geographic region affect security in the sense of relieving our dependence on an adversarial supply source or on a potential interdictor of supply? Does the change allow for relieving allies' dependence on that source of supply and therefore affect their security relations within the alliance and with potential adversaries? How do the differences in various political perceptions of changing access to a natural resource affect security relations among states in that region? What is the desirability, in terms of indirect military advantage, of denying access to potential adversaries or of offering access to allies? Similar questions can be raised and analyzed with respect to their impact on security relations with neutral nonaligned states. All these questions and more can be raised about a wide variety of items other than natural resources.

For the purposes of concise presentation, a highly simplified exposition of the concept and dimensions of strategic value has been given here. Ascertaining strategic value and changing strategic value according to worth and access are, in reality, quite complex undertakings. The concept is advanced not for its apparent simplicity but for the clarity it brings to an understanding of threat assessment and the use or control of military force in the current international strategic environment. As some of the illustrations imply, such clarification does alter the kinds of threat assessments made—now and in the recent past—by the United States. It also provides a more realistic and practical approach for making choices among available policy options and the available means of implementing security policy.

Notes

1. These problems are treated at length in the following two sources: Robert O. Keohane and Joseph S. Nye, *Power and Interdependence* (Boston: Little, Brown, 1977). Klaus Knorr and Frank N. Trager, eds., *Economic Issues and National Security* (Lawrence, Kan.: Regents Press of Kansas, 1977).

2. A statement by Dr. Frank Barnaby, director, Stockholm International Peace Research Institute as quoted in Murray Thomson, *A Time to Disarm* (Montreal: Harvest House, 1978), p. 17.

3. I. Kende "Dynamics of War, of Arms Trade and of Military Expenditure in the Third World 1945-1976," *Research on Peace and Violence* 7, no. 2, 60.

4. Glenn H. Snyder *Deterrence and Defense: Toward a Theory of National Security* (Princeton, N.J.: Princeton University Press, 1961), p. 33.

Defining Strategic Value

Snyder's definition reads as follows: "The strategic value of a particular piece of territory is the effect which its loss would have on increasing the enemy's *capability* to make various future moves, and on decreasing our own capacity to resist further attacks" (emphasis in the original).

5. In the multilateral case, V can include self or only allies; X includes only neutrals and nonaligned; Y includes only adversaries; Z represents any mixture of the previous categories (including self) with the stipulation that at least two different categories of identity are included. Where appropriate, access by multinational corporations can be included in Z.

6. In the case where the analyst is endeavoring to assess another state's view of the strategic value of an item, the other state is "self," and the other state's perception of allies, neutrals and adversaries is used in the identity categories. Depending on the security relationship, the analyst's own state becomes an ally, neutral or adversary.

7. Although these factors have obvious economic connotations, one can think of non-economic items in such terms. Let us say, for example, that the analyst wishes to assess the scarcity of and degree of dependence on a particular strait which is part of an ocean-going transportation link and is used by military and commercial vessels. The "type" of the item can refer to whether the strait is in a state's internal waters, or is an international strait. The "quality" of the item would lead to an analysis of the level of usage by the military and commercial vessels of "self", allies, neutrals and adversaries. "Future demand" leads to an analysis of trading and deployment patterns, security relationships involved in the transportation link and future levels of demand for the most significant commodities that are transported through the strait. The availability of substitutes and other sources of supply would include the availability of other ocean-going routes as well as land or air routes where appropriate.

8. The double lines emphasize discontinuity, or the distinction, between unilateral and multilateral access on the one hand, low scarcity and high scarcity on the other. The access distinction is reinforced by the use of latin and greek alphabet subscripts, whereas the scarcity discontinuity is reinforced by the nonsequential ordering of subscripts in both alphabets. As the only natural sequence of increasing strategic value is related to degree of dependence, this has been reinforced by the use of sequential numerical subscripts.

9. *B.P. Statistical Review of the World Oil Industry, 1977* (London, 1978), pp. 8, 10.

10. *Oil and Gas Journal* 75, no. 30 (25 July 1977):141.

11. All statements concerning Iran, Saudi Arabia, and China in this and the following four paragraphs are made on the basis of the situation in September 1978.

12. If the same cases are analyzed from the perspective of strategic value of the oil to Israel and the potential adversaries are specified Arab states, the conclusions and the comparative assessment would be quite different.

13. As the access component has yet to be brought into the discussion, it should be noted that the assessment of scarcity and dependence are from the perspective of the analyst or policy-maker in the state concerned. Oil, for example, is plentiful in Kuwait but has a high scarcity in Japan. Therefore the strategic value of oil for Japan in worth terms alone, will come under the quadrant 4 limiting case, where as the strategic value of oil for Kuwait will belong in an intermediate range between quadrants 1 and 2.

14. Although the Wp level of worth has a fossil-fuel oriented definition for the degree of dependence dimension in the earlier example, for the purpose of this and subsequent discussion, it represents the high scarcity of and maximum degree of dependence—appropriately defined on any item.

15. All letter designations for access type and identity are derived from figure 3-2. In addition to those specified, designations are: C = unilateral neutral or nonaligned; V = multilateral allies; X = multilateral neutral or nonaligned; Y = multilateral adversaries; Z = multiform.

16. A table of the 59 changes in access can be constructed as an aid for making such assessments. If a plus sign is used to designate an advantage (or increase) in capability to make, resist or deter various future moves and a minus sign corresponds to a disadvantage, examples of cases for the table are as follows:

Access Change	Effect on		CSV
	SV_i	SV_{ii}	
$D \rightarrow A$	− (high)	+ (high)	highest in own favor
$A \rightarrow D$	+ (high)	− (high)	highest in adversary's favor
$A \rightarrow V$	+ (slight)	− (slight)	slight in adversary's favor
$Y \rightarrow Z$	− (slight)	+ (high)	high in own favor
$Z \rightarrow X$	− (slight)	− (slight)	negligible

It should be noted that advantages and disadvantages of the same order for SV_i and SV_{ii} do not cancel each other out. Advantages and disadvantages of different orders have a differential effect on the cumulative CSV, whereas advantages of the same order for each, or disadvantages of the same order for each result in negligible CSVs. As a general operating principle, it is assumed that in any change from any unilateral category to any multilateral category the possibility of exploiting divisions within the multilateral group by either the potential adversary or us is a factor in assessing changing strategic value. A second assumption concerns identities: the designation of ally, neutral, or adversary is issue specific, and enough information is available to be certain of the choice in designation.

17. See p. 58.
18. See p. 58.
19. More precise conclusions depend on an analysis of the specific items and location in question, but it should be noted that the concepts and dimensions of strategic value, worth, and access provide the analytical tools for such an undertaking.
20. Melvin A. Conant and Fern Racine Gold, *The Geopolitics of Energy* (Boulder, Colo.: Westview Press, 1978), p. 3.
21. See note 16.
22. See note 16.

Part II
Selected Problems in American Security Policy and Policy-Making

4 Arms, Arms Control, and Alliance Relationships: The Case of the Cruise Missile

J.I. Coffey

Introduction

At times it seems that the North Atlantic Treaty Organization (NATO) lurches from crisis to crisis, its gait much like that of a tortoise on an uneven beach trying to return to the comforting tranquility of the ocean. Some of the crises that confronted NATO in the past, like that over the European Defense Force of 1954, were largely political while others, like the bitter debate on the doctrine of flexible response (which stimulated the withdrawal of France from the integrated command structure) were more markedly military in nature. NATO may now, however, be confronting a new crisis, with both political and military overtones, that is at least as crucial as any it has encountered previously, centering around the issue of whether, how, and under what circumstances the alliance should deploy cruise missiles in Western Europe.

This issue arises in part because the cruise missile is a technological innovation of unparalleled (if unproven) potentialities, which can be fired from aircraft, ships, submarines, and a variety of ground launchers; which can hit with extreme accuracy targets of all kinds at ranges of 2,000 nautical miles or more; and which can carry not only onboard sensors and electronic jammers, but also conventional or nuclear warheads. For all these reasons, the cruise missile could become not only a useful adjunct to tactical forces but also a valuable addition to strategic or regional nuclear forces, with the United States projecting the former and some among the allies arguing for the latter.[1] Since this is so, it is understandable that Soviet leaders in particular, and some proponents of arms control in general, have sought to limit the range, the deployment, and the utilization of cruise missiles. Thus the stage is set for a bruising struggle between those within the western alliance who would make extensive use of cruise missiles, in a variety of roles, and those who would seek to inhibit, if not to preclude, certain roles—a struggle that finds Americans and West Europeans in both groups.

In this chapter, I will describe the cruise missile and outline some of the missions the several versions now under development could carry out. I will then examine some of the military implications of possible deployments, assess their impact on alliance relations, and look at some of the implications for arms control. I will suggest an approach that may enable us to pass between the Scylla of untrammelled deployment and the Charybdis of complete denial—if indeed the latter rock is really close and solid enough to be threatening.

The Cruise Missile: Characteristics and Capabilities

Although cruise missiles in one form or another have been in arsenals since the Germans invented the V-1, or "buzz bomb," during World War II, the particular missile (or set of missiles) concerning us represent a quantum jump in military technology. Basically, the cruise missiles that the United States has under development (such as the Air Force's AGM-86A and the Navy's BGM-109, or Tomahawk), are small, light, highly accurate, and comparatively inexpensive air-breathing missiles of short to medium ranges (300-1,200 nautical miles, with the possibility of doubling the latter figure). Both smallness (these missiles are 14-18 feet long and 21 inches in diameter, and weigh only 3,200 pounds, fully loaded) and range are achieved by coupling a new and very efficient turbofan engine with a high-energy, high-density jet fuel.[2] In the strategic version, accuracy is achieved by a combination of inertial guidance and a terrain contour matching system (TERCOM), which can achieve CEPs on the order of 50-100 feet, while in the tactical versions TERCOM may be supplemented or replaced by infrared, radar, electro-optical and radiation-homing systems, thereby further enhancing accuracy.[3] Moreover, both strategic and tactical versions can be preprogrammed to make course changes (to avoid defended areas or unsuitable terrain) and to reorient themselves on particular landmarks, as well as to skim the ground, adjusting as necessary for changes in elevation, thereby making the task of defending against them complex, difficult, and expensive.[4]

When one considers that the several cruise missiles now under development by the United States can be fired from torpedo tubes, launched from both bomber and transport aircraft, started from the decks of ships, or ignited from a variety of ground-based platforms, including missile erectors, flatbed trucks, and simple guiderails, it is obvious that the cruise missile can be an asset to the Army, Navy, and Air Force. And when one considers that the Tomahawk cruise missile is, as shown in figure 4-1, designed in modular form so that it can carry different payloads of munitions and equipment, can utilize different propulsion systems, and can be equipped with a variety of guidance packages, it is obvious that this is a versatile as well as a potentially formidable weapons system.

The Case of the Cruise Missile

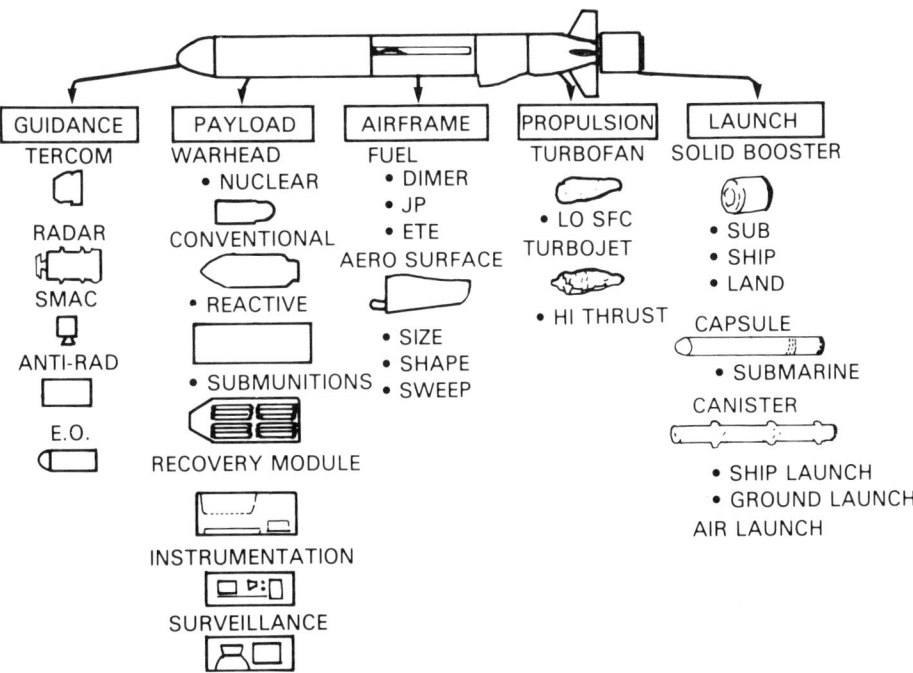

Source: Robert L. Pfaltzgraff and Jacquelyn K. Davis, "The Cruise Missile: Bargaining Chip or Defense Bargain?" *NATO's Fifteen Nations*, June/July, 1977, p. 33.

Figure 4-1. Tomahawk Vehicle Modules.

Cruise Missiles in Europe: Roles and Missions

Although the cruise missile was initially designed for strategic missions, our concern here is not with that role but rather with its utilization in the European theater of operations. It is obvious that cruise missiles could, like other remotely piloted vehicles, scout for enemy units, monitor targets, detect (and jam) air defense radars, and perform a number of important missions in the field of reconnaissance and surveillance.[5]

Another role for the cruise missile would be to replace manned aircraft and short-range ballistic missiles (SRBMs) such as Lance and Pershing in a variety of strike missions, using conventional munitions such as concrete-penetrating warheads, armor-seeking cluster bombs, grasshopper mines, and fuel air explosives.[6] These missions could include attacking fields on which Warsaw Treaty Organization (WTO) fighter-bombers were based; inhibiting the deployment for combat of Warsaw Pact tank and motorized divisions; striking at troop concentrations or artillery batteries; and attempting to cripple the logistical structure supporting WTO combat forces.[7] Moreover, cruise missiles with controllable guidance systems could, like fighter bombers, deliver heavy ordnance on moving targets that are within the range of vision of forward observers, or which have been spotted by remotely piloted vehicles, by observation aircraft, or even by other cruise missiles equipped with devices for target identification and designation. (In fact, if and as onboard guidance systems are installed on successive generations of cruise missiles, these could strike at mobile land targets, such as SAM batteries, troop trains and convoys, even as their naval counterparts are currently programmed to strike at enemy ships.)

Finally, it should be noted that cruise missiles offer new ways of attacking enemy naval vessels; of coping with amphibious operations, such as might take place in northern Norway; and of interdicting coastal shipping used to bring forward supplies. And cruise missiles could, of course, be used to deploy antisubmarine mines in waters through which Soviet hunter-killer and ballistic missile submarines would have to pass, as well as to block initial egress from their home ports.

Last—but by no means least—is the possibility of using cruise missiles in a theater role, that is, for striking at targets 500 or 1,000 miles from the front lines—wherever those may be. Medium-range cruise missiles (MRCMs) could, like short-range ones, be used to destroy point targets on Warsaw Pact lines of communication, to render airfields inoperable, to knock out fuel dumps, depots, and so forth, and to interdict the forward movement of supplies and reinforcements. More significantly, their range and their accuracy would allow them to attack targets within the Soviet Union, to include bomber bases, naval airfields, and even hardened sites such as communication centers. And they would, even more significantly, enable cruise missiles to launch counterforce strikes against Soviet MR/IRBMs targeted on Western Europe and, in a future timeframe, perhaps to locate, identify, and strike at mobile missiles inside the Soviet Union.[8]

Obviously, all these strike missions could be carried out using nuclear warheads in lieu of conventional ones, with consequent increases in effectiveness—and, presumably, higher risks of escalation. Thus, the first question to be answered is whether some of or all the missions projected for cruise missiles are sufficiently useful militarily to warrant their deployment and, if so, whether the missiles allocated to Western Europe should be equipped with conventional munitions, nuclear warheads, or both.

The Cost-Effectiveness of Cruise Missiles

Some of the missions that cruise missiles could carry out (such as ship-to-ship operations) are likely to be decided on an overall basis rather than in terms of NATO requirements, and may, in any case, have only a secondary impact on alliance relations and/or arms control. Others, such as reconnaissance and surveillance, may be determined on purely technical grounds, such as the relative costs and effectiveness of cruise missiles and other RPVs (remotely piloted vehicles)[9]; here again, a U.S. decision not to utilize cruise missiles for such purposes is unlikely to have serious military or political consequences. The same cannot, however, be said with respect to the use of cruise missiles for strike missions; hence, it is necessary to evaluate both short-range cruise missiles (SRCMs), that is, those with ranges under 600 kilometers, or 375 nautical miles, and MRCMs, those with ranges of 1,200 miles or more, in both nonnuclear and nuclear roles.

At the beginning, one must note that the variety of ways in which SRCMs could supplement or replace fighter-bombers and SRBMs makes them extremely promising. For one thing, they are likely to be considerably more accurate than either, which would make them more effective in attacks on point targets, whether military or civilian. For another, they may be less vulnerable to Warsaw Pact defenses than aircraft would be, for reasons already given. For a third, they may (in their tactical versions) be considerably cheaper in terms of missions undertaken than either of their competitors.[10] For a fourth, their deployment in either a conventional or a tactical nuclear role would enable the diversion of fighter-bombers currently programmed for interdictory and suppressive strikes to battlefield support, thereby enhancing NATO's defensive posture. And for a fifth, this deployment would, given the multiple launch modes previously described, increase the number of targets at which the Warsaw Pact would have to strike should it seek to neutralize NATO tactical delivery vehicles.

All this does not mean that SRCMs are such an unalloyed military blessing that they should be welcomed, like the Pope's benediction in St. Peter's Square. For one thing, cruise missiles may not be the best way of augmenting tactical nuclear forces in Europe for some missions; in fact, a mobile truck-mounted version of the NIKE Hercules air defense weapon, modified to attack ground targets, might be clearly superior for battlefield usage. For another, cruise missiles are not only potentially vulnerable to advanced air defense systems, especially those incorporating look-down, shoot-down capabilities, but also could be knocked down at the low altitudes at which they approach targets by exotic means such as balloon-supported steel nets and barrages of scrap metal fired from simple cannisters. For a third, submarine-launched cruise missiles can be easily detected by the enormous burst of bubbles accompanying their launch, and those with solid boosters that are fired from the surface give out not only clouds of smoke but lots of noise—which is readily identifiable.

Furthermore, if the ground-launched cruise missile is itself to be kept relatively invulnerable, measures will have to be taken to deploy it widely (with consequent difficulties in command, control, and communication) as well as to disperse, under guard, the nuclear warheads that are now kept in a limited number of fixed storage sites in Western Europe.[11] Whether this is on balance desirable depends not only on doctrine for the employment of tactical nuclear forces in Europe but on the political and psychological implications of such a dispersal.

This latter issue arises because, as already noted, cruise missiles come in a variety of ranges, up to and including those necessary to strike at targets in the Soviet Union. Whether the military value of interdictory operations with conventionally armed cruise missiles would warrant the allocation of the necessary resources is problematical; even if the great majority of these MRCMs survived and achieved their designed CEPs, it is doubtful that knocking out a dozen bridges, or blasting a score of marshalling yards, would have that much impact on operations in Central Europe. Attacks on airfields might have more of an effect on Soviet capabilities for both air strikes and airborne operations; however, it is questionable whether conventionally armed cruise missiles could, despite their high accuracy, knock out appreciable numbers of Soviet MR/IRBMs.

The picture would change considerably if the allies possessed nuclear-armed MRCMs, which would greatly enhance the effectiveness of interdictory operations and attacks on airfields, naval bases, and so forth. More importantly, as Kosta Tsipis points out, the extreme accuracy of the nuclear-armed cruise missile gives it a kill probability of one, even against superhardened targets such as missile silos.[12] With such weapons the NATO allies would, for the first time, be themselves able to strike, with high accuracy and considerable assurance, at the Soviet MR/IRBMs and medium bombers, which pose such a massive threat to Western Europe and which so greatly overmatch the regional nuclear forces currently at the disposal of the West Europeans (see table 4-1).[13]

Whether such a capability is militarily necessary is again largely unanswerable, since that answer depends on detailed knowledge of the strike plans of U.S. strategic nuclear forces. What is clear is that this capability could enable even those allies not having nuclear warheads of their own to extend the area of conflict and/or to change the types of targets being attacked, once the president of the United States had authorized the employment of nuclear weapons—thereby loosening markedly that tight control over the conduct of any nuclear war that the

Table 4-1
Regional Nuclear Forces (Europe)

Launch Vehicle Type	Britain and France	Soviet Union
Medium-range ballistic missiles (MRBMs)		400[a]
Intermediate-range ballistic missiles (IRBMs)	18	150[a]
Sea launched ballistic missiles (SLBMs)	128[b]	374[c]
Bombers	33[d]	374[e]
Total launch vehicles	179	924
Deliverable warheads	340	1498
(of which independently targetable)	(212)	(1498)
Deliverable megatonnage	262	2365
Megaton equivalents	250	1911

[a] Assumes that 100 of the 500 Soviet MRBMs and 40 of the 190 IRBMs are not targeted against Europe.

[b] To be increased by 1979 to 144 SLBMs, as France completes a missile-submarine now under construction.

[c] Soviet SLBMs are counted under global forces, Soviet submarine-launched cruise missiles (SLCMs) under tactical nuclear forces.

[d] Exclusive of 18 French Mirage IVA bombers in reserve, and 48 British Vulcan B2 bombers assigned a tactical role but which could attack strategic targets in the Soviet Union.

[e] Includes 136 Tu-22 Blinder strike aircraft assigned to the Long-range Air Force, but excludes 280 Tu-16 Badger and 30 Backfire aircraft in the Naval Air Force, configured for attacks on shipping but which could in theory carry nuclear weapons.

United States has sought to maintain.[14] And it would enable Britain and France (who do possess warheads not subject to U.S. control) to strengthen and to upgrade their regional nuclear forces if they chose to do so, either by arming their hunter-killer submarines with SLCMs, by equipping aging bombers or modern transports with ASCMs, or even by deploying GLCMs; after all, it is less than 1,200 miles from Strasbourg to Kiev and only slightly more from Dover to Leningrad.

Furthermore, even the refusal of the United States to provide MRCMs could not preclude this development. For one thing, Britain and France are already studying cruise missile technology on their own. For another, short-range missiles can be converted into medium or intermediate-range weapons, by substituting a module containing the turbofan engine of the strategic variant for that holding the turbojet engine of the tactical version; moreover, range could be further extended by substituting (the lighter weight) nuclear weapons for conventional warheads and/or by coupling in an additional fuel tank. Thus, once tactical cruise missiles are deployed, strategic ones can be developed or improvised—with results in terms of hard target kill capability dependent only on whether the allies had access to, or could build independently, the TERCOM guidance system.

The Cruise Missile and Alliance Relationships

These latter possibilities lie at the heart of any decision to deploy cruise missiles in Europe. Few would argue against the deployment of SRCMs, whether for purposes of reconnaissance and surveillance, for nonnuclear combat missions, or even as additions to NATO tactical nuclear forces. Nor would the problems of installing "two key" systems on nuclear warheads, of devising adequate command and control systems, or of integrating cruise missiles into plans for the use of tactical nuclear forces in time of war pose any greater difficulties than those now extant in assuring the readiness, the survivability, and the responsiveness of the several components of those forces.

However, the West Europeans, although they might accept cruise missiles in a tactical role, are much more interested in employing them in a theater role, that is, as a psychological and military counter to Soviet regional nuclear forces. Thus, the NATO ministers of defense, at the October 1977 meeting of the NATO Nuclear Planning Group, "expressed a strong view that it is important to keep open options for the cruise missile of intermediate range, for these serve as a counterweight to the massive Soviet build-up."[15] The same point has been made by British and West German delegations to the United States, who reportedly stressed the potential of nuclear-armed cruise missiles in "redressing a growing imbalance favoring

Soviet medium-range missiles and bombers which threaten Western Europe" and came out strongly against both range limitations and numerical constraints.[16] Similar views can be found in editorials, articles, and official statements in virtually all the NATO countries and among individuals of almost every political persuasion,[17] many of whom, like West German Defense Minister Hans Apel, are concerned about the possibility that the "theater missile gap" may expose Western Europe to military and political blackmail.[18]

Obviously, failure to respond to such concerns, to perpetuate what one West German analyst called "a chronic ethnocentrism in . . . strategic outlook," would adversely affect American relations with the European allies.[19] More significantly, it might induce at least some of the allies to "go it alone"; a move that the British and French would find feasible, if costly. It could also put the West Germans in a double box, since they not only would be affected more directly by a U.S. refusal to deploy MRCMs but also would find it most difficult, for political reasons, to proceed to build their own cruise missiles, with all that this might imply concerning the future development of their own nuclear capabilities.

Both for these reasons and for purely military ones, some in the United States favor acceding to the requests of the allies to "keep the options open"; indeed, the Pentagon is allegedly considering both a MRCM and an MRBM for the European theater.[20] Unfortunately, the deployment of such missiles would, whatever their military utility, have disadvantages in other fields. For one thing, the deployment of MRCMs is likely to arouse violent Soviet opposition, especially if these missiles are in a land-based mode, the one most suited to give all the allies an opportunity to participate in their manning. (Some wags already translate GLCM as "German-launched cruise missile.") And whereas one might regard such opposition as both self-serving and, given the size of Soviet regional nuclear forces, somewhat sanctimonious, the implications for détente must be considered.

Another disadvantage is that such a deployment could raise from their uneasy sleep doctrinal questions about the proper role of tactical nuclear forces in Europe. In the past, the European allies (especially the West Germans) have tended to emphasize the deterrent role of such forces, and especially the linkage between their use and the threat to employ the U.S. strategic deterrent; for this reason, they have pressed for initial strikes at targets deep in Eastern Europe—if not in the Soviet Union itself. Conversely, the Americans have tended to stress the war-fighting role of nuclear forces in Europe and to oppose targeting plans that would run a high risk of provoking a strategic nuclear exchange. In this debate, they have had the advantage, since they controlled virtually all the delivery vehicles capable of making deep strikes.[21] If, however, MRCMs (or MRBMs) were deployed, this would no longer be true, and the United States could expect renewed efforts to alter its doctrine (and its concepts of deterrence) to conform more closely to European views.

Whether this would in itself be bad is hard to say; there is nothing sacrosanct about U.S. concepts of deterrence—which have, moreover, not always met the perceived needs of our NATO allies. Such a change (in weaponry, in doctrine, or in both) would, however, diminish to some extent the ability to control escalation in time of war, an ability that successive U.S. officials have regarded as crucial. Furthermore, this would be true even if only SRCMs were deployed, inasmuch as these could be converted into longer range weapons as described previously, or placed on aircraft, aboard ships, and in submarines, which could carry them closer to European strategic targets. And although the likelihood of this happening is small, the possibility of so doing will exist—with the British and the French able to mate warheads under their control with missiles provided by the Americans. Thus, the United States must recognize that cruise missile deployment can ultimately enhance European freedom of action—whether or not the United States so desires.

Cruise Missiles and Arms Control

It is, of course, the possibility that new weapons capable of hitting the USSR may be introduced into Western Europe that has aroused the concern of the Soviet Union and has stimulated its efforts to prevent the NATO allies from acquiring such weapons. To date, these efforts have been only partially successful; whereas the (3-year) Protocol to the SALT II treaty bans the deployment of ground- and sea-launched cruise missiles with ranges over 600 kilometers (375 nautical miles) it does not preclude their development and flight testing. And although the United States has undertaken not to circumvent the provisions of the Protocol (by helping its allies to deploy medium-range GLCMs and SLCMs within the next 2 years), there is nothing to preclude it from providing either information now or weapons after December 31, 1981—except the potential consequences for SALT III.

One such consequence could, of course, be a reluctance on the part of the Soviet Union to proceed with the further reductions in, and constraints on, strategic nuclear forces that are envisioned following the conclusion of SALT II. Another could be Soviet insistence that such negotiations cover not only cruise missiles in Europe but other forward-based systems, ranging from U.S. fighter-bombers stationed in England to French IRBMs deployed

The Case of the Cruise Missile

in the Rhone Valley. And while there may well be value to expanding both the scope of SALT III and the number of participants in the process, such changes are not likely to make for rapid progress on strategic nuclear issues.

Perhaps more importantly, cruise missiles may provide an obstacle to agreement as well as a stimulus to negotiations. As noted previously, short-range and medium-range missiles are identical in external configuration and (at least in the ground- and sea-launched versions) readily changeable from one range to another by substituting a different propulsion module. Alternatively, or additionally, range can be further extended by inserting extra fuel modules into those types that are not length-limited—and GLCMs are not. Finally, it is, as mentioned earlier, easy to change from a conventional to a nuclear warhead. These factors mean three things:

1. As cruise missile technology diffuses, which it inevitably will, many more countries will acquire the ability to deliver effectively nuclear weapons, even against distant targets. (To give a perhaps extreme illustration, Bulgaria, with four obsolete coastal submarines and a few production reactors, could qualify as a strategic nuclear power!)

2. It will be extraordinarily difficult to verify whether any range limitations placed on cruise missiles in Europe are in fact being observed.

3. Even if they are, these limitations could be overcome in short order, through converting essentially tactical weapons into ones with theaterwide capabilities. And since both verification of agreed restrictions and inhibitions to upgrading would presumably have to apply to the Soviet Union as well as to its neighbors to the west, the possibilities of effectively monitoring any arms control agreement covering cruise missiles seems small indeed.

"To Do or Not to Do"

Under these circumstances, one interested in preserving stability might well wish that the cruise missile had never been invented; it will, like the atom bomb and gunpowder before it, profoundly affect military capabilities, introduce uncertainties into calculations, and intensify the effect of perturbations in the military balance. Since what has been invented cannot be uninvented, we must, however, attempt to cope with the consequences. The question is: How?

One alternative would, of course, be to develop MRCMs carrying U.S. nuclear warheads, and to deploy land- and/or submarine-launched versions of these. This would have the advantage of providing a European-based counter to existing and projected Soviet regional nuclear forces, thereby redressing—at least in part—the military and political imbalances that are of such great concern to many among the NATO allies. Given, however, the relatively slow response time of cruise missiles, hundreds, or even thousands, of these could not prevent the Soviet Union from devastating Western Europe, either in a preemptive strike or through a launch on warning. Furthermore, their deployment would certainly increase tensions between East and West, could jeopardize further progress in SALT, and might well stimulate the USSR to take countermeasures, such as the deployment of more of its powerful, mobile SS-20 IRBMs, with their accurate MIRVed warheads. Hence, even aside from the fact that the United States might not be totally happy with an option that diminished its ability to control the course of a conflict in Europe, or the allies with one which smacked so strongly of theater nuclear war, such an option might not be the best.

An alternative would be to limit the ranges of any cruise missiles deployed in Europe to 600 kilometers, thereby reducing drastically their effectiveness in a European strategic role. This would enable the upgrading and the expansion of NATO tactical nuclear forces as well as the allocation of cruise missiles to conventional operations—both of which may be useful militarily. It would probably not alarm the Soviets to the same degree as would the deployment of MRCMs nor jeopardize progress in SALT to the same extent—although it would pose almost insuperable problems in verification, especially if any understanding also applied to Soviet missiles, as it should. Needless to say, this option would by no means satisfy the NATO allies, who are much more interested in medium-range missiles than in short-range ones. Nor would it preclude their creating a European strategic capability of their own, by installing SRCMs on submarines, ships, or aircraft, by making adaptations to GLCMs which would extend their range, or by developing their own MRCMs, which several countries are now considering. Thus, this alternative might be better, but not good enough.

Nor can the United States simply refuse to provide cruise missiles at all—even if such a move were feasible in view of domestic politics. For one thing, this would undoubtedly exacerbate relations with the NATO allies, who have been very concerned lest the Americans do just that—if not now then 2 years hence when the Protocol to SALT II would expire. It would almost certainly stimulate West European production of cruise missiles, even though these might lack the high accuracy which TERCOM provides. Nor would such a refusal make sense if done unilaterally, since any incumbent administration would thereby lay itself open to charges of giving the USSR something for nothing—if not to more serious allegations of weakness and vacillation.

Fortunately, there is a further alternative, that of attempting to negotiate limitations on European-based cruise missiles, which can at least influence, if not substitute for, decisions on their deployment. I refer, of course, to the conversion of SALT III into a forum for dealing with cruise missiles, MR/IRBMs and other "gray area" weapons, as well as with (or in lieu of) the strategic delivery vehicles which have been the object of negotiations so far.

Admittedly this would be, as I said earlier, an arduous and time-consuming process. For one thing, there is the problem of establishing a forum that will give appropriate recognition to the views of the NATO allies (and of the East European members of the Warsaw Treaty Organization) without becoming so large as to be unmanageable or so encumbered by procedures for consultation as to be immovable. For another, there is the problem of inhibiting, during the course of the negotiations, other arms build-ups that would either generate intense pressures for the deployment of cruise missiles (as could the large-scale production of Soviet SS-20 IRBMS) or that could render meaningless any agreed constraints on cruise missiles—as could intensified programs for the modernization of NATO and WTO tactical nuclear forces. And for a third, there is the problem of reconciling divergent Allied interests, force postures, and concepts of deterrence to which I have alluded earlier.

Fortunately, it may be possible to finesse this latter problem (to which any solution is unlikely) by eating one's cake while still baking it, that is, by conducting West-West negotiations on doctrine for the employment of cruise missiles and on questions concerning their development even as one conducts East-West negotiations on measures for their limitation. Equally fortunately, there are indications that a number of the potential participants (such as President Carter, Chancellor Helmut Schmidt of the Federal Republic of Germany, and Secretary General Leonid Brezhnev of the CPSU) are interested in such negotiations—although in the case of Schmidt, at least, there seems to be some doubt as to whether deployment of new weapons in Europe should await the outcome of negotiations or, on a limited basis, proceed in parallel with them. Given the impact of weapons deployments on both the process of negotiations and their outcomes, I would, however, suggest an alternative: an immediate ban, for a 2-year period, on the introduction of any new nuclear delivery systems, Eastern or Western, into Central Europe, coupled with a similar ban on the further deployment of SS-20 IRBMs in the western military districts of the USSR, in effect a variant on Mr. Brezhnev's call for a ban on western modernization which would also place limitations on the upgrading of Soviet weapon systems.[22] If negotiations on the limitation of "gray area" weapons are to succeed, we need a pause in the build-up of those weapons—and, because of their overlapping roles, in shorter range weapons as well.

As of November 1979, it seems doubtful that such a pause will occur, as many leaders in the West are seemingly insistent on pushing ahead with programs for the deployment in Europe of Pershing II's and nuclear-armed cruise missiles.[23] Even if NATO decides to go ahead with these programs, I would, however, urge that these same leaders proceed simultaneously to create the machinery for negotiations. Since these will affect weapons now in the hands of, or destined for, West Europeans, they must determine for themselves what their role would be. At the risk of being considered a "great power chauvinist" I would urge that the NATO allies not follow the pattern of the negotiations on mutual force reductions, which features a twelve-nation NATO delegation with elaborate procedures for caucusing at Vienna, for deriving positions within the NATO headquarters in Brussels, and for linking both of these with "backstop" delegations in the countries' capitals. Consultation (and sometimes formal agreement) is undoubtedly necessary, and some European representation in the actual talks is certainly desirable, but the latter should, if practicable, be limited to one or two members on a rotating basis, along with an American delegate.

Whether such negotiations would be productive is perhaps doubtful, for all the reasons given earlier; to give just one illustration, either all GLCMs must be counted as nuclear-armed (which would mean virtually ruling out conventional missiles) or some means of demonstrating that conventionally armed missiles are not carrying nuclear warheads must be devised. Nevertheless, it is at least conceivable that the participants could, before the Protocol to SALT II expires, agree to trade off inhibitions on NATO MRCMs for reductions in Soviet MR/IRBMs, to modify SRCMs in ways that would differentiate them from their long-range brothers (as has been done with ALCM carriers under SALT II); to arrange for the exchange of reassuring information concerning alterations that could extend the range of SRCMs, and perhaps even to allow a limited number of inspections of deployed missiles, as is provided under the Comprehensive Test Ban Treaty. An eminent European once said, "If Austria did not exist, it would be necessary to invent it." The same can be said of the proposed conference on limiting cruise missiles in Europe; the need is to act on the statement.

Notes

1. Following the definition used in the Strategic Arms Limitation Talks (SALT), strategic nuclear forces include heavy bombers, intercontinental ballistic missiles, submarine-launched ballistic missiles, and other launch vehicles with effective ranges of over 3,000 miles—or with carriers, such as the submarine, which can enable them to strike targets at that distance. Regional nuclear forces consist of medium or light bombers, medium-range or intermediate-range ballistic missiles, and similar launch

vehicles with ranges of 1,000-3,000 miles. The targets for either set of forces may include weapons sites, military installations, industrial facilities, governmental centers, and/or populated areas, depending on the doctrine and the capabilities of the country employing such forces.

2. For details, see A.A. Tinajero, *Cruise Missiles: U.S. Programs*, Issue Brief no. IB76018, The Library of Congress, Congressional Research Service, Major Issues System, 29 April 1977.

3. CEP stands for circular error probable, the radius of a circle within which one-half of the missiles can be expected to hit.

4. News briefing by Dr. William J. Perry, Undersecretary of Defense for Research and Engineering, 14 November 1978, subject: Cruise Missiles and Defensive Systems.

5. For a longer listing and some discussion, see Robert Kennedy, "The Cruise Missile and the Strategic Balance," *Parameters* 8, no. 1 (March 1978):7.

6. Fuel air explosives are devices employing a mixture of jet fuel and compressed air, which, when detonated near ground level, produce overpressures sufficient to crush trucks and aircraft, damage missiles and artillery pieces, and kill or injure individuals within range.

7. One author notes that "the presently perceived threat of a rapid armor/mobile infantry thrust into Europe diminishes when one considers that all known Soviet fuel depots, ammunition storage sites, transportation nets, communication sites and even headquarters could be struck by accurate, low-flying cruise missiles within two hours of the outbreak of hostilities." Lt. Commander Edward J. Ohlert, USN, "Strategic Deterrence and the Cruise Missile," *Naval War College Review* 30, no. 3 (Winter 1978):28.

8. The problem of target identification and missile direction could be solved using space satellites, other prelaunched cruise missiles or, if they could survive, remotely piloted vehicles. In the longer run, cruise missiles could be fitted with internal sensor and guidance systems, which would make them self-contained, but these are certainly some way into the future.

9. See, for example, Jonathan E. Medalia, "Remotely Piloted Vehicles" (Paper delivered at the 1976 Annual Meeting of the International Studies Association, Toronto, Canada, February 25-29, 1976), mimeo.

10. Desmond Ball, "The Costs of the Cruise Missile," *Survival*, 20, no. 6 (November/December 1978):246-247.

11. G. Philip Hughes, "Cutting the Gordian Knot: A Theater-Nuclear Force for Deterrence in Europe," *Orbis* 22, no. 2 (Summer 1978):327-329.

12. "The Long-Range Cruise Missile," *Bulletin of the Atomic Scientists* 31, no. 4 (April 1975):20.

13. Although the British and the French do, as shown in table 4-1, have independent nuclear forces, the weapons at their disposal are neither numerous enough nor accurate enough to allow them the luxury of pro-

gramming counterforce strikes against Soviet delivery vehicles even if they should choose to do so—which they have not. To the extent that such counterforce strikes are envisioned the allies now have to rely on the SLBMs allocated to Supreme Allied Commander, Europe (SACEUR) (currently, as in the past, an American general) and/or on ICBMs based in the United States.

14. It is, of course, possible that technology could solve the problem that technology has created, either by enabling the installation of tamper-proof guidance systems or by making possible differential weapons releases, such that the warheads on some cruise missiles were armed and those on others were not.

15. *The New York Times*, 13 October 1977, p. 8.

16. *The Boston Globe*, 27 March 1977, p. 21.

17. See for example, the references in Christopher Makins, "European Security and the Theater Nuclear Balance," *Arms Control Today* 8, no. 11 (December 1978):1-4.

18. Interview in the *Bremer Nachrichten*, 28 August 1978, translated and excerpted in *The German Tribune*, no. 855, 10 September 1978, p. 1.

19. Hans Ruhle, "Cruise Missiles, NATO and the European Option," *Strategic Review* 6, no. 4 (Fall 1978):48.

20. Testimony of Undersecretary of Defense William J. Perry, reprinted in *The Defense/Space Daily*, 28 November 1978, p. 124.

21. Although tactical aircraft available to NATO are in theory capable of reaching targets 1,000 miles or more away, operations at such extreme ranges are both difficult and uncertain; thus, the American SLBMs in the Mediterranean constitute the bulk of the forces available for such missions.

22. *The New York Times*, 7 October 1979, pp. 1, 12.

23. At the NATO Ministerial Meeting of December 12, 1971, members agreed to the deployment of 108 Pershing IIs and 464 GLCMs to be based in Belgium, Britain, the FRG, and Italy. (Because of a prior vote in the second chamber of the Estates General, the Dutch delegation did not accept the 48 GLCMs earmarked for Holland.) Two days later U.S. Secretary of State Cyrus Vance, speaking for the Allies, called for negotiations on these and other long-range theater nuclear-delivery vehicles, but without specifying either a procedure or a timetable for negotiations.

5 NATO Defense: The Problem Is Not More Money

Steven L. Canby

NATO's forces today are incapable of coping with a serious Warsaw Pact attack. Yet NATO's population and GNP are considerably greater than those of the Warsaw Pact. Moreover, even in peacetime, NATO spends more on its military forces than the Warsaw Pact;[1] if France is included, NATO has nearly a quarter million more men in its peacetime air and ground forces stationed in the NATO Guidelines Area (NGA) than has the Warsaw Pact.[2] The fact that a (conventional) solution on the central front has eluded and continues to elude us for the last two decades does not mean a solution does not exist. It may only mean that the problem has not been approached from the right perspective. Indeed, the solutions suggested during that period were generally of the same generic breed—that of a system view, an approach central to the analytical methodology developed in this country in recent years. For the problem in Europe, this approach can be aptly summarized from a recent Defense Department report to Congress: "If our goal is to improve the combat effectiveness of our forces, we should improve the basic functions which must be performed to produce combat power in war and readiness in peace. An examination of those functions and how they are performed should improve the evaluation of the forces' combat capability."[3] This approach is plausible and a valid technique for component analysis. But being a subset of economics, it can be addressed in those terms and recognized as microanalysis. In economics, macrologic does not follow from, and cannot be derived from, aggregated microanalysis. Correspondingly if NATO's conceptual approach to armored warfare in Europe is invalid, the systems approach will not solve the problem by component analysis. It will only refine the manifestations of the approach in vogue, regardless of its validity. It also follows that if NATO's approach to organizing its forces is conceptually dated, comparisons like percent of GNP spent on military forces (which NATO spends so much rhetoric on) are only indicators of relative monetary burden, not military effectiveness and the efficacy by which a society generates its military forces. Sweden and the Netherlands spend roughly the same percentage of GNP on their military (3.7 and 3.4, respectively). Yet the smaller Swedish nation with a population of 8.3 million generates a much more credible defense force than Holland with a population of 13.9 million. Similarly Finland with a population of 4.7 million spends relatively only a third (1.1) that of the Dutch and Belgians (3.0), but yet has developed and demonstrated (in World War II) a credible defensive capability.[4]

NATO's much touted Long Term Defense Program (LTDP) suffers on both accounts. It is but a grandiose extension of earlier United States-sponsored initiatives like the Alliance Defense 70 (AD-70) and European Defense Improvement Program (EDIP). These programs have all sought component or functional area improvement, without recognizing that the real problem was the logic by which these components were being organized and used. Normally this approach—although unduly expensive for the military benefits obtained—nevertheless leads to some increase in military capability. In the case of the LTDP, however, NATO's conventional capability may actually be slightly reduced, even though requiring compounded budgetary increases of 3 percent for 15 years, totalling $50-80 billion. This surprising paradox results from (1) the program's low overall effectiveness caused by addressing across-the-board functional areas in lieu of binding constraints; (2) promotion of certain sophisticated technologies that induce counter-productive behavior (for example, sophisticated data processing communications (C^3) can negate proper usage of armored forces); and (3) paying for the program's high-cost technology by trading off force structure and slipping newly conceived reserve unit mobilization plans as in the case of the Federal Republic of Germany (FRG).

The Divergence in NATO Strategy

The loci of possible conflicts (that is, destruction) largely explain the divergences in views between the two sides of the Atlantic. The U.S. strategic and tactical nuclear monopoly once offered a one-sided advantage, whereby the United States could wield NATO's military power without undue cost and retaliatory burden on itself. For the Western Europeans, this was the best of all worlds: low-cost defense in peacetime and the opportunity to be the "eye" of any war storm, whose destructive forces would fall primarily on the Soviet homeland. Strategic parity has ended this idyllic world. The American homeland is now equally exposed to destruction, possibly even more so given the Soviet civil defense program. The Europeans for their part have become mesmerized by the fear of a tacit Soviet-American deal refocusing the destructive forces of war onto the European homelands and by the possibility of a U.S. withdrawal that would leave Western Europe defenseless and exposed to Soviet political coercion.

The European interpretation of the NATO strategy of flexible response remains that of the nuclear tripwire. Their concept of a stalwart defense does not mean a true conventional fighting capability.[5] Its meaning is in the context of crisis management: conventional forces are to be strong enough to provide options during crises, to provide a cordon for the purpose of preventing excursions and nibbling actions on the part of the Soviets, and, most important, to provide time and inducement for the United States to initiate nuclear weapons as pressure builds on the cordon defense. Its practical import is similar to the French view. The role of conventional forces is to test enemy intentions. Ambiguous aggression is to be countered with a conventional response, and serious aggression is to be met with an automatic (French) nuclear response (as in the old strategy of massive retaliation).[6]

Only the United States is seriously interested in a *true* conventional capability. European NATO has only limited interest in conventional forces. Their concern—which pervades all their thinking—is in the degree of American commitment to use strategic nuclear weapons. Their interest in the LTDP is that the United States after years of easing out of Europe, is now committing itself further in the defense of Europe. By whom, when, and how nuclear weapons are to be first used and employed remain the core of European-NATO strategy. The United States has seen a conventional defense as an attainable goal requiring only marginal adjustments. The Europeans have always seen a large disparity in conventional capabilities. Thus while expensive adjustments of the AD70 variety have been seen as closing the gap by the United States, they have often been viewed as counterproductive by the Western Europeans. In their view these adjustments are expensive, do little to close the actual gap, and have (in the past) undercut deterrence. For the Western Europeans, conventional forces serve primarily to satisfy the United States in peacetime and to provide a "good show" in wartime, to justify escalation—first to the (symbolic) use of tactical nuclear weapons and then quickly to the use of U.S. strategic weapons against the Soviet Union.

Deterrence works in two ways: by the threat of punishment if a hostile act is initiated or by denying the aggressor the objective of his act. Strategic forces pose the threat of punishment on one's homeland; conventional forces pose the denial function against ground-seizing forces. Tactical nuclear forces as they exist today perform neither of these functions; theirs is a linkage function. By definition, tactical nuclear weapons are not targeted on the Soviet homeland (most lack the range), and they cannot defeat enemy ground forces except by heavy use of destructive firepower. Denial forces that are inadequate can weaken deterrence, since their very existence may lead the defender into attempting to defend with them first, thus providing an aggressor with time. Time can be used for territorial grabs to induce long-term demoralization. Or it can be used for the rapid movement of armor along the axes of advance, to unravel the cohesion of the defending military system, particularly that of a coalition—with its tendency to shatter at points of stress.

Even with a true denial capability, NATO would still require strategic coupling and linkage between the two. NATO's strategy of graduated response is correct in the abstract; its problem is in implementation. A true conventional defense enhances its version of deterrence and reduces the possibility that the use of nuclear weapons might have to be initiated by the defender should deterrence fail. Conventional forces must also be designed for nuclear operations. But for the sake of alliance cohesion, the United States should also visualize tactical nuclear weapons only as a link to strategic nuclear weapons. In-theater tactical nuclear warfighting is not a politically viable NATO option. Neither the United States nor Western Europe should have to bear the prospect of nuclear devastation alone. If this burden is not explicitly surfaced and shared, alliance friction will continue to fester, presenting a fissure for the Soviets to exploit.[7] This, of course, means West Europeans for their part must reduce the likelihood of nuclear devastation on the United States by generating strong conventional forces.

Western European willingness to develop a true conventional balance is dependent on three conditions: (1) undiminished deterrence, (2) costs at roughly today's real levels, and (3) contained destruction. The last condition rules out war-fighting with tactical nuclear weapons, and also sustained conventional warfare of the kind practiced in World War II. Considerations of cost rule out anything more than a stalwart conventional defense given the current posture of NATO forces. A true conventional defense would require considerably more divisions than NATO has today, and obtaining them with formations as currently deployed would require proportionate increases in budgetary outlays. Continued deterrence always requires a meaningful strategic capability. Changes in conventional forces have two effects on deterrence: curve-shifting from the perceived change in the political-military milieu accompanying changes in conventional forces and movement along a "U-shaped" curve. The U-shape implies high (although unstable) deterrence with weak conventional forces (that is, their being a trip-wire for automatic response), declining deterrence as conventional forces are increased to give a semblance of conventional defense capability (the so-called nuclear pause), and then with climbing deterrence as the adversary perceives that a true conventional war-fighting capability has been created. Curve shifting relates to the degree of perceived U.S. commitment. These effects can be reinforcing or at cross-purposes. In the past, American efforts to increase NATO's conventional forces have been in the perceived context of unilateral U.S. withdrawal, and the effects have had reinforcingly downward effects on deterrence. Present efforts are in the context of enhanced U.S. interest and commitment and have countervailing effects on deterrence. West German demands for forward deployments and a forward defense are largely keyed to the dangers of the nuclear pause. They are fully aware of the pitfalls of a brittle and therefore fragile forward linear defense. On the other hand, in the period of unambiguous U.S. strategic superiority, the cordon strengthened NATO's immediate capabilities to resist incursions and *faits accomplis*, while at the same time lowering the nuclear threshold and enhancing deterrence because of its obvious (to NATO/European and Soviet military observers) vulnerability to major assault. (Indeed, it is the collapse of this delicate balance that now makes the West Germans so anxious).

NATO's Military Problem

NATO's military deficiency derives from this discrepancy in military thought: its conceptualization of modern war in the European theater is more akin to that of Douhet than Guderian.[8] Douhet argued that the attrition of modern war could be circumvented by attacking the adversary's national will directly through the air, with one's own army minimizing its casualties by foregoing the offense and holding to a static defense. NATO's approach to war is similar, as reflected in General Goodpaster's statement: "What can be assured is that any attacking force would be subjected to heavy, continuing and increasing losses with no certainty of tactical success, and with rapidly escalating threat to rear areas and to the aggressor's homeland."[9] Ground forces are thus to hold and, in the process, attrit enemy ground forces; their larger rationale, however, is to gain time for escalatory decisions against the enemy's rear and homeland areas. NATO's force structure corresponds to this thinking: strong tactical air forces oriented toward offensive air capability (nuclear strike and conventional ground support) and ground forces deployed in cordonlike national corps sectors across the front.

Douhet's is a firepower approach to war; Guderian's is a maneuver approach. This distinction drives the design of armies and tactical air forces and accounts for NATO's low "teeth-to-tail" ratios (that is, combat to support elements). A bombardment approach in ground warfare leads to the practice of applying strength against strength and to the physical destruction of the opponent. A maneuver approach seeks to beguile the opponent, focusing strength against weakness. In the first case, war is attrition on the battlefield; in the second, war is the avoidance of costly battle with the operational aim of unraveling the opponent's ability to organize himself and to act. The first becomes a protracted conflict; the second seeks a quick victory.

NATO could achieve conventional parity on the central front, but only by generating additional forces to man its ramparts or by concentrating present forces into an operational reserve. Whereas forward "walls" could, in principle, stop armored attacks, such linear (cordon) defenses have not been successful in the past and are unlikely to be successful in the future, even with the advent of the new defensive technologies.[10] If discontinuities develop in a cordon defense—which is highly likely given the inadequate size of today's forward-deployed forces—the defense can be readily defeated by an opponent geared to find and exploit such discontinuities. (And that is exactly the aim of the present Soviet operational scheme.) If the ramparts can resist, they still remain vulnerable to echeloned battering-ram tactics (characteristic of old-style Soviet offensives). On the other hand, for all its compelling military virtues, an elastic defense built around a strong operational reserve is politically unfeasible for NATO without a corresponding forward wall. The Germans demand a forward defense to offset the adverse effects of the nuclear pause, to commit their allies (for deterrence), and to counter ambiguous incursions as well as territorial seizures.

In armored warfare the key to a successful defense has historically been the maintenance and use of operational reserves. A fortiori, if tactical nuclear weapons are used: static, positional, defenses are obviously more targetable than elusive mobile forces. For Westerners defending against Russians the use of mobile warfare and operational reserves has additional virtues. First, it must be recognized that positional warfare implies a certain passivity on the part of the defense, whose emphasis is on firepower and attrition warfare. Mobile warfare, on the other hand, depends on maneuver and command flexibility. Second, it is to be noted that the Western and Eastern military establishments have opposite characteristics: the East has numbers but lacks initiative, while the West lacks numbers and prides itself on individual initiative. That is, the West depends on tactical brilliance and fine coordination to offset inadequate resources and reserves—characteristics that can only be obtained by wide-open maneuver warfare. The command rigidity of Soviet formations may make them susceptible to maneuver counterattacks. But that is quite distinct from attrition losses to firepower and the inability to replace losses at critical points in time and place. The West as now organized cannot absorb such losses; the Soviets can. Traditionally, Russian forces function amidst high losses. The size and organizational pattern of the Soviet army allows it to field a military system that is hydralike. As in the fable, the Soviet system may similarly be immune to losses, unless its command-brain subsystem is itself damaged and thrown off its "program." This calls for dislocation, not attrition.

NATO has deployed its divisions by national corps sectors, each corps more or less fighting its own battle independently (hence the term "layer-cake"). NATO's forward forces are so thinly deployed that there is no defense in depth (in the sense of physical occupation by many units, as opposed to movement through an area—or occupation of alternative positions—by a single unit). Nor can NATO units be leap-frogged to the rear to give respite and as a precaution against the unforeseen. Reserves in some corps sectors amount to less than a brigade. Each of NATO's two army groups retain only one earmarked German division for reserve. Thus NATO can neither sustain a serious positional defense, nor stage a serious counterattack.

NATO's shortage of divisions cannot be made good by the United States. The United States could reinforce considerably faster than at present, but only up to the ceiling of absorption capacity, a function of in-theater personnel and equipment stocks. However, the binding constraints are organizational and doctrinal rather than material. Greater prepositioning of equipment (POMCUS) stocks and enhanced airlift are expensive and address the apparent limitations rather than the organizational problems within the army that are the real limits to rapid reinforcement and field deployment. In any case U.S. forces can only form a small part of total alliance requirements; they can become a meaningful addition only if the Western Europeans themselves increase their reinforcement capability—in which case it will be found that NATO can in fact field a more than adequate number of divisions for its defense—and do so within present budgetary constraints.

Analysis of the German *blitzkrieg* and of the present Soviet operational scheme clearly indicates that programs that do not address the central issue of maneuver warfare and the need for strong operational reserves are not viable solutions in themselves. It should be noted in this regard that standardization and interoperability for ground forces cannot achieve very much so long as NATO retains its present compartmentalized national corps sector ("layer-cake") deployment. The Soviet operational scheme will reinforce the natural tendency of each national corps to view itself as the target of a principal thrust. Rather than releasing brigades (in themselves inadequate forces) to adjacent sectors, each corps is more likely to demand brigades from adjacent corps sectors. Sophisticated command, control, and communication systems (C^3) will do little to correct this anomaly: they will simply aggregate and transmit the perceptions of subordinates to their seniors.

Standardization and greater readiness are not substitutes for greater numbers of combat forces. The value of readiness fades with prolonged warning. An emphasis on the criterion of readiness can mask the importance of and preclude the funding for reserves. If, in addition, readiness is interpreted to mean forward billeting in peacetime to reduce movement times to war positions, readiness can even be counterproductive by compromising the viability of a defense against a well-executed surprise attack.

Standardization by contrast is of military value if it leads to major savings in equipment procurement and logistics and to force interoperability. Savings produce the wherewithal for additional forces; force interoperability can to some extent substitute for force size and reserves by making formations of one corps sector available for use in another. Unfortunately, standardization produces little savings and force interoperability is nearly moot for ground forces. Major equipment items suitable for standardization amount to only 14 percent of the NATO country budgets. Even assuming a nonexistent ideal world of free trade and comparative advantage, equipment savings in production could at most only lead to overall savings of 2 to 3 percent.[11] Similar savings in research and development (R and D) and logistics are only possible if nations (for example, the United States) were willing to foreclose future options (particularly in the critical aerospace and electronic areas) and if standardization is across the board so that national logistic systems could be folded into a larger NATO system.

Ground force interoperability has little practical meaning for three reasons: (1) of NATO's eight corps sectors, only German corps I and II have uncommitted formations (that is, reserves) of any significance. Except for the Dutch corps (which has special problems of its own), NATO's remaining corps have virtually no reserves. Thus, there are few formations presently available for transferring from one corps sector to another. (2) German forces can already operate throughout the German territory, by virtue of their territorial commands, their peacetime billeting, and the location of their five interspersed corps and division sectors (the three corps, plus 6th Panzer Grenadier and 12th Panzer divisions). (3) Even if reserves were available for shifting to another national corps sector, there is still no real requirement for interoperability as long as the NATO deployment calls for a cordon defense. In a cordon defense, since subtle national differences will always remain even if equipment and doctrine were overtly similar, it remains easier to form national reserves by shifting corps boundaries. It can thus be paradoxically argued that interoperability comes into its own only if NATO had more combat units and were to use them in a maneuver mode of warfare; however, it is also apparent that if NATO had these forces and adopted this form of warfare, NATO would have already resolved its most pressing military problems (conventional).

**Military Solutions at Less
than Present Costs**

The common features of the possible solutions to Central Europe's defense are (1) a large operational reserve, (2) protection against surprise attack, and (3) the political imperative of a multinational forward defense. Other force characteristics acquire their desirability from their effect on these features. The cordon, for instance, may be desirable for deterrence, but it puts units on line rather than in reserve. Restructuring for greater teeth-to-tail ratios is mainly to generate the wherewithal to create large reserves and to counter surprise (as well as to create a mind-set and streamlined units more suitable for armored warfare).

Only programs that address the central issues of maneuver warfare and strong operational reserves are viable solutions. This means that the defense must be keyed to large mobile reserves; but it does not mean that all forces must be homogeneous, in-being, or of high quality. (This certainly was not a German characteristic in World War II, even when executing highly successful ripostes against quantitatively superior opponents.) The focus on maneuver and operational reserves also indicates that NATO's problem is conceptual and organizational. It is not one of resources, or of attaining economies or improvements from the prescripts of economic theory. Recognition that the problem is structural and not incremental means that the demanding conditions of undiminished deterrence, costs at roughly today's real levels, and contained destruction can in fact also be satisfied.

One solution that satisfies the military conditions for a true conventional defense is the concentration of NATO's active forces into operational reserves while the forward space is defended through a territorial defense scheme based jointly on static defense of villages and the outer crust of forward cities. The advantages of a territorial defense are organizational simplicity and cost effectiveness. Territorial defense can be based on reservists, and they do not require expensive equipment. However, they cannot be expected to resist full-scale combined-arms attacks armed with the entire range of weapons and equipment available to regular forces. They must be considered auxiliaries, capable of coping with regular forces only in secondary sectors and only in special terrain conditions where they can engage the attacker without becoming readily targeted and destroyed. Operationally, it should be noted that territorial defense (and the defense of built-up areas) can only serve as adjuncts to the regular-force defense. Against opposing forces as large as those of the Warsaw Pact, which are too large to be defeated by attrition alone, territorial forces by themselves cannot be decisive. Victory can only be obtained by the maneuver of heavy regular forces to break down the attacker's own cohesion. However, the importance of territorial defense forces derives from their ability to be more effective against surprise than normal readiness measures and that they can tie down large numbers of opposing forces, if they are integrated into an overall scheme whereby territorial defense forces complement the regular forces. In addition, territorials can relieve expensive regular formations, allowing the latter's concentration into an operational reserve, and also provide screening forces, to mask the positioning of reserves for flanking counterattacks against Soviet thrust lines.

While territorial defense may be politically unacceptable because it imposes a qualitative distinction between Germans and non-Germans and would thus undermine the NATO "layer-cake," two other solutions, restructuring of NATO forces and the Dutch Rechstreeks Instromend Mobilisabel (RIM) are available. These retain the political attributes of the "layer-cake," while obtaining the essence of the mobile defense. Both solutions accept the political imperatives of deterrence and forward defense. But they do so in a way that remains militarily viable, as opposed to

NATO's present plans. Although taking different routes, both exploit already trained European reservists, thereby generating large numbers of suitably trained divisions to thicken the forward crust and to provide the operational reserves. The essential difference between the two is that restructuring requires large-scale reorganization to release personnel to man cadres of new reserve divisions, whereas the RIM solution does not require these wrenching changes. Instead it focuses on replicating active units by a system that in effect places entire units on extended leave. The RIM solution requires very small cadres, in fact so small that they can be provided in large part by "double hatting" the personnel overhead normally associated with a peacetime military establishment. The anomaly of the RIM solution is that its (present) formations are to be used in a framework of armored warfare, while in fact the formations remain structured for an infantry-with-tanks approach to warfare. This can be made to work, but it obviously follows that the optimum solution is to combine the two: NATO units should be restructured specifically for armored warfare and the (Western European) reserve should be generated by a RIM solution, although with larger cadres than those provided by the Dutch (a consideration of particular concern for the Germans because of their uniquely demanding and high quality tactical system).

The trained manpower for large Western European reserves already exists. But their equipment procurement and their proper organization into structured units has been inhibited by the NATO adoption of the Anglo-American concept of sustainable combat, and by SHAPE's (Supreme Headquarters Allied Powers Europe) fear that anything less than expensive standing forces would lead members of the alliance to be remiss in their commitments. NATO has failed to recognize the utility of structured reserves. It has allowed its reserves to be organized into replacement pools geared for sustaining active units by individual replacement in lieu of the traditional continental system of forming large numbers of units designed for impact in a war of spaced campaigns. Echeloned forces—the way armor ought to be fought—reduces logistical and readiness requirements and facilitates replacement absorption; each readiness echelon (for example, Categories I-III if a cadre system is used) need only block until the next readiness echelon can mobilize and deploy; forward echelons can be active while rearward echelons retrofit themselves; and echelons can operate in a nonorganic support framework, the amount of support provided being a function of combat activity. This, of course, capsulizes the Soviet system; but it is in reality nothing more than an adaptation of the post-1870 continental mobilization system to the natural contours of armored warfare.

The cost advantage of reserves is apparent. Personnel and operating costs (roughly 75 percent of all-service military cost) are sharply reduced. No research and development is required (5 percent), and equipment (1⁻

NATO Defense

percent) and construction (3 percent) costs are generally low, since reserves have habitually been assigned older equipment with little market value. The costs of reserve units in many countries can therefore be quite low, amounting to only a small percentage for Home Guard, territorial defense-type units, and those field units mobilized from equipment holding detachments. On the other extreme, reserves of the Israeli model with extensive in-service and refresher training are demanding on civilians and relatively expensive. But they are also as effective as their active counterparts.

The challenge with reserves is (1) to contain their monetary costs and (2) their demands on the citizenry while making them (3) rapidly mobilizable and (4) militarily effective on mobilization. Israeli-like solutions with repeated call-ups satisfy criteria 3 and 4, but not criteria 1 and 2. Cadre systems—like those of the Soviets—straddle these criteria. For territorial defense systems, criteria 2 conflicts with 3 and 4. The Dutch reserve system (RIM) satisfies all four criteria.

The Dutch RIM system matches reserve battalions with an equal number of identical active units. On release from their active unit, conscripts pass in company-sized organic units (to retain intraunit and interpersonal training and familiarity) to "short" leave for 4 months and then to their parallel reserve unit for 16 months. The innovation in the Dutch system is that rather than assigning former conscripts to equipment-holding or cadre units, structured active units are placed in toto on "leave," complete with equipment. Accordingly, all the relationships of personnel that develop with each other and their equipment are retained for a period short enough before atrophy of skills becomes serious. Figure 5-1 graphically

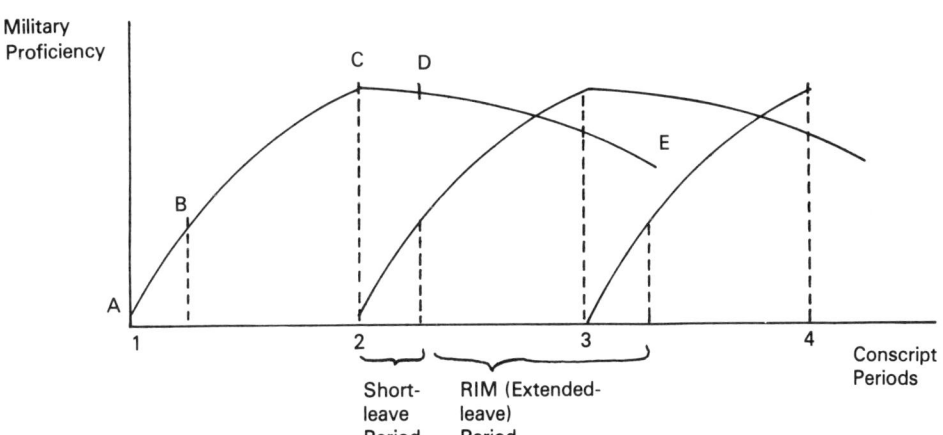

Figure 5-1. The Dutch Innovation.

compares the Dutch system with that of the standard NATO conscription system. The vertical axis represents military proficiency; the horizontal, conscript periods. The (integrated) area under the proficiency curve represents military effectiveness. In the standard system, conscripts enter service, become trained, and at the peak of training are dismissed from service. The cycle is then repeated for the next younger age cohort. For most countries, the period of actual usefulness (BC in figure 5-1) is somewhat less than the full conscription period (AC). Personnel are usually assigned to a training unit for 4 months (AB), then placed in a combat unit. RIM introduces two variations. Full use of a conscription period is obtained by the concept of the short leave (or standby reserve in the new West German system). That is, conscripts follow the same assignment pattern as in the standard system. The difference is that at the normal termination of service, a period of short leave (CD) equal to the initial training time (AB) is tacked onto military service. In a crisis, they return from leave and replace those undergoing initial training. The second variation is another full use of a conscription period from the same conscripts, obtained by extending the concept of short leave into a full conscription period (DE). The differences between short and extended leaves are that personnel in the latter are no longer legally constrained to reside in a specified area of the Netherlands and that the company-size units no longer return to their parent battalion. Instead they are grouped into a reserve (RIM) battalion from units sequentially flowing from the original parent battalion. (Thereafter reservists can be grouped in normal equipment-holding cadre formations.)

The result is that at the cost of an additional set of first-line equipment, of civilian maintenance personnel representing roughly 1.5 percent of unit strength, and of a regular officer and senior NCO cadre of around 7 percent, the Dutch can field an additional combat battalion that is equal in quality to that of a standard conscript battalion. It should be specifically noted that this is a dominant mobilization system for field forces. By reducing the size of the required cadre, costs are lower than comparable cadre systems. No additional demands are placed on the citizenry for refresher training. Units can be mobilized as rapidly as that of any reserve system. Units are effective almost immediately after their assembly, as compared to the cadre system, which always requires some integration of reservists and personnel familiarization.

It thus comes about that, whether by restructuring or RIM, the West Europeans could triple their division count for about a 30 percent increase in army costs. Half this increase would consist of high-quality mobile formations; half would consist of antitank blocking divisions. Their combination would provide a long-war hedge and a measure of (physically occupied) defense in depth. NATO could retain the form of the layer-cake but at the same time NATO could be creating the operational reserves needed for a viable defense and, as a byproduct, for establishing a new conventional deterrent to help offset the loss of American nuclear superiority. Given the European budget ratios of 50:30:20 for ground, air, and naval, a very robust and true conventional defense is accordingly obtainable for a 15 percent increase in total Western European military budgets.

Through structural specialization and revamping of present reserves, this cost can moreover be reduced to less than that of the present posture. Since the budgetary ratio in the Western European military establishment is 50:30:20 for ground: air: naval, a 30 percent army increase implies a corresponding decrease in Western European air and maritime budgets and capabilities. For tactical air forces, a 30 percent reduction in Western European assets could be replaced at virtually no cost by the United States, resulting in no loss in overall air capability. Only a portion of U.S. air assets are deployable to the European theater. Forty percent are siphoned off by the navy and marines for service-oriented missions, most with little relevance to a conflict with the Soviet Union. Nor can the full strength of the USAF be deployed to Europe, due to secondary commitments, sustaining base training requirements, and the limited supporting (beddown) capacity in Western Europe itself. The result is that if a war in Central Europe were to last only several weeks almost two-thirds of U.S. tactical airpower would not have been brought to bear, a force double that of the Western European air forces.

A similar shift is possible with naval forces. If the United States were to restructure its forces for armored warfare and posture them for fast reinforcement, it could structure its (1973) authorized European equipment stocks into 11 divisions. These divisions would equal only 7.5 division equivalents in peacetime but could be immediately deployed in wartime and fully manned within 14 days, requiring only the seating capacity of commercial aircraft. The reinforcement problem is not that of lift capacity and reception facilities. Rather, it is organizational within the Army. In the context of a three-fold increase in Western European divisions, and of the removal of a possible emotive charge of the United States using Europeans as cannon-fodder, no further U.S. ground reinforcements are likely to be required for a conflict on the Central European front. Additional U.S. ground forces would be needed only as a protracted war hedge. Accordingly, these divisions need not arrive for many months, removing the requirement for that part of the air/sealift and sea-lane protection force justified by rapid reinforcement to the central front. These redundancies could be partially cashed in for a U.S. saving (or converted into greater combat capabilities elsewhere) and partially shifted to pick up that part of Western European naval responsibilities released by their shift in focus to greater efforts on the ground.

A shift from balanced national contingents toward (partial) alliance specialization—the Americans to air and naval power, and the Western Europeans to land power—indirectly leads to greater equipment standardization as a side-effect of the implied dominance of countries in specified functions. This presents a structural argument for standardization in addition to those of interoperability and economies of scale in procurement. This approach to alliance rationalization would preserve a favorable U.S. trade balance in military equipment and also the long-run viability of the peacetime presence of U.S. troops in Europe.

In short, while it can be agreed that the present emphasis on a conventional balance in Western Europe is rightly placed, it must nevertheless be recognized that current programs (that is, the LDTP): (1) do not meet our goal of strengthening NATO's conventional defenses, (2) work against the objective of easing the Europeans from enervating dependence on the United States and into assuming a greater share of the overall world defense burden/responsibility, and (3) undercut our trade balance. In the long run, it must be remembered that if the Europeans will not buy our goods and will not hold our dollars, how are we to finance our troops abroad (the modern version of history repeating the 1920s debate on German reparations)? Finally by the proper solving of NATO's long-standing military deficiency and with the management attention and resources released therefrom, U.S. security planning can be cast wider than that of a continental strategy.

Notes

1. According to *The Military Balance*, NATO outspent the Warsaw Pact in 1976 by $160 to $136 billion. (In fact, due to the index number method of converting Soviet budgets to dollar terms, the differential is larger.) In military manpower, NATO again had more men under arms (4.82 to 4.75 million). In estimated reservists the Pact led NATO 6.1 to 5.1 million. (However, if estimated reservists were commonly defined versus institutionally defined by law) as all men or all men with formal military training within specified age brackets, NATO's number would again be the larger.) International Institute of Strategic Studies, *The Military Balance, 1977-1978* (London: 1977), pp. 82, 84.

2. The statistic normally cited for the NGA is (in thousands) 782 NATO versus 935 Pact (ground) and 193 NATO versus 204 Pact (air). The French have an additional 280,000 ground and 104,000 air, the bulk of which are stationed in Northeast France. Ibid., pp. 22, 23, 110.

3. *A Report to Congress on U.S. Conventional Reinforcements for NATO*, Office of the Secretary of Defense, June 1976, p. VI-7.

4. International Institute of Strategic Studies, *Military Balance*, pp. 82-83.

5. See for example, the British *Statement on the Defense Estimates 1977*, pp. 9-10; The German *White Paper 1975/1976 (the Security of the Federal Republic of Germany and the Development of the Federal Armed Forces)*, pp. 48, 84, 85; and a report to the Assembly of the Western European Union, *Rational Deployment of Forces on the Central Front*, April 1975, p. 22 by General U. de Maiziere.

6. Géneral d' Armée Adrienne M. Fourquet, "The Role of the Forces," *Survival* (July, 1969):206-210.

7. So far the Soviets have never much exploited this divergence in NATO alliance interests. It is, of course, central to the French withdrawal from NATO, and to the present alliance imbroglios over the cruise missile in SALT and the "neutron bomb." Contrary to the impressions of the code words used in these debates, the Western Europeans always view tactical nuclears for their political impact. Thus whereas the United States may see enhanced radiation weapons as increasing deterrence through their more efficient fighting impact, the Western Europeans would see them as enhancing deterrence by increasing the nuclear commitment of the American ally and by lowering the nuclear threshold, thereby increasing the credibility of their use and of their concomitant linkage to strategic weapons.

8. Guilio Douhet, *The Command of the Air* (London: Faber & Faber, 1943); Heinz Guderian, *Panzer Leader* (London: Michael Joseph, 1952).

9. "NATO Strategy and Requirements 1975-1985," *Survival* (September/October 1975); p. 212.

10. For a brief and brilliant discourse on the merits of a cordon defense, see Carl von Clausewitz, *On War* (Princeton, N.J.:Princeton University Press, 1976), Book 6, Chapter 22, pp. 453-455. A cordon defense is consistent with the European interpretation of the NATO (14/3) strategy of forward defense and flexible response, but it is not consistent with the American interpretation.

11. See for example, David Greenwood, *Measuring Certain Economic Benefits from Increased NATO Standardization: Production Economies, Alternative Methods of Acquisition and Their Budgetary Impact* (Potomac, Md.:C & L Associates, September 1978), pp. 166-167.

6

Population Defense Reconsidered: Is the ABM Really Inconsistent with Stability?

Jerome Slater

Ever since the effective abolition of antiballistic missile (ABM) systems in the Salt I Treaty, both the United States and the Soviet Union necessarily have had to rely entirely on deterrence rather than defense to prevent nuclear catastrophe. The overall strategic posture of the United States is explicitly based on establishing and maintaining a balance of terror, or, more officially, mutual assured destruction.

The time has come to make explicit and to reexamine what has heretofore remained largely implicit in the doctrine of mutual assured destruction—MAD—namely that the greatest threat of war, of mutual nuclear catastrophe, is a deliberately instigated attack by the government of one superpower against the armed forces or population of the other. If in fact this is the central threat, then MAD is quite appropriate. Indeed, the madder MAD is (the more insanely destructive), the better it works, since it can hardly fail to deter deliberate all-out war. But, it will be argued here, such a war is highly unlikely, and MAD is not only irrelevant to the far more likely threats of nuclear catastrophe, it is worse than irrelevant, since it threatens to make nuclear attacks of some kind more likely to occur and more destructive if they do occur.

The central argument of this chapter will be that the underlying rationale of the U.S./Soviet strategic arms control negotiations—to stabilize and institutionalize MAD, primarily by eschewing defensive measures and stabilizing offensive weapons at some (very high) level of rough parity—is fundamentally wrong and dangerous. Instead, it will be proposed, MAD should be modified to allow for mutual defense against various kinds of light attacks, which can be done without reducing deterrence against heavy attacks.

To provide the context for the central argument and proposed modifications in both U.S. and Soviet doctrines and weapons systems, a brief historical review is in order. As a result of the prevailing doctrines and their underlying assumptions, the major "success" of the SALT negotiations to date, the only important ongoing weapons system that has actually been curtailed by mutual agreement has been the ABM. That is to say, the single

101

weapons system meaningfully constrained in 12 years of serious arms control negotiations has been the single weapons system that was defensive, that actually had some promise of saving lives rather than destroying them.

Of course there have been understandable and superficially plausible—although ultimately unpersuasive—reasons that have brought about this sorry state of affairs. Recall the various shifting and unpersuasive rationales for ABM systems when they first became potentially operable in the mid-1960s. Initially, it was hoped, ABMs could provide a meaningful defense against a full-scale Soviet attack against U.S. cities. But it soon became apparent that since the only effective defense of cities would have to be 100 percent perfect, any city-defense ABM system could rather easily be overwhelmed by a superpower determined to do so. The dominant view of U.S. strategists, moreover, was that an American effort to protect its cities against a full-scale Soviet attack would inevitably be seen as part of a potential offensive strategy, in which the Soviets would fear the United States was intending to attack its retaliatory forces in a disarming first-strike and shoot down those it missed with its ABM system. Since both superpowers, then, would interpret such ABM systems as a threat to MAD, and could easily counter them, the attempt to construct antisuperpower city defenses would generate new offensive systems to overcome them and would end by being costly, futile, and perhaps even dangerous.

As the fatal defects of heavy population defense systems gradually came to be appreciated, at least by American strategists, new ABM rationales were devised. In a famous speech in 1967, Secretary of Defense Robert McNamara announced that the Johnson administration had concluded that there were "marginal grounds" for deploying an ABM system against the hypothetical sort of intercontinental ballistic missile (ICBM) attack that China might be capable of mounting in the mid-1970s.[1] This rationale (which McNamara himself evidently had doubts about) was no more persuasive than its predecessor, however. It was based on the premise that China might attack the United States with a few nuclear missiles despite the fact that it would be utterly destroyed in retaliation. The argument assumed, in other words, that the leadership in Peking was quite literally mad, an assumption completely at variance with China's highly cautious behavior over the years.[2] Indeed, about the only remotely conceivable situation in which the Chinese might fire nuclear missiles at the United States would be in response to an all-out *American*-initiated attack. Thus, a modified ABM system could hypothetically be employed to support a surprise attack by the United States against China, a prospect that did not endear the ABM system to many Americans who were already deeply worried (thanks to escalating U.S. actions in the Vietnam war) about their *own* government's rationality. Moreover, it was quickly understood that a thin anti-China ABM system could become an entering wedge for a heavy anti-Soviet system, as many

Pentagon officials were openly advocating. In any case, the Soviets were almost bound to assume the worst and to take countermeasures. Finally, with the waning of the Vietnam war and the rapprochement with China, the anti-China rationale disappeared, an embarrassment safely interred.

By 1969, when the new Republican administration took office, critics of the ABM had succeeded in making their point, but rather than drop the system Richard Nixon undertook to change the rationale once again. The new "Safeguard" system was designed not to protect populations but land-based ICBMs. In some respects this was an improvement over earlier rationales, since it avoided the hypothetically destabilizing features of all-out city defenses. As the administration pointed out, in the paradoxical "logic" of nuclear deterrence, protecting missiles would not—or at least should not—trigger fears of a first-strike capability, which inevitably would lead to a new escalation of the arms race, dangerous international tensions, or conceivably even preemptive attacks.

On the other hand, while avoiding the worst defects of earlier ABM systems, Safeguard had its own impressive flaws. Was it really necessary to spend billions of dollars to protect ICBM complexes when the Soviets, even with the most devastating first strike worst-case theorists could imagine, could not totally destroy even our land-based systems, let alone make more than a dent on our extensive bomber and submarine missile forces? Moreover, would not the Soviet worst-case planners undoubtedly see Safeguard as just another maneuver to keep alive the possibility of the United States later shifting to a heavy population defense, and react accordingly? More and more the ABM appeared to be a pyrrhic technological victory, a weapon in search of a rationale. Former Senator J. William Fulbright eloquently summarized these objections: "The deployment of this dubious new weapons system, virtually certain as it would be to destabilize the present arms balance and to initiate a costly and futile intensification of the arms race, would be the antithesis of prudence, at best wasteful, more probably prodigal, and quite possibly disastrous."[3]

Unfortunately, lost in all the chaff had been the germ of a good idea: ABM protection of U.S. cities against accidental, unauthorized, or third-party (other than Chinese) attacks. Both Johnson's anti-China and Nixon's Safeguard systems had indeed included this kind of protection, but distinctly as a secondary matter, and neither proponents nor critics of the proposed systems made much of the matter. The unpersuasiveness of the primary rationales for ABM systems, then, as they were presented in the late 1960s and early 1970s, had the effect of precluding serious discussion of the one rationale that actually made some sense.

By the early 1970s, the tide of opinion in the national security community, Congress, and in the informed public had decisively swung against ABMs of any kind. Not only had all the major rationales of the ABM been effectively rebutted, but the ABM had become a symbolic issue. Growing frustrations about the Vietnam war and a generally antimilitary shift in public and congressional opinion had made it even more difficult to consider the ABM on whatever merits it might have had. In the Senate, the ABM became a surrogate for congressional futility over rising military expenditures and the Indochina war.[4] Thus, in 1970 Congress rejected the Nixon administration's request for a twelve-site ABM system to defend four ICBM complexes, and failed by only one vote (the Senate divided 50-50) to eliminate ABMs altogether, authorizing funds for just two ABM installations.[5]

Thus, faced with effective congressional opposition to all but the most minimal ABM system, and in imminent danger of losing even that, the Nixon administration was compelled to seek a negotiated abolition or strict limitation on ABMs in Salt I. Liberals had won their single major victory over military expenditures since World War II; it was a sign of how ideological the ABM issue had become that in the end only a handful of conservatives, particularly Donald Brennan and Herman Kahn, were left to point out the moral ghastliness of MAD, which the ABM, at least in principle, had some possibility of mitigating.[6]

As is well known, though, it took some time to convince the Soviets that defense against ICBMs was bad. The initial Soviet position was the rather old-fashioned, commonsensical one that, as Premier Alexei Kosygin put it: "Defensive systems, which prevent attacks, are not the cause of the arms race, but constitute a factor preventing the death of people. . . . Maybe an anti-missile system is more expensive than an offensive system, but it is designed not to kill people but to preserve human lives."[7] Eventually, though, the Soviets were persuaded to abandon such simplistic views, their thinking grew "more sophisticated," the American negotiators succeeded in "raising their learning curve."[8] Of course, it might have been less a matter of a new Soviet appreciation of the greater subtlety of the U.S. position than a resigned realization of the fact that they were on the wrong end of a self-fulfilling prophecy: the American arguments that "neither side" would allow the other to create a theoretically effective defensive system and that defensive systems always could and inevitably would be overwhelmed by simply adding sufficient numbers of new offensive systems, were not, after all, merely hypothetical arguments but a concrete warning of what the United States would in fact do if the Russians sought to build a heavy ABM system. Thus, the Americans had the unquestionable capability to ensure they were right in predicting that deployment of ABM systems would only stimulate an offensive arms race, create dangerous new tensions and interacting fears, and end by being futile and extremely dangerous to boot. Still, for a time the Soviets sought to salvage at least some defense, proposing a thin ABM system to protect each nation against accidents, unauthorized launchings, or third-party attacks. For reasons that were never made clear, the United States rejected this proposal, except for the eventual minor compromise of allowing an ABM site to protect Moscow and Washington.[9] Evidently the Nixon administration had never taken very seriously its own earlier arguments over the desirability of thin population defenses.

Thus, the 1972 SALT ABM treaty limited each superpower to a maximum of two ABM sites with 100 launchers each, one of which could protect the national capital, the other an ICBM complex; an amendment to the treaty in 1974 reduced the permissible sites to one each, and since then the United States has phased out its single ABM site, which had been providing meaningless "protection" of the ICBM complex at Grand Forks, North Dakota. The result of this process is that both sides are now defenseless, not only against a full-scale attack from the other, but against *any* kind of missile attack from *any* country or group.

Perhaps it should be reemphasized that the ABM treaty was not supposed to be an end in itself. It was not based on the rationale that defense per se was bad but rather that the abolition of defenses was a necessary means to an undeniably desirable end: meaningful cutbacks of offensive systems.[10] For some time, indeed, the United States had refused to sign an ABM-only SALT agreement, successfully putting pressure on the Soviets to agree also to an interim offensive weapons accord. Moreover, after signing the SALT agreements, the U.S. government officially stated that if a permanent offensive arms agreement was not reached within 5 years, "it would constitute a basis for withdrawal from the ABM treaty." Evidently, though, the United States has abandoned the reasoning that led to this qualification, for in December 1977 it joined in an executive agreement with the Soviet government reaffirming the ABM treaty, even though no permanent offensive weapons limitations were in sight, not even the practically meaningless ones that the United States and the Soviets were currently talking about.

The ABM Treaty, the Arms Race, and MAD

So the abolition of ABMs left both the Soviet Union and the United States unambiguously hostage to each other, institutionalized mutual assured destruction, and by so doing, it was widely argued, eliminated the last remaining rationale for a continuing arms race. Somehow, though, it has not been generally noticed that in this crucial respect the ABM treaty has miserably failed! The *rationale* (such as it was) for a continuing offensive arms race may have been eliminated, but the race itself goes on. Indeed, it has substantially escalated since 1972.

Since the SALT agreements, the United States has added about 3,300 warheads to its existing ICBM and SLBM force, bringing the total up to some 9,000 warheads, has greatly increased the accuracy and yield of those warheads, has deployed longer range missiles on its submarine force, is planning to deploy the larger, more deadly Trident submarine force in the 1980s, is beginning work on a mobile land-based missile that will be far larger and more accurate than any existing U.S. ICBMs, and will begin the first of a planned 11,000 force of air-launched cruise missiles in 1980 or 1981. Similarly, the Soviets have also greatly expanded their nuclear force, mainly by quadrupling their ICBM warheads (through MIRVing) since 1972, giving them a force of over 5,000 warheads today. All this suggests a paraphrase on Talleyrand's famous remark on the difference between "intervention" and "nonintervention": "arms race" and "arms control" are two phrases that mean precisely the same thing.[11]

What went wrong? In retrospect, it is clear that McNamara and other proponents of the action-reaction cycle theory of the arms race exaggerated the importance of that factor and, as a result, failed to realize that the ABM agreement would hardly suffice to meaningfully brake continued offensive weapons acquisitions. It is not just the interaction between defense and offense that drives the arms race but also such untouched but equally or more powerful forces as the underlying Soviet-U.S. political conflict or security dilemma; the implementation of particular strategies, such as counterforce; worst-case reasoning in the national security bureaucracy; technological determinism (what can be done will be done); bureaucratic politics, interservice rivalries, domestic politics, and vested interests; the desire for negotiating advantage in future arms control talks ("bargaining chips"); and finally, perhaps, sheer mindless momentum.

Here are the fruits of some 12 years of serious, intensive arms control negotiations: we have all been deprived of some measure of protection against certain kinds of attacks, but little or nothing has been done to inhibit the arms race or stabilize mutual deterrence. Thanks to this lamentable situation, it is apparent that in the past few years a growing disillusionment with MAD has set in within (for want of a better phrase) the national security community. Whereas criticism of MAD formerly was primarily associated with the right, this is no longer the case, and there is now widespread agreement about the grave defects of MAD.

First of all, MAD is a doomsday machine, a high-risk, all-or-nothing strategy. As long as it works it is fine, but if it fails it guarantees apocalypse. More specifically, MAD provides excellent deterrence against large-scale nuclear wars deliberately initiated by the government of either superpower, but this is the least likely danger of nuclear catastrophe in the years to come. Like the famous doomsday machine, it certainly reduces the risk of war, but equally certainly it does not reduce the risks to zero, and that is what is decisive.

Secondly, MAD is an independent variable in international conflict, it is a cause as well as a consequence of superpower tension, it is akin to two scorpions in a bottle. It is at least possible to imagine an international future in which ideological or nationalistic conflicts have faded, but interstate conflict and even war persists, largely because of the weapons themselves. Indeed, not long ago Fred Iklé argued (somewhat prematurely, perhaps) that this absurd situation already existed: "Toward each other as a people, Americans and Russians harbor practically no feelings of hostility, but by our theories they must indefinitely face each other as the most fearful threat to their future existence."[12]

Third, MAD, if actually carried out, would be grotesquely immoral. We threaten to slaughter tens or even hundreds of millions of civilians in response to an action of their government over which they have no control. No remotely rational purpose could be achieved by implementing the threat of mass destruction on which MAD rests, perhaps not even retaliation and punishment pure and simple, since the government officials whose aggression (actual, expected, or imagined) precipitated the response are among those most likely to escape the retaliatory blow. Of course, some argue (or hope) that MAD is perhaps only a necessary bluff that would not actually be carried out should deterrence fail. But this seems like wishful thinking. To bluff, it would be necessary to plan—or at least systematically think about—how *not* to strike back; such plans would run too high a risk of being discovered by the other side, which would, of course, gravely undermine deterrence. The entire military system is geared to strike back in certain contingencies; therefore it is only too likely that it actually *would* strike back in those contingencies, however mindless and murderous retaliation would be.

What might cause MAD to fail? The three most worrisome possibilities are generally thought to be:

1. Strategic asymmetry between the superpowers, in which one side comes to believe it has the capability of destroying the other side's retaliatory forces—or enough of them to make the ensuing retaliation "acceptable"—in a disarming first-strike. This is currently the prime worry of many U.S. strategic analysts, who fear the Russians may be aiming for such a first-strike capability in the mid-1980s; others note that the increased accuracy of U.S. warheads combined with their sheer numbers already must be deeply worrisome to Russian planners. In the well-known logic of deterrence, strategic asymmetries run the risk, in theory anyway, of precipitating not only a surprise attack by the stronger side on the weaker but also a preemptive attack by the weaker against the stronger.

2. Technological breakthough, in which one or the other superpower suddenly develops some superweapon, offensive or defensive, that it believes allows it to strike the other side's nuclear forces with impunity.

3. Accidents (inadvertent missile launchings, for example); unauthorized actions by lower level commanders of nuclear weapons; terrorist attacks by irrational political leaders of national governments ("crazy states") or even of subnational groups: a nuclear-armed Quadaffi or the PLO, and so forth.

The dangers of the first two contingencies are probably exaggerated, but the last is very serious indeed. As long as we assume, as deterrence requires, even minimal rationality on the part of Soviet and American leaders, they are not likely to see a theoretical asymmetry or some new technological miracle as making a full-scale attack reasonable—not when merely one of the opponent's submarines, if it escaped attack, could destroy over one hundred cities, one surviving bomber could destroy up to twenty cities, and so on. Nothing has changed, or is likely to change, the basic strength of MAD: only a 100 percent successful disarming strike could rationally be even contemplated, but a guaranteed 100 percent successful strike is utterly impossible. Thus, the balance of terror—defined to mean the state of mutual deterrence between each superpower's government—has not been delicate since at least the mid-1950s, is not delicate now, and will not be delicate in the foreseeable future, at least against any currently imaginable developments. To my knowledge, no one has taken issue with McGeorge Bundy's famous observation: "In the real world of real political leaders—whether here or in the Soviet Union—a decision that would bring even one hydrogen bomb on one city of one's own country would be recognized in advance as a catastrophic blunder; ten bombs on ten cities would be a disaster beyond history; and a hundred bombs on a hundred cities are unthinkable."[13]

But: what about the accidental launching, the unauthorized launching by a certifiably insane lieutenant, the acquisition of nuclear weapons by irrational governments, terrorist organizations, or even criminal groups? All these science-fiction nightmares of the past are now increasingly an unhappy reality, and they will become considerably more so as each superpower builds more and more nuclear weapons, as weapons-grade material proliferates around the world as a by-product of peaceful nuclear energy programs, and as the knowledge of how to build nuclear weapons becomes increasingly diffused. Of course major efforts have been made to improve top-level command and control over nuclear weapons, to prevent the spread of weapons to other countries, and to limit the capabilities of nuclear reactors producing energy to also produce weapons-grade materials. But it would indeed be optimistic to believe that these efforts will be fully successful into the indefinite future. Given the sheer amount of nuclear weapons and weapons-grade material already around, let alone what will become available in the next few decades, and given the endless possibilities of human error, systems breakdowns, ideological or criminal fanaticism, and just plain malevolence, the odds are mounting that a catastrophe will occur.[14]

Against such catastrophes, MAD is not merely useless—it is *worse* than useless, for it threatens to turn an accident or some other kind of limited attack into apocalypse. And even if it did not, even if the superpower leaders did not respond to an attack with a spasm of total destruction, the prospects are not very comforting. Consider this: a single American nuclear submarine with MIRVed missiles can today target 160 separate Soviet cities; the Soviets will soon have a comparable capability; and the projected Trident submarine of the 1980s will be able to strike at 240 cities. Thus, an unauthorized attack by a single submarine, even if it did not precipitate an all-out war, would not be much less destructive than a deliberate, full-scale assault some 20 years or so ago.

Are there any alternatives to MAD? The major alternatives that have attracted the attention of nuclear strategists are minimum deterrence and counterforce. As the debate over these proposed strategies is well known, perhaps a few summary observations will suffice here. Minimum deterrence is politically unacceptable, does not solve the moral problem, and is potentially more unstable against deliberate superpower attacks than MAD (the fewer the weapons, the greater the likelihood that a technological breakthrough could create the temptation of a disarming first-strike).

Similarly, counterforce as a solution may be worse than the problem. As many critics have pointed out, the notion of limited nuclear exchanges with military (and industrial?) installations as the primary targets suffers from some fatal defects. Given the enormous destructiveness of nuclear weapons and the likelihood that military targets will be defined broadly, civilian devastation will be widespread; by requiring far more nuclear weapons than assured destruction, counterforce would be extremely costly and would add additional fuel to the arms race; counterforce strategies may make nuclear war more likely by making it appear, however illusorily, as more rational and controllable. Given the well-known limitations on human and organizational rationality, limited nuclear exchanges are likely to quickly escalate into all-out war; and counterforce is likely to increase international tensions, the adoption of launch-on-warning strategies, and possibly even the prospects of preemptive attacks, since the accuracy and sheer weight of nuclear weapons required for a counterforce retaliatory strategy are quite indistinguishable from the capabilities necessary for a pure first-strike strategy.

The argument here is not for some grand change in overall strategy, but only for a reasonably modest shift in emphasis—in doctrine and weapons systems—toward defense, to mitigate the most undesirable consequences of the balance of terror. The major premise underlying the argument is that MAD overdeters and underdefends; therefore what is proposed is the reintroduction of ABM city defenses, perhaps along with some kind of civil defense against radioactive fall-out, to provide substantial protection against light, unauthorized, accidental, or third-party attacks.[15] The reintroduction of ABM city-defense systems should be done only through formal agreement with the Soviet Union, in which each side agrees to deploy enough ABMs to provide a meaningful defense against various sorts of light attacks, but nowhere near enough to successfully defend (thereby undermining deterrence) against full-scale deliberate superpower attacks. The precise numbers of such ABMs, their locations, and so forth, would have to be worked out in detailed negotiations, but a rough figure of some 1,000 launchers covering the entire national territories of the United States and the Soviet Union would seem about right.[16] At the same time, agreed-on deployments of fall-out shelters might also be considered. Unlike the city-evacuation civil defense measures currently being considered by the Carter Administration (and said by some to be already in effect in the Soviet Union), fall-out shelters would be useful only against light attacks and would not raise suspicions of first-strike intentions.

No doubt some will argue that even a relatively small-scale ABM/civil defense capability, when combined with the first-strike capabilities that each side will have against fixed, land-based ICBMs by the mid-1980s, would increase the risk of a full-scale deliberate disarming strike. However, given the huge numbers of bombers, submarines, cruise missiles, and, probably, mobile ICBMs that will be available in the 1980s, no such first-strike temptation would be remotely rational, no matter what the level of ABM defenses, let alone the relatively modest levels proposed herein. To further reduce first-strike fears (as well as for other, equally good reasons), it would be desirable for the superpowers to mutually reduce their offensive forces, particularly those accurate and powerful enough to be used for first-strike purposes against hardened ICBMs, and negotiate limitations on antisubmarine warfare and bomber defense systems. The reductions should be to levels that would substantially diminish first-strike fears, but not so low as to drastically undercut second-strike retaliatory forces.

Thus, although it could be argued that these proposed changes in the strategic posture of both superpowers in theory would weaken deterrence against deliberate attacks, they would do so *only* in theory, and only slightly. Since we already have a redundancy of deterrence by large orders of magnitude against any even minimally rational opponent, the trade-off between slightly-less-but-still-more-than-sufficient deterrence against the least likely kind of nuclear war for some kind of defense against the most likely kind of catastrophe would seem to be sensible.

To be sure, the light city-defense systems proposed here could cause some problems. Perhaps the most important is the possibility that France, Great Britain, and China might fear that Soviet defensive systems would undercut their minimum-deterrent forces; if so they might respond with a major nuclear arms buildup. However, it is also possible that they would conclude that they could overcome light city defenses with concentrated attacks against key Soviet cities, thereby preserving some significant minimum deterrent capabilities and obviating the "need" for a tremendously costly expansion of their existing forces.

How likely would the Soviets be to negotiate limited ABM systems? This would seem unlikely to be a major problem, given the well-known historical defensive orientation of the Russians, their earlier reluctance to abandon ABMs, their current civil defense measures, and their lively concern (however misplaced) over China.

Would a light, national population defense work? Even at the time of the first ABM debate in the late 1960s, many prominent scientists opposed to ABM systems conceded that an effective defense against limited attacks was feasible. For example, Abram Chayes and Jerome Wiesner wrote: "We conclude that an ABM system, if it performed reliably, could provide some protection against some kinds of accidental missile launches.[17]"; similarly, George Rathjens, a prominent physicist and nuclear strategist, estimated that all the United States could be defended from light attacks from perhaps a dozen interceptor missile sites.[18] In general, though, there was little serious discussion about such a system, in part because of the assumption that a light system would "inevitably" be expanded to a heavy defense, in part because of the assessment (or, rather, assumption) that the costs of such a system relative to the dangers it sought to guard against did not warrant the construction of an ABM system "on the basis of its performance of this mission alone."[19] It is precisely the argument of this chapter, of course, that the dangers now existing from various kinds of light attacks do warrant light defensive systems.

It is also possible that future ABM—or, rather, ballistic missile defense (BMD)—systems may be based on entirely different principles than earlier technology permitted. In the 8 years since the ABM was banned, both the Soviet Union and the United States have had active research and development programs seeking major breakthroughs in defensive technologies.[20] One of the major efforts has been on high-energy laser beams and, more recently, nuclear particle beams. At the same time, with the extensive deployment of satellite systems and the development of over-the-horizon radars, it is now possible to detect almost immediately the launchings of missiles in other countries. If the laser or particle-beam technology proves effective—although this is still very much an open question—incoming missiles could be destroyed within minutes after launch, thousands of miles from their targets. Moreover, the speed and accuracy of new-technology ABMs might be such that they could be armed with nonnuclear warheads, thereby eliminating two of the more serious defects of earlier ABM systems: the widespread destruction that nuclear ABMs themselves might inflict, and the erosion of presidential control over nuclear weapons (stemming from the time-urgent necessity to delegate operational control over the firing of ABMs to lower level field commanders). All this may sound a bit like science fiction, but successful testing of improved ABMs has continued since 1972, there are reports that the United States will be testing laser and/or particle beam antimissile systems in the early 1980s, and a number of military scientists believe that effective nonnuclear defensive systems could be operational in less than a decade.[21]

Finally, what about the costs of a light nationwide defensive system? In earlier years the estimated costs of such ABM systems ran from $10-20 billion, or $2-4 billion annually for about 5 years, but as any future systems may be based on radically new technology, it simply is not possible at this point to make even an educated guess. It is possible, of course, that the costs could prove prohibitive, but given what is at stake this seems unlikely, especially if the costs of construction of defensive systems were offset by substantial cuts in offensive systems.

Over the long run, the end we should aim at is the progressive dismantling of the doomsday machine we have created and its replacement by more defensive strategies and weapons systems. This is not the place to discuss major alternatives to MAD, but we should not assume that it is beyond our moral, intellectual, or technological capacity to devise saner doctrines and weapons systems. In the meantime, the modest changes discussed here would provide a reasonable measure of both deterrence *and* defense against light attacks.

Notes

1. *The New York Times*, 19 September 1967.

2. McNamara conceded this, in describing the hypothetical attack against which the United States was preparing to defend itself as "insane and suicidal." Ibid.

3. In Ralph Lapp, *Arms beyond Doubt* (New York: Cowles Publications, 1970), p. 85.

4. As Elizabeth Young put it, congressional debate "fastened on to the ABM question as if it contained all folly, all the arms race, all guilt for previous connivances. Oppose the ABM and your sins will be forgiven you." In *A Farewell to Arms Control?* (London: Penguin Books, 1972), p. 188.

5. For discussion on Congress and the ABM, see Alton Frye, *A Responsible Congress: The Politics of National Security* (New York: McGraw-Hill, 1975).

6. The major works defending the ABM include Donald G. Brennan, "The Case for Missile Defense," *Foreign Affairs* 47 (April 1969); Brennan,"When the SALT Hits the Fan," *National Review* 24 (27 June 1972); William R. Kintner, ed., *Safeguard: Why the ABM Makes Sense* (New York: Hawthorn Books, 1969); Johan J. Holst and William Schneider, Jr., eds., *Why ABM?* (New York: Pergamon Press, 1969).

7. Quoted in Clark Murdock, *Defense Policy Formation* (Albany, N.Y.: SUNY Press, 1974), p. 135.

8. John Newhouse, *Cold Dawn* (New York: Holt, Rinehart & Winston, 1973), pp. 3, 4.

9. On the SALT negotiations over thin ABM systems see: ibid.; John Barton and Lawrence D. Weler, eds., *International Arms Control* (Palo Alto, Calif.: Stanford University Press, 1976), p. 186; and Raymond Garthoff, "Negotiating with the Russians," *International Security* 1 (Spring 1977).

10. Note, however, the remark of Gerard C. Smith, chief of the U.S. delegation to SALT I, that the ABM treaty had ended "one-half of the nuclear arms competition," as if the abolition of defensive weapons to save lives was in and of itself desirable and an end value on the same plane as ending offensive arms competition. See Smith, "A Double Standard," *International Security* 2 (Summer 1977):62.

11. In this connection, in 1972, Jerome Kahan warned that if an ABM treaty was not negotiated, "the United States would almost surely take actions to increase the survivable power of its deterrent force by deploying new generation offensive systems. . . . The level of United States strategic spending could rise by as much as $3 to $5 billion annually. The Soviet Union, in turn, would probably increase its offensive missile deployments well beyond the present levels and emphasize advanced MIRVs." From Jerome Kahan, "Limited Agreements and Long-Term Stability; A Positive View toward SALT," *Stanford Journal of International Studies* (spring 1972); reprinted in U.S. Senate, Committee on Foreign Relations, *Hearings on Strategic Arms Limitation Agreements*, 92d Congress, 2d Session, 1972, p. 421.

Not a word of Kahan's prediction needs modification despite the fact that the negotiations succeeded.

12. In "Can Nuclear Deterrence Last Out the Century?" *Foreign Affairs*, 51, no. 2 (January 1973):282. This justly famous article has precipitated much of the current reevaluation of MAD, including my own.

13. "To Cap the Volcano," *Foreign Affairs*, no. 1, 48 (October 1969):10.

14. For a similar argument, see Ikle, "Nuclear Deterrence."

15. To be sure, ABMs would provide defense only against missile attacks, not against every possible form of nuclear weapons delivery. However, although terrorist or other deliberate attacks of course could circumvent any ABM system by finding other means of delivery, missiles would be the most likely form of accidental or unauthorized attack.

16. Kahan, "Hearings," p. 418. It has been pointed out that even relatively limited ABM launcher capabilities would require an extensive radar system that could provide the basis for a heavy ABM system. However, I assume that the ease with which a heavy system—one that aimed for population defense against full-scale superpower attacks—could be overcome would act as a major deterrent against its deployment and that the negotiated limitations on numbers of ABM launchers in a light system could be relatively easily verified.

17. Abram Chayes and Jerome B. Wiesner, eds., *ABM* (New York: Harper & Row, 1969), p. 42.

18. George Rathjens, "ABCs of ABMs," *Bulletin of the Atomic Scientists'* 27 (March 1971):15.

19. Chayes and Wiesner, *ABM*, p. 42.

20. The plain language of the 1972 ABM treaty apparently banned various qualitative improvements in ABM systems or the development of "exotic" new technologies, but both sides have "interpreted" this part of the treaty into meaninglessness, and neither has objected to the other's ongoing research, development, and testing programs.

21. The most authoritative source on continuing U.S. and Soviet ABM programs is *Aviation Week and Space Technology*. For detailed articles on recent developments see the issues of April 22-May 6, 1974; April 21, 1975; December 8, 1975; September 6, 1976; June 4, 1978; August 7, 1978; August 14, 1978; and a 6-part series on particle-beam technology, October 2-November 13, 1978. For other discussions of new-technology ABM systems see U.S. House of Representatives, *Evaluation of Fiscal Year 1979 Arms Control Impact Statements*, Report of the Committee on International Relations (Washington, D.C.: Government Printing Office, 1978); Richard Garwin, "Effective Military Technology for the 1980s," *International Security* 1 (Fall 1976); Steward W.B. Menaul, "The Military Balance and Its Implications," *Strategic Review* (Summer 1977). A more skeptical assessment of the military applications of particle-beam technology is found in John Parmentola and Kosta Tsipis, "Particle-Beam Weapons," *Scientific American* 240 (April 1979), although their skepticism is primarily directed against the feasibility of particle-beam defense against large-scale, deliberate launches.

7 Arms Control through Communication and Information Regimes

Davis B. Bobrow

Introduction

The value of arms control measures depends on the answers to two questions. Do they make the world better than it would be otherwise? Do they make the world better than it was? Strong nays to the second question make yeas to the first of little comfort. By almost any standard—destructiveness, diffusion of ownership, financial expense, hair trigger readiness, speed of use—the arms postures of the superpowers and of the world as a whole have become increasingly terrifying.

There is little credible prospect for a reversal of this trend solely through currently emphasized arms control approaches. Their emphases are familiar by now: (1) forces only capable of defensive or second-strike effectiveness; (2) force-sizing limits on numbers and types of weapons prevalent in (SALT) and (MBFR/MFR) forums; (3) military expenditure limitations; (4) deployment constraints; and (5) supplier cartels to withhold militarily relevant technology. Arms acquisition and development continue to substantially outdistance arms control accomplishments.

This chapter argues for greater attention to communication and information regimes as a central element of arms control efforts. These regimes apply to national and alliance military postures conceived as forces embedded in a system of communication, command, and control, and intelligence (C^3/I), to information sharing and communication between adversaries, and to observational and communication capacities of third parties potentially or actually involved as providers of guarantees, sanctions, or mediation. The third parties may be other governments or international organizations. Pertinent technologies enable multiple-indicator observation of many militarily relevant activities anywhere in the world under many conditions. They can provide real-time communication of messages from and to many points on the globe with little need for specialized local facilities.

This research was supported in part by the Defense Advanced Research Projects Agency of the U.S. Department of Defense and was monitored by the Office of Naval Research under Contract No. N00014-75-C-0846. Views expressed are those of the author and should not be interpreted as necessarily representing the official policies, either expressed or implied, of the Advanced Research Projects Agency or the U.S. Government. Robert D. Warrington provided helpful research assistance.

Unilateral C^3/I steps contribute to arms control by reducing the dangers of: accidental war by human or equipment failure; inadvertent war due to the activities of mischievous, catalytic third parties; destabilization of quantitative or qualitative force ratios; escalation of limited conflicts; acute tensions conducive to runaway uses of force; misunderstandings of adversary intentions (policy objectives, triggering thresholds, targeting objectives) leading to destabilizing actions.[1] Progress in the C^3/I domain has marked arms control successes since World War II.[2] Particularly significant are the SALT-related agreements between the United States and the USSR on noninterference with national means of verification and on communications and querying/confirmation modalities.[3] Verification capabilities have already slowed arms procurement.[4] For regional conflicts, the most familiar example of what the Israeli leader Shimon Peres has called "modern peacekeeping" is the thin United States-operated sensor capability emplaced between Israeli and Egyptian forces in the Sinai.[5]

Nevertheless, steps to date for information and communication regimes supportive of arms control are clearly marginal and fragmentary in a number of important respects. These include coverage of militarily significant parties and locations, of indicators of operational intentions, of the variety of signals, queries, and messages between the superpowers and other parties, and of the background comprehension necessary for the provision of information and communication in times of heightened tension. These information and communication arrangements provide no ready basis for third-party participation or for treating problem situations not previously recognized. They are not commensurate with the range of parties, situations, and incentives pertinent to arms acquisition and use. They fail to provide for the unfolding processes of learning and bargaining that arms control durability and momentum require.[6]

Before turning to each of the three related arenas of information and communication regimes (within a national or alliance security system, between adversaries, and responsive to third parties), at least cursory mention must be made of two general sets of issues. The first deals with the part played by communication and information matters in the initiation, escalation, reduction, and termination of war and preparations for it, and in crisis avoidance, management, and resolution. The second concerns the U.S. stake in improved information and communication regimes for arms control.

General Considerations

C^3/I systems are to weapons as nerves are to muscles. They provide a critical capability for potential strength to be used according to higher purposes and for the consequences of prior and current uses of force to inform subsequent action. Appeals for greater attention to communication, command and control, and intelligence within and across national lines are often rejected almost reflexively. These appeals are said to lack understanding of the realities of force, to divert resources from weapons, to rest on unwarranted assumptions of trust or at least mutual peaceful intent, and to sacrifice attractive options for surprise and deception. Such criticisms are largely uninformed, without theoretical foundation, and pernicious in their implications. These failings hold at least for situations in which the parties are heavily armed and lack a basis for confidence about securing desirable outcomes through the use of force. The premises for automatic rejection of the directions of arms control effort under discussion do not apply to most contemporary situations of central interest.

Historical illustrations come readily to mind, including estimation of an opponent's irrevocable intent to attack and speed of implementing that intent (World War I), inattention to warnings (Pearl Harbor and the Chinese intervention in Korea), missed opportunities to avoid war (the United States and Japan in 1941), and unnecessary escalation (the Mayaguez incident). Governments have repeatedly found themselves in wars and crises they did not want and were unable to limit, interrupt, or terminate according to high policy. The reasons often lie in deficient ability of high officials and their staffs to know in a timely and accurate fashion the behavior of their own forces and to get them to engage in desired conduct and refrain from unwanted conduct. Deterrence has often failed in spite of large military inventories when adversaries perceive that another's C^3/I systems make an effective military response impossible or dilatory[7] or imply first-strike intentions. Governments also have repeatedly found themselves unwittingly inducing war because of misunderstandings about an adversary's reading of their capability and intent. And nationally disastrous wars for all parties have continued because of an inability to engage in sufficiently clear communication to bargain effectively about the level and termination of violence.[8]

The "realists" have not found any convincing way to avoid a substantial number of surprises, so-called intelligence failures, in spite of high levels of vigilance. Approximately one-third of the crises involving the United States since World War II have come as surprises, and another third were not clearly anticipated.[9] There are conceptual and pragmatic reasons to doubt that full warning through unilateral means is a feasible objective.[10] Nor have the realists proposed any effective set of measures for a necessarily surprise-ridden world short of limitless expenditure and a cool-headed approach. In the absence of trust, gaps in information and communication hardly allow prudent decision-makers to do anything else but prepare for those worst-case possibilities within the limits of political feasibility, economic wherewithal, and psychological tolerance.

Information and communication regimes are most needed in an international environment of mistrust and where actors operate with limited foresight and control. They offer one necessary way to deal with the security dilemma often characterized in prisoner's dilemma terms.[11] Even if one accepts this characterization of strategic situations, and there are good reasons to be skeptical in this respect[12], information and communication regimes should appeal as ways of weakening the constraints on arms control that prisoner's dilemma formulations imply.[13] To the extent that such regimes lower the likelihood of hostile surprises without time for a damage-limiting response and of escalation, they lay the foundation for most other confidence-building measures to break threat spirals.[14]

It should be understood that the regimes necessary to enable arms control to proceed should not be limited literally to observations of military preparation and activity but must also extend to analysis of observations and appraisals of their implications.[15] In part, this is because of the lack of binding interpretive significance inherently associated with any particular observation.[16] More fundamentally it is because of the importance of the parties' judgments about violations of rules of the game or conventions, the triggering thresholds mentioned earlier.[17] The role of communication is to enable mutual discovery of what conventions and rules the parties believe applicable and what are for them violations. These matters need to be clarified in the course of evolving strategic interaction.[18] Also, pertinent technologies for information and communication must be readily available and operate in a timely fashion to control military moves. Those conditions are generally met by modern computer, communications, and remote sensing equipment.[19]

It is true that informing and communicating with adversaries and opening oneself to observation by third parties, or sharing unique observation capabilities with them, weakens efforts to surprise or deceive adversaries. Transparency replaces secrecy. While it would be foolish to argue that such changes are always desirable, the net loss they involve is easily overrated for many security situations.[20] The loss can be mutual between adversaries or even advantageous for bargaining and deterrence purposes. There is no loss if the existing capacity for surprise and deception is weak or irrelevant. There is little reason to believe that substantial weakness in military capability can be kept hidden from a determined adversary. Increased transparency may well do little to worsen the position of the weak but do much to limit misunderstandings among the strong including misunderstandings of intentions or miscalculation about adversary moves. In an era of notable first-strike advantages and "gray" weapons systems, it may contribute to what will otherwise be a diminished capacity to verify military preparations. Of course, clarifying for others the capabilities and limitations of one's C^3/I systems may make it easier for them to engage in surprise and deception. This possibility should not be ignored but should be kept in perspective. All warning estimates and force control resources and procedures need not be disclosed. Some significant elements of disclosure may well be desirable for deterrence.

As for third parties, superpower arrangements to police the world often are not feasible or desirable. Only third-party actions can deal with many international flash points. Many adversaries are critically dependent on third-party evaluations of their behavior. Transparency can contribute to reliable guarantees and timely steps by other governments to limit regional conflicts and to bring pressure against arms buildups which pose increased local dangers. Transparency to third parties can help make safeguards workable instruments of security rather than only wishful pieces of paper. Information and communication regimes in and of themselves are, of course, insufficient to these purposes. And the third parties must not be biased in favor of any particular adversary.

Rejecting information and communication arms control measures often becomes heated when one recommends such emphases for the United States. After all, some argue, the United States is already handicapped relative to the USSR, because it is an open society where military tidbits frequently appear in "Aviation Leak" exposing the nation to deception and exploitation. The problem is not new, as Pericles reveals: "Our city is thrown open to the world and we never expel a foreigner or prevent him from seeing or learning anything of which the secret revealed to an enemy might profit him. We rely not on management or trickery but on our own hearts and hands."[21]

Experience with partial reliance on transparency, for example, the "national means" to verify SALT, has not been reassuring. The Soviets limit their transparency as much as possible by encoding telemetry from missile test shots and developing antisatellite weapons.[22] Those who defend the record of compliance, by asserting the adequacy of U.S. verification or denying the need for precise observations, are held to be naive for several reasons.[23] As a largely status quo power committed to international legality, the United States and by extension its allies in Europe, Asia, and the Middle East are not the governments likely to initiate the use of force or to violate arms control agreements. As allegedly decadent, soft societies with weak leadership, the Western democracies—and the United States in particular—are unlikely to pay the monetary, human, and political price associated with the prompt and decisive use of force to defend or bolster allies or innocent parties.[24] Much of the world is fundamentally hostile to the United States or at best naive about the Soviets and their friends. Aggression by them is ignored, and independent democratic governments are attacked.

In my view, those who find these statements valid should also find strong U.S. initiatives for information and communication arms control regimes with substantial elements of transparency attractive. Rejection by others should provide particularly clear evidence of their pursuit of military advantage, first-strike and surprise attack options, and policies of the aggressive extension of force by themselves or their proxies. The identity of those truly committed to military solutions and imposed hegemonial fait accompli will be harder to overlook. If the information and communication arms control initiatives are accepted, the disadvantage of the asymmetries allegedly burdening the United States may well become smaller rather than greater.

Even if U.S. initiatives for joint regimes are rejected, unilateral imposition of greater transparency and appropriate C^3/I may be in the American interest. First, technically feasible steps may increase the credibility of U.S. deterrence and security commitments. Second, they may decrease the attractiveness to others of surprise attack attempts and measures to violate arms control agreements and to intervene in third areas. Third, they may provide to American publics, including important political and bureaucratic groupings, convincing evidence of the aggressive intentions and actions of nations that directly threaten the United States or governments favorable to U.S. interests. To the extent one finds these general arguments persuasive, some urgency arises when we recognize the mounting threats even to maintaining the current degree of transparency of national security postures. These include antisatellite weapons and sovereignty claims with regard to the use and control of space and space-based technologies. Fourth, C^3/I regimes increase the availability to high U.S. officials of information about potential and ongoing incidents with improved prospects for avoiding and acting appropriately in crises that may not be under the full control of any foreign central government.

Specific Possibilities

In this general context, different measures and goals merit serious consideration for each of the three arenas of information and communication arms control regimes mentioned earlier.

National and Alliance C^3

There is no necessary association between weapons systems conducive to stability at the strategic level or to controlled escalation and termination at other levels of war and C^3/I systems with similar effects.[25] The problems with the rationale for and current state of U.S. C^3/I systems are numerous from an arms control perspective.[26] The problems posed by differences between adversaries in their attention to C^3/I as a critical element of capability and signal of intent are also adverse to arms control progress.

Arms Control

The design and acquisition by the United States of manifestly dependable second- and subsequent strike C^3/I systems seem imperative. The general properties of such systems are clear in the abstract, featuring survivability through redundancy and hardening and the assurance of clear political lines of authority. When U.S. officials proclaim a doctrine of flexible response, they incur the obligation to establish C^3/I systems compatible with that doctrine in terms of ability to adjust military objectives and interrupt and terminate conflict short of inventory exhaustion. The absence of credible enduring C^3/I tempts an adversary to launch a beheading first-strike, that is, an attack that eliminates the policy and command centers and the communications needed to relate weapons use to national policy. Also, absence can be read as indicating first-strike intent. Emerging doctrines and weapons systems, unless accompanied by enduring C^3/I, are likely to generate severe pressures for a launch-on-warning posture, a stance that brings us closer to a doomsday machine nuclear situation.[27] Given the stakes and the historical record of governmental performance referred to earlier, the doomsday stance hardly seems desirable.

Second, with respect to alliances such as NATO, important objectives include significantly integrated C^3/I, including the delegation of appropriate authority to alliance institutions. From a deterrence point of view, such integration and delegation are crucial for a credibly coordinated military posture in contrast to a contingent and cumbersome legislative process for arriving at a military response. From a war-fighting point of view, significant C^3/I integration across alliance member lines provides some of the necessary conditions for timely and adaptive actions that are not bypassed by events. Failure to have appropriate C^3/I entitles adversaries and alliance members to doubt whether in the time of need there will in fact be an operational military alliance, that is, a multinational force committed to timely, coherent action, with any reasonable prospect for success. Resistance by alliance members to an integrated C^3/I posture is a clear sign of lack of commitment to alliance actions and of the desire to reserve options for unilateral policies. Lack of connectivity and delegation have the same de facto consequences as a lack of policy commitment to an alliance. Of course, one cannot create mutual interests simply by positing joint C^3/I arrangements. However, lack of commitment to such arrangements indicates the fallacy of estimates, doctrines, plans, and force procurements that assume such arrangements exist. NATO members may not accept truly joint C^3/I and have not done so historically. This state of affairs at least calls for a drastic reexamination of U.S. views on NATO to bring them into line with the current fragmented C^3 realities or to achieve an integrated C^3/I posture. It is inconsistent to expect the Soviets to forego opportunities presented by the disjuncture between weapons and C^3 and at the same time to proclaim the need for a NATO military buildup.

Third, sound crisis avoidance and management preparations impose still another set of C^3/I requirements on the United States and its allies. Three sorts of technological and institutional capacity stand out. First, capacity must be flexible and usable for any part of the world, that is, it should be applicable to unexpected situations in what are most of the time geographic areas of little interest. Second, capacity must exist to provide high officials of the United States and associated governments with clear and timely descriptions of what the other parties to a crisis are doing and what they themselves are doing as visible to the other participants in the crisis and their supporters. Third, the United States and its allies should have the option of communicating and exchanging information with any involved authoritative institutions elsewhere in the world clearly and quickly. The last point implies the capacity to net together at will diverse sets of parties in international affairs. Unilateral steps by the United States can provide these capacities to a very substantial extent.

All three areas of need (national, alliance, and crisis) will be best met by C^3/I postures that exist, are widely known to exist, and are in fact exercised before times of critical use.

Between Adversaries

The diversity of sets of adversaries in the contemporary world makes it difficult to generalize about C^3/I measures and goals. Nevertheless, if one believes that governments often outwit themselves and have at best imperfect consensus among their components (institutions), some common points stand out.

First, information and communication regimes should warrant confidence in warning far enough in advance of an attack to provide the adversaries with feasible options other than striking first or accepting a politically if not necessarily militarily decisive attack. Appropriate regimes will embody conventions about the notice times that meet these conditions and the treatment of the cost of alarms. For situations of high mobilization and direct confrontation, for example, the two Koreas, Israel and the front-line Arab states, possibly the Central front in Europe, warning that distinguishes normal from abornmal situations is extremely difficult. But it is possible if the parties are willing to make themselves transparent in depth and to make their C^3 observable as well as their deployed force and logistics systems. Even if an adversary is perceived as implacable, committed to the use of war as an initiative policy, and unlimited in its war aims, such arrangements may improve deterrence under assured destruction conditions. When both parties distrust each other's intent and are at least uncertain about the net consequences of war, the proposed steps may provide a welcome safeguard.

Second, the regimes should provide for assured prompt and wide-ranging communications at all times including during hostilities. These should not be limited to narrow, highly structured exchanges shaped by preceding accords between adversaries for contingencies that may bear little relation to the crisis condition before them. Agreements before a crisis should instead develop flexible arrangements capable of adaptation to the fluid and largely unforeseen circumstances implied by the term crisis.

Third, the information-sharing arrangements must enable each adversary or involved third party to establish to what extent actions by others do or do not follow from deliberate and calculated national policy. It is important to provide correctives for the possibility that particular individuals and institutions are in fact pursuing not national policy but their own policy preferences. Examples include the possibly unauthorized U.S. bombings during the Vietnam War and the actions by security institutions in the United States and the USSR during the Kennedy administration, which injected elements of conflict into the relations between those two governments while their highest officials were seeking to do the opposite.[28] In addition to such authorized but intentional acts, the sequences of action and reaction between adversaries may become unsynchronized. Institutional systems may have different leads and lags in decision-making and implementation. Judgments may err in treating action by an adversary as a response to a particular action or set of actions by an opponent. At some points, the opponents may even come to react primarily to their own anticipations of adversary reaction and the adversary's actual behavior can become almost irrelevant in the policy process. Communication and information regimes should recognize these sources of interpretive error and allow for some clarification. Fourth, the provisions of the information and communication regimes must have a significantly self-enforcing quality, which minimally implies previously established standards of compliance and costly response to violations of those standards.[29]

Finally, information and communication regimes between adversaries may be managed through tolerated and reciprocal unilateralism, third-party governments and institutions, or joint action. While the first is the easiest to achieve at least between the superpowers, it leaves much to be desired. The second implies that adversaries share a belief in the even-handedness and good will of the third party—a hard set of conditions to meet. Shared, jointly operated information and communication systems are most likely to meet the conditions stated and to move from observation to appraisal, although they are the hardest to achieve.

Responsive to Third Parties

Effective third-party actions for arms control have as one necessary condition timely and credible information and communication systems. Because the information and communication systems should serve collective interests in arms control and peace, it is important that they not be under the control of particular nations with their own private interests in selective observation, dissemination, interpretation, and message transmission. The painful experience of the Japanese in using the USSR as an intermediary in attempting to terminate World War II well illustrates this point. Proposals that international organizations rely on information from their national members are insufficiently sensitive to such problems.[30]

At least some public utility information and communication regimes for arms control should then be owned and operated by regional and international organizations. This principle applies to all the elements of such information regimes: collection and processing technology, institutions that provide direction and priorities, interpretation centers and their associated data bases, cadres of analysts and their organized memories, and military experts who supply hypotheses and make judgments about them in the light of the information acquired. Analogous requirements hold for communication systems. Current and potential adversaries will have some of the same doubts about international organizations as about national third parties. These doubts may be less severe as diverse interests are represented in the international organizations that have much less of an intervention capability.

International organization communication and information regimes for arms control have recently received substantial attention, and the subject is not likely to lose interest.[31] With particularly strong initiatives by France, the First Committee of the General Assembly adopted a resolution on December 27, 1978 for expert planning of an "international satellite monitoring agency." The resolution followed after a number of other French proposals, which spelled out the uses such a U.N. capability would have including monitoring compliance with international disarmament and security agreements, investigating crisis and tensions situations at the request of any member government or the Security Council, and building international confidence. The agency would evolve in three stages: a data processing center drawing on national satellites; data receiving stations directly linked to national satellites; and, ultimately, ownership of its own satellites.[32]

Interestingly, both the USSR and the United States abstained from voting on the French-initiated draft resolution. The U.S. position has been reserved about information regimes under UN control. The United States has skirted the sharing of satellite as contrasted with aircraft and ground sensor collected observations, emphasized that all involved parties must consent to observations being shared with the UN, and shunned general commitments to share technology and sensor control with others. The Soviets have not even supported such partial measures.

It may well be the case that both superpowers fear loss of their technological superiority in satellite development, the possible targeting

Arms Control

uses of satellite observations, and the possibly adverse UN positions based on independent observations. The French proposal would also operate to lessen market and military assistance advantages, which the superpowers currently possess. While the details need careful scrutiny and thought, some of the arguments made earlier about the U.S. stake in "openness" and factual appraisal of conflict situations suggest the need for an appraisal of international organization information and communication regimes on arms control and political grounds that goes well beyond concern with current relative advantage. An important part of that appraisal obviously should involve the extent to which international public utilities will have the ability to observe C^3 as well as military force and logistics-related matters, and safeguards to insure the balanced interpretation and dissemination of the information they may collect and generate.

Relatively wide exploration and discussion of these matters may not have the drama of specific arms control negotiations and agreements and may involve dropping some tattered curtains of secrecy. It clearly will involve dealing with the problems of background understanding necessary to interpret sensor observations meaningfully and accurately. And it will also involve seeing to it that the incentives to the personnel in an international organization on balance favor even-handed observation and interpretation. These complexities suggest the wisdom of turning first to regional rather than global international regimes.

Concluding Perspective

The arms control measures emphasizing information and communication do not all call for substantial transfers of authority from national governments or complete departures from precedents established albeit tenuously between the superpowers. Unilateral measures can go forward in the absence of complex political arrangements. Multilateral measures can be urged to clarify the realities of security alliances. And joint and international organization measures need not in the first instance involve the dismantling of national communication and information capabilities. Of course, arms control progress through information and communication measures is neither simple nor a panacea. The security asymmetries, political obstacles, and decision-system characteristics that limit the wisdom of action regardless of information and communication remain. And the technical feasibility provided by modern information, communication, and remote sensing technologies leaves complex problems of practical application to specific situations and institutions.[33]

Yet it still seems past time for the most serious and substantial attention to these heretofore second-class dimensions of arms control. Attempts to limit forces through current arms control priorities have served only poorly to build confidence or provide safeguards. We increasingly face the situation well summarized by Winston Churchill many years ago: "Death stands at attention, obedient, expectant, ready to serve, ready to shear away the peoples *en masse*."

Notes

1. Clark C. Abt, *Theoretical Aspects of Unilateral Arms Control* (Bedford, Mass.: Raytheon Co., 1963).
2. F.A. Long, "Arms Control from the Perspective of the Nineteen-Seventies," *Daedalus* 104 (1975):1-14.
3. U.S. Arms Control and Disarmament Agency, *Arms Control and Disarmament Agreements* (Washington, D.C.: U.S. Government Printing Office, 1975).
4. Lawrence Freedman, *U.S. Intelligence and the Soviet Strategic Threat* (Boulder, Colo.: Westview Press, 1977).
5. United States Sinai Support Mission, *Report to the Congress* (1975), mimeo; ibid., *Second Report to the Congress* (1976), mimeo.
6. R.H. Kupperman and R.H. Wilcox, "Interactive Computer Communications Systems," *Proceedings of the International Conference on Computer Communications*, Stockholm (1974), mimeo.
7. Arnold L. Horelick, "The Cuban Missile Crisis: An Analysis of Soviet Calculations and Behavior," *World Politics* 16, no. 3 (April 1964):363-389.
8. James L. Foster and Garry D. Brewer, "And the Clocks Were Striking Thirteen," *Policy Sciences* 7 (1976):224-243.
9. Leo A. Hazelwood and John J. Hayes, *Planning for Problems in Crisis Management* (Arlington, Va.: CACI, 1976).
10. Richard K. Betts, "Analysis, War, and Decision," *World Politics* 31, no. 1 (1978):61-89; Michael I. Handel, "The Yom Kippur War and the Inevitability of Surprise," *International Studies Quarterly* 21, no. 3 (1977):461-502; Avi Shlaim, "Failures in National Intelligence Estimates," *World Politics* 28 (April 1976):348-380; Abraham Ben-Zvi, "Hindsight and Foresight: A Conceptual Framework for the Analysis of Surprise Attacks," *World Politics* 28, no. 3 (1976):381-395; Richards J. Heuer, Jr., "Cognitive Biases in the Evaluation of Intelligence Estimates," *Proceedings of the 10th Annual Conference, American Institute of Decision Sciences* (St. Louis, 1978), mimeo.
11. Robert Jervis, "Cooperation under the Security Dilemma," *World Politics* 30 (January 1978):167-214.
12. Russell Hardin, "Mutually Expected Rationality," paper presented at the annual North American meetings of the Peace Science Society (International) (Chicago, 1978), mimeo.

13. Davis B. Bobrow, "Information Systems to Constrain Conflict," in J. Ben-Dak, ed., *Peace Thinking and the Arab-Israel Conflict* (Ramat-Gan: The Turtle-Dove Press, in press).

14. David Astor and Valerie Yorke, *Peace in the Middle East* (London: CORGI, 1978).

15. Raymond Cohen, "Threat Perception in International Crisis," *Political Science Quarterly* 93, no. 1 (Spring 1978):93-107.

16. Roberta Wohlstetter, "Cuba and Pearl Harbor: Hindsight and Foresight," *Foreign Affairs* 43, no. 4 (July 1965):671-707.

17. Dean G. Pruitt, "Definition of the Situation as a Determinant of International Action," in Herbert C. Kelman, ed., *International Behavior* (New York: Holt, Rinehart and Winston, 1965); Thomas C. Schelling, *The Strategy of Conflict* (New York: Oxford University Press, 1963); Davis K. Lewis, *Conventions* (Cambridge: Harvard University Press, 1969).

18. R.H. Kupperman and S.C. Goldman, "Towards a Viable International System," in Nathaniel Macon, ed., *Computer Communications* (Washington, D.C.: International Council for Computer Communications, 1975).

19. T. Greenwood, "Reconnaissance, Surveillance and Arms Control," *Adelphi Paper 88* (London: Institute for Strategic Studies, 1972); SIPRI, *World Armament and Disarmament, SIPRI Yearbook* (Stockholm: Almqvist and Wiksell, 1974); Pierre-Marine Adrian and Marion F. Baumgardner, "Landsat, Computers and Development Projects," *Science* 198, no. 4316 (November 1977): 466-470; Joseph N. Pelton, *Intelsat* (Mt. Airy, Md.: Lomond Books, 1974); Herbert F. York and G. Allen Greb, "Strategic Reconnaissance," *Bulletin of the Atomic Scientist* 33, no. 4 (April 1977):33-41.

20. S.J. Brams, "Newcomb's Problem and Prisoner's Dilemma," *Journal of Conflict Resolution* 19 (1975):596-612; Steven J. Brams, Morton D. Davis, and Philip D. Straffin, Jr., "The Geometry of the Arms Race" (1977), mimeo.

21. Harvey A. DeWeerd, "Verifying the SALT Agreements," *Army* 28 (1978):15-18.

22. Carnes Lord, "Verification and the Future of Arms Control," *Strategic Review* 6 (1978):24-32; Colin S. Gray, "SALT I Aftermath," *Air Force Magazine* 58 (1975):28-33.

23. SIPRI, *Strategic Disarmament, Verification and National Security* (New York: Crane, Russak, 1977); Mark M. Loewenthal, *SALT Verification* (Washington, D.C.: Congressional Research Service, 1978).

24. Julian Critchley, *Warning and Response* (New York: Crane, Russak, 1978).

25. John D. Steinbruner, "National Security and the Concept of Strategic Stability," *Journal of Conflict Resolution* 22 (September 1978):411-428.

26. Davis B. Bobrow, "Communications, Command and Control," in Ellen P. Stern, ed., *The Limits of Military Intervention* (Beverly Hills, Calif.: Sage Publications, 1977).

27. Herbert York, *Race to Oblivion* (New York: Simon and Schuster, 1970); Herman Kahn, *On Thermonuclear War* (Princeton: Princeton University Press, 1961).

28. Amitai Etzioni, "The Kennedy Experiment," *Western Political Quarterly* 20, no. 2 (June 1967):361-380.

29. Fred C. Iklé, "After Detection—What?" *Foreign Affairs* 39, no. 2 (January 1961):208-220.

30. A. Myrdal, "The International Control of Disarmament," *Scientific American* 231, no. 4 (October 1974):21-33.

31. M. Callahan and K. Tsipsis, "The Crisis Management Satellite," (Cambridge, Mass.: Program in Science and Technology for International Security, M.I.T., 1978), mimeo; United Nations General Assembly, "Review of the Implementation of the Recommendations and Decisions Adopted by the General Assembly at its Tenth Special Session—Monitoring of Disarmament Agreements and Strengthening of Security." (1978) Ac 1/33/L.13; *Department of State Bulletin*, "U.N. Special Session on Disarmament" 78 (1978):31-35, 42-57.

32. Permanent Mission of France, "Adoption of a Programme of Action on Disarmament," Note Verbale dated 30 May 1978 addressed to the Secretariat, United Nations General Assembly, A/S-10/AC.1/7.

33. Bobrow, "Information Systems to Constrain Conflict."

8

Harmonizing Policies across Arms Control Domains: Dilemmas and Contradictions

Robert E. Harkavy

Introduction

Whereas during the bulk of the postwar period, arms control had served as a somewhat peripheral and certainly subordinate aspect of national security strategy (and was viewed by many as more often than not essentially in contradiction to it), it has by now clearly come to occupy a pivotal position in American foreign policy priorities.[1] Some might claim that it has become a near dominant "ideology" for an articulate, influential segment of the foreign policy elite and its adjuncts in academe. As one sympathetic commentator recently put it:

> The idea and institution of arms control have become assimilated in U.S. strategy. Arms control is no longer thought of as a special category. Rather, it has become an integral part of U.S. diplomacy no matter whether the subject is NATO, strategic weaponry, economic development, or energy policy. Indeed, so much momentum has gathered behind the need for coherent arms control policies that they would be impossible to suddenly stop.[2]

By no means all observers are happy with the increasing centrality of arms control. Some have come to perceive it as a subtle displacement or rationalization of national weakness and lack of will, and decry the extent to which it has become nearly superordinate rather than subordinate to grand strategy.[3] Strong critics of the current emphasis had even begun, amid the post-Vietnam strategic malaise, to refer ironically to the "mad momentum of arms control."

Surely, the diverse array of arms control efforts in which the United States and other nations have been engaged has become numerically impressive. Indeed, a review of the recent and current arms control agenda, as reflected, for instance, in the annual reports of the Arms Control and Disarmament Agency (ACDA) and also in the summary statement that emerged from the UN's 1978 Special Session on Disarmament (SSOD), reveals an almost bewildering number of arenas that are now, recently have been, or

---

The author wishes to thank the Peace Studies Program at Cornell University and its director, Franklin Long, for assistance in connection with this chapter.

are about to be, the subject of formal negotiations—in a variety of negotiating formats and locales.[4] The arenas include strategic arms limitations (SALT); nuclear test bans (LTB and CTB); Mutual and Balanced Force Reductions (MBFR); chemical (CW), biological (BW), and radiological (RW) weapons; environmental modification (ENMOD); nuclear weapons in outer space and on the seabed; "inhumane" conventional weapons; conventional arms transfers (CAT); regional naval deployments and associated basing limitations (Indian Ocean); nuclear proliferation (including regional nuclear weapons free zones—NWFZs); "no first use" of nuclear weapons; military expenditure limitations (MEL); antisatellite weapons; "cut-off and transfer" of nuclear materials; "hot lines" and accident measures; missile test notifications; the control of terrorism; and still others. The scope and variety of such efforts is certainly extraordinary, rivalled earlier only by the ambitious agenda of the lengthy preparations for the Geneva Disarmament Conference, which extended from the mid-1920s to the early 1930s.

Hopeful about what appears a favorable tide after decades of relative inactivity, many arms control proponents seem convinced that across-the-board, full-tilt pursuit of formal controls arrangements in all or most of the aforementioned categories is inherently desirable and that, in combination, their contributions to peace and/or conflict control (however defined or measured) must be complementary and additive, if not synergistic. Success in any one area is assumed to add forward momentum toward a distant, hoped-for disarmament (as distinct from arms control) millenium that, most centrally, would see the elimination or significant reduction of nuclear weapons.

Amid this still cautious euphoria, very little attention has been paid, either in the scholarly or policy-making milieus, to the myriad, important causal relationships among the various arms control domains.[5] Specifically, there has been little attention to what some might claim are inherent and profound contradictions in the simultaneous pursuit of numerous, related arms control goals, wherein progress in one area might actually impede or negate progress in others.

Needless to say, the problems of delineating these interrelationships, and of dealing with the corresponding cost-benefit calculi in situations of multiple choice, constitute a mere microcosm of those involved in fashioning a coherent, overall national security strategy. Ideally, arms control ought to be one major integrated element of a national grand strategy. And, of course, all the arms control arenas are closely related to crucial issues in the broader strategic context. For example, SALT is deeply enmeshed in America's China and NATO policies; nonproliferation policy is inextricably connected to those for the Middle East, southern Africa, and Korea; and there is an obvious nexus between arms transfer policies and those for overseas bases, and oil and other raw materials acquisitions.

Then, too, there is the question of how diverse clusters of arms control policies affect overall policies with respect to particular geographic regions. What, for instance, is the combined impact of American SALT, test ban, nonproliferation, and CAT policies on Western Europe's military security, on the evolving Far East diplomatic alignments, or on the Middle East?

The following discussion, therefore, to the extent it is somewhat narrowly focused on relationships primarily between arms control domains, is necessarily somewhat abstracted from a broader focus and is intended primarily to be illustrative of dilemmas and contradictions at that one level. It is done so with the assumption that problems of multiple advocacy in arms control have heretofore been abnormally immune from analysis, or even recognition.

The Arms Control Agenda: An Overview Typology Applicable to Arms Control Interrelationships

The by now rather massive literature on arms control exhibits a dearth of typologies or classificatory frameworks that might provide some ordering of arms control issue areas and hence a start toward a "comparative arms control." The literature consists of chronologies of successful and failed negotiations in discrete areas; aggregate histories portraying the ebbs and flows of overall progress toward disarmament; some use of game theory to explain diplomatic bargaining strategies; and much emotional polemics, pro and con.[6]

As an underpinning for an analysis of regime interrelationships, a simplified typology may be utilized that encompasses such criteria as weapons or force types involved, numbers and types of nations, and the geographic locus of political/military interests engaged. It will be immediately apparent that it is not easy to put all the regimes and associated negotiations in separate boxes and that some amount of overlap is unavoidable—for instance, where initially bilateral or two-bloc agreements are subsequently extended to a more global basis. That caveat aside, the following classification may be useful in ordering the mix of arms control issues that have been of recent interest (see also table 8-1).

1. Issues of an essentially bipolar (United States-USSR) or bi-bloc (NATO-Warsaw pacts) nature, involving a debatable mix of zero-sum and variable-sum bargaining relationships, and variously, the stabilization, adjustment, reflection, and so forth of the central military balance. Such arrangements are not intended to add additional adherents and involve essentially questions of "vertical" proliferation of arms by the major powers.

2. Issues similar to those mentioned, but where initially bilateral or two-bloc agreements may subsequently be expanded to near-global adherence, even if what is proscribed, circumscribed, or spatially demarcated may

Table 8-1
Typology of Arms Control Domains

	Predominant Vertical Proliferation	Mixed Vertical and Horizontal Proliferation	Predominant Horizontal Proliferation
Bilateral, bi-bloc arrangements	SALT, MBFR, Indian Ocean, antisatellite, "hot lines," "no first use," missile test notification	"Cut-off and transfer"	
Effectively bipolar, but extended to multilateral adherence	Seabed, outer space	CTB, MEL	
Universal banning of baneful weapons or geographic demarcations on weapons deployments—multilateral	ENMOD Antarctica	CW, BW, RW, NWFZs "inhumane" conventional weapons	Nonproliferation (NPT), anti-terrorism
Supplier-recipient market transactions—"Spread" (supplier oligopolies)			CAT, nuclear exports controls (London Suppliers)

Note: "Horizontal" proliferation here used to denote increased military capability for small states, including enhancement of systems already possessed. Vertical refers to increased superpower capabilities, arsenals, and so forth.

currently be beyond the capabilities of more than a few major states. Here, the superpowers have foresworn areas of activity both to insulate them from their own competition and to provide demonstrations of their arms control bona fides for a global audience.

3. Further along a spectrum, those arrangements that aim at global proscribing and elimination of certain "unacceptable" or particularly pernicious weapons classes or modes of waging warfare. In some of these areas, numerous nations may now have the capability for significant weapons development.

4. Those areas of arms control essentially involving supplier-recipient market transactions; basically, involving issues of technology transfer or "spread," that is, "horizontal" proliferation, both of conventional and nuclear weapons.

This classification deals primarily with arms control issues hitherto subject to bilateral and multilateral negotiations and formal agreements aimed at bans, limits, reductions, and balances. Beyond that, of course, one might further cite the importance of nonformal (tacit) agreements and of unilateral restraints and "demonstration effects."[7] The United States, for example, has recently attempted unilateral restraints with respect to both its own weapons deployments and external transfers. In the former category, at least for the present, the deployment of neutron bombs has been curtailed. Unilateral restraints in arms transfers have been exemplified, for instance, by the Carter administration's annual sales ceilings; curbs on concussion bombs, phosphorus shells, and so forth; embargoes on South Africa and Libya; and denial of sales of attack aircraft to sub-Sahara Africa. Such unilateral restraints, particularly to the extent that they may only be temporary, are related to the broader context of formal arms control negotiations, as witness, for instance, the American threat to remove its arms transfer ceilings if matching restraints and/or formal agreements involving other suppliers are not forthcoming.

Crucial to the foregoing typology is the division between issue areas respectively involving East-West and North-South loci of political interests and bargaining, revolving about the matters of "vertical" and "horizontal" expansions of power and proliferation of weapons types and inventories. The two superpowers (and sometimes their close allies) have bargained over serious although often marginal advantages in SALT, CTB, MBFR, the Indian Ocean, and so forth, while remaining conscious of pressures to demonstrate some seriousness in slowing vertical proliferation, to provide in turn justifications for pressures against horizontal proliferation, which might narrow the overall gap in military power between the developed and developing nations.

Conversely, the developing nations have utilized the threat of horizontal proliferation, particularly nuclear, to prod the major powers into doing something about vertical proliferation. The Seabed Treaty, for instance, demonstrated the pressures on the superpowers about not appropriating areas of the world for themselves where they alone now have the wherewithal to deploy military technology.[8] Then, too, third world revisionism has generally dictated some recalcitrance in the face of efforts such as the London Suppliers' arrangements and the U.S.-Soviet CAT talks, which, their "collective goods" benefits and accompanying United Nations rhetoric notwithstanding, represent threats to freeze the power gap between the currently strong and weak. Generally, recent arms control efforts have involved a curious and complex juxtaposition of head-to-head bargaining between the superpowers (SALT, MBFR, and so forth), some convergence of superpower interest in preventing overall shifts in the North-South division of power or the development of minimum deterrence capability in newer locales (NPT, BW, CW, RW), and conflicting motives involving the latter consideration but also that of the continued use of competitive instruments for achieving political influence and strategic access (CAT). As such, a coherent overall arms control policy has come to require the orchestration of numerous goals and requirements, involving very different audiences and global interests.

The Critical Arms Control Interrelationships:
Pros and Cons

Space does not permit a full analysis of the myriad relationships spanning pairs of arms control issue areas, much less of more elaborate chains of cause and effect involving several of them in combinations. Hence, the focus here will primarily be on the crucial two-way interrelationships among nonproliferation, strategic arms, and conventional arms transfers, each analyzed as a dependent and independent variable in relation to the others (see table 8-2). Some additional attention will be paid to the lines that extend from these issues to other arms control domains such as test bans, MBFR, and Indian Ocean demilitarization.

The most widely discussed set of interrelationships has involved nuclear proliferation as a function of SALT, CTB, and CAT. There are serious disagreements over the strength and significance of these relationships, at a time when nonproliferation has appeared to have achieved a position of relative primacy among the various arms control problems—both for consistent arms control advocates and their usual opponents.[9]

The so-called "doves' dilemma" involves the role of CATs in providing incentives or disincentives for nuclear proliferation.[10] On one side of the issue are those who take this dilemma seriously, claiming that to the extent some seriously threatened nations are denied the weapons necessary for them to maintain regional balances (in some cases involving sheer survival), that an obvious incentive to acquire an "equalizer" will result, perhaps even in the face of sanctions and/or the embargoing of peaceful nuclear materials and technology. The dilemma is taken very seriously in the cases of such "pariah states" as Israel, Taiwan, South Korea, and South Africa, all of which face the spectre of unfavorable conventional balances and the absence of assured, credible big-power support in times of crisis. This has also been well illustrated by recent American efforts to forestall Pakistani nuclear development by a mix of sticks (economic and military aid cutoffs) and carrots (offers of additional fighter aircraft).[11] Still other states—Spain, Chile, Iran, Yugoslavia—are also habitually noted as having potential nuclear security incentives for, at the present, still less compelling reasons.

Some arms control advocates tend to deny the reality of this CAT/proliferation nexus and claim that nuclear aspirations, to the extent they exist, cannot at any rate be bought off by increased or maintained conventional arms supplies. They resist the notion that some smaller states should be allowed to practice an implicit "nuclear blackmail." Referring sarcastically to a "methadone treatment" for proliferation, these arguments usually stress the potential enhancement of nuclear delivery capabilities through arms transfers to countries whose nuclear ambitions may not easily be deflected by political disincentives. It is important to note

Table 8-2
Arms Control Interrelationships

	Dependent Variables			
Independent Variables	CAT	Nonproliferation	SALT	CTB
CAT		Controls enmeshed in "doves' dilemma," increasing nuclear incentives in "pariah" states. Controls threaten facilities for monitoring nuclear activities. Economic link between "two-way street" and nuclear exports.	Controls threaten facilities for ASW, verification intelligence.	Possible implications for overseas verification facilities.
Nonproliferation	Increased demands for conventional arms in threatened states.		NWFZ's limit strategic deployments. Intended to limit upward pressures on U.S.-USSR strategic weapons, reduce strategic complications of a more proliferated world.	Intended to halt new entries into club—may result in clandestine programs ("bombs in the basement")
SALT	Parity, degradation of U.S. nuclear umbrella increases demands for arms—Nixon Doctrine.	U.S. acceptance of parity, degraded nuclear umbrella increases incentives. ABM lowers "entry price." Detente lessens incentives for proliferation by lowering tensions.		Impact on testing of new warheads allowed by agreement.
CTB		Demonstration effect dampens incentives, delegitimizes tests by aspirants.	Precludes testing some new systems. Reliability problem, verification problem regarding low-yield tests.	

that opinions on either side of this argument are usually ideologically predictable, with the "arms controllers" normally aligned on the side that denigrates the reality of a nexus between these two domains. The same analysts, incidentally, are the most likely to downgrade related arguments that CAT controls may unintentionally lend impetus to indigenous conventional arms development programs and hence ironically result also in an expanded number of factors in the arms supplier markets. That argument has arisen in response to recent conventional arms development activities in India, Brazil, Israel, South Africa, South Korea, and Egypt, among others. Similar arguments have arisen over the possibility that the restrictions on export of nuclear technology embodied in the London Suppliers' arrangements might encourage indigenous nuclear development in nations such as Pakistan or South Korea.

Some analysts have further suggested that some of the newer long-range precision-guided weapons systems might be considered, if transferred abroad, as effective surrogates for nuclear weapons, providing both for area and point destruction capabilities.[12] Here, considerations both of defense and deterrence are involved. The CAT/proliferation connection may be important in still other ways, albeit indirectly. To the extent arms transfers and/or arms aid may often be a required trade-off for the major powers' acquisition and retention of overseas bases, controls may in some cases result in jeopardization of facilities needed to monitor suspicious nuclear activities through air sample collection and seismological techniques.[13] We shall later discuss a parallel connection involving CAT and SALT. Then too, there are myriad economic linkages between CATs and nuclear export policies, for instance, with the use of reactor deals as "sweeteners" for arms sales.

The assertion that halting nuclear proliferation depends crucially on the superpowers' demonstration of seriousness about SALT and CTB is stated as follows in the most recent ACDA annual report, with respect to CTB (and by extension to SALT):

> A comprehensive test ban treaty, by freezing nuclear weapons technology and constraining further improvements in existing nuclear weapon stockpiles, would make a major contribution to curbing the nuclear arms competition between the United States and the Soviet Union. It could also be expected to improve the climate for a reduced reliance on nuclear weapons throughout the world by demonstrating that the nuclear powers are committed to nuclear arms control. A treaty that attracted broad support among non-nuclear weapons states would be an important tool in strengthening international efforts to prevent the proliferation of nuclear weapons.[14]

The existence of the SALT/nonproliferation relationship is tenaciously asserted by arms control proponents, no doubt in part because it has been underscored by numerous (and perhaps in some cases disingenuous) statements from nations such as India, Brazil, and Yugoslavia, which have complained about the discriminatory impact of NPT and its still unfulfilled promise about big-power denuclearization. Hence also, the potential impact of a CTBT on proliferation is taken even more seriously than that of SALT, just because the former would be less discriminatory in promising a universal ban on testing even if some states are already beyond the nuclear brink. There is some evidence that belief in the validity of these relationships has had some convergent impact on the U.S.-Soviet SALT and CTB negotiations, particularly given the well-advertised Soviet concern with proliferation, which, given the locations of the most obvious potential proliferators, may be objectively stronger than that of the United States.[15]

On the reverse side of the argument are those who claim that assuming a causal nexus between SALT/CTB and nonproliferation involves merely superficial, wishful thinking, or a case of taking one's own propaganda too seriously. Why, they would ask, would the nuclear decisions of Israel, Taiwan, South Korea, South Africa, and so forth (aside from the serious threat of sanctions and other objective political and economic costs) be at all dependent on what occurs in the SALT and CTB negotiations, the outcomes of which may impinge on small powers' security interests only to the extent that they merely reflect Soviet achievement of parity and hence produce a reduced American military credibility abroad? The vertical levels of arms mutually agreed to in SALT, and the accompanying qualitative restrictions, would appear virtually irrelevant to most small states in any objective sense. To the extent such arguments are at all meaningful, objectors would claim that they apply, rather, in a "moral," "world order" sense primarily to cases such as Brazil or Argentina, where status considerations presumably outweigh those of security and survival in the hierarchy of proliferation incentives. It might be conceded, however, that a finalized CTB could create some pressures against nuclear testing by aspirant proliferation states, perhaps in some cases constraining them to clandestine programs without actual tests.

In a much broader sense, of course, the history of the SALT negotiations (and the overall trends of the U.S.-Soviet nuclear strategic arms race) may have had—or may yet have—a profound impact on nuclear proliferation. This too has, however, been argued in distinct, contrasting ways. On one side, it is argued that the evident relative decline of U.S. power, and the now formal acknowledgement of strategic parity, will have reduced the sense of security of many nations (including some not even informally allied with the United States), diminished the credibility of U.S. nuclear guarantees, and hence enhanced the incentives for proliferation in some threatened countries.[16] This applies particularly to many countries around the Eurasian rim, where the Soviets may have a growing geographical advantage in conventional intervention capability and where a previously offsetting U.S. long-range logistical advantage is now rapidly diminishing. Earlier able to rely on at least the threat of a hitherto superior U.S. nuclear deterrent, many countries in near proximity to the USSR may have come to realize that the latter may now act with greater freedom beneath the umbrella of an approximate nuclear stand-off, increasingly perceived as involving a slight Soviet advantage. Such considerations apply, of course, not only to SALT but to the aggregate of arms control negotiations that affect the superpowers' relative military balance, that is, MBFR, the Indian Ocean, and so forth. And, if nations such as Taiwan or South Africa should go nuclear for these reasons, the resulting nuclear "chain effect" could involve nations initially not directly affected by such considerations.[17] Then too, there looms the problem of Japanese rearmament, possibly with an eventual nuclear dimension.[18]

As most of the nations considered potential proliferators are outside the Soviet influence orbit, the reverse of these propositions—concerning the possible impact on proliferation of U.S. strategic superiority—seems not particularly applicable. Cuba and North Korea are perhaps potential hypothetical exceptions.

Restrictions on ballistic missile defenses, formalized in the ABM treaty, may also have had—or may yet have—some impact on nuclear proliferation, and as one writer has noted, this relationship does not seem to have been widely canvassed either before or after the signing of the treaty.[19] While serving to maintain and stabilize some second strike capability for the British and French deterrents against the USSR (along with assisting China's deterrent), ABM may also have reduced the future "entry price" to a deterrent relationship with one of the superpowers or both for some additional middle-range powers. Then too, mutually agreed ceilings on offensive strategic systems by the superpowers might provide incentives for future vertical proliferation among the lesser nuclear powers, say France, which might seize the opportunity partially to close the gap with the former.

Still, arguments are made on the contrary, that SALT will assist the nonproliferation effort, not only by partially keeping the superpowers' promise written into the NPT but also to the extent that a stabilization of their strategic competition might somehow restrain the nuclear ambitions of others. That argument, of course, is based on hopes for the success of the "linkage" element in détente, whereby the resulting web of relationships is hoped to restrain further Soviet adventures in areas such as the Middle East, Korea, and southern Africa.

An addendum to these relationships involves the possibilities for a "no first use" agreement or mutual pledge on nuclear weapons among the major powers, whether formal or based on separate declaratory statements. Such an agreement has been trumpeted for its potential value in restraining the nuclear ambitions of others, who might then worry less about a superpower nuclear intervention in a regional conflict. On the other side is the argument that such an agreement involving the United States might enhance proliferation incentives, for example, in South Korea or in Western Europe, where there has long been reliance on the American nuclear umbrella in the face of conventional military insecurities.

In reversing these lines of causation, nuclear proliferation may also be demonstrated to act as an independent variable in relation to other arms control domains, particularly SALT and the test ban, but perhaps also to biological, chemical, and radiological weapons. Needless to say, every addition to the "nuclear club" may serve to complicate the U.S.-Soviet strategic nuclear negotiations, as have already the British, French, Chinese, and Indian programs. The impact on ABM has been noted, and we may not have heard the end of that, as future proliferation could later force either or both superpowers back toward consideration of enhanced ABM coverage under certain circumstances, perhaps even on a negotiated basis.[20] Earlier, of course, SALT I itself was originated in the immediate wake of the NPT, once the German problem had been resolved to the Soviets' satisfaction after the wrangling over Euratom and the aborted NATO Multilateral Force.[21]

Very recently, there have been faint hints of emerging U.S. military contingency planning for a more proliferated world despite the surface reluctance publicly to concede such a grim eventuality. There have also been some hints of consideration of joint U.S.-Soviet planning for some foreseeable circumstances involving small powers' nuclear threats or use.[22] If such planning were moved further to a stand-by capability, it might involve some additional upward pressures on the superpowers' nuclear force levels (perhaps only the retention of delivery systems that might otherwise be scrapped), some retargeting of weapons systems, or even some new overseas deployments of nuclear weapons. The Soviets' apparent deployment of nuclear-armed Scud missiles in Egypt during the 1973 war illustrates such possibilities.

Otherwise, in outlining the possible impacts of proliferation policy on SALT, it is apparent that the establishment of some NWFZs, for example, in the Indian Ocean, the Pacific, or Latin America, could have some impact on the U.S. strategic posture, particularly if they precluded stationing or transiting of U.S. nuclear submarines in some areas. However, the introduction of the longer-range Trident submarine missiles should later largely alleviate whatever degradation of the U.S. deterrent posture might now result from such arrangements.

Although there is yet little evidence of a strong connection between nonproliferation, on the one hand, and BW and CW proliferation, on the other, such relationships ought perhaps be taken more seriously than they have been. The question here is whether, in some cases, the use of sanctions or other leverage by the big powers to thwart nuclear proliferation might lead to overt or clandestine surrogate mass casualty deterrent postures. Some observers have suggested that the speed with which the U.S. and the USSR steered the BW Convention through the CCD bespoke of heightened superpower anxieties about the ease with which some small nations might develop a dangerous BW pandemic capability. Egypt's widely reported development of a significant nerve gas stockpile to match, asymmetrically, Israel's assumed nuclear arsenal, may be one straw in the wind.[23] (And to the extent the latter was impelled by insecurities about conventional arms supplies, it provides an illustration of the extended chain-effect possibilities.) Relative to the cost of a militarily significant nuclear infrastructure, BW and CW activities may both be very cheap as well as difficult to detect. The earlier massive Soviet efforts in both areas, relative to the United States, might have been indicative to the extent they could have been interpreted as offsets to the then existing U.S. nuclear advantage at both the strategic and tactical levels.

On the face of it, the impact of CAT on SALT would appear rather negligible. However, there are some fairly important connections here, albeit somewhat indirect. For, just as arms transfers may affect nonproliferation through the connecting link of overseas bases, likewise, the loss of overseas bases that may result from restraints on arms sales (or other blockages of an arms transfer influence relationship), may also degrade U.S. nuclear strategic capabilities. The apparently only temporary loss of Turkish facilities reportedly had a significant negative impact on U.S. verification capabilities in connection with SALT, among other things involving telemetry monitoring of Soviet missile tests. In that case, part of the loss was apparently compensated for by back-up facilities in Iran, which have now been lost.[24] Although many ground-based facilities for these activities are being superseded by satellite technology, it is apparently the case that full use of the satellites (including that for early warning of missile launches) depends on still other overseas facilities used to communicate with them and to retrieve the information they gather. Arms sales policies involving numerous other clients besides Turkey may be subject to such considerations, which, for the most part, are shrouded in secrecy.

Further links between CAT and SALT may be discerned in the requirement for antisubmarine warfare (ASW) facilities (P-3 Orion staging bases, SOSUS terminals, and so forth), and also Omega and Loran navigational and positioning facilities for SSBNs, which depend on arms sales policies with such diverse clients as Portugal (the Azores), Spain, Iceland, Liberia, Singapore, Indonesia, Norway, and others. Further, the U.S. B-52 strategic bomber force still utilizes overseas recovery and tanker facilities in Spain and elsewhere, which are subject to alliance relationships hinged on arms transfers. Overall confidence in the U.S. triad is here at stake, yet little attention has been paid to this chain of relationships running from arms transfers to overseas facilities to the strategic nuclear balance.

Two major aspects of the SALT/MBFR nexus have been commented on.[25] First, to the extent the United States has now formally accepted the principle of parity at the strategic nuclear level, there has been a reduction in whatever credibility once might have existed for a massive American strategic nuclear response to a Soviet conventional assault on Western Europe. This, in turn, has enhanced the necessity for achieving a credible conventional balance in Central Europe, particularly as the recent Soviet build-up of theater nuclear forces may also have reduced the deterrent value of NATO's own tactical nuclear weapons. (Parity at the strategic level has increased American fears about the dangers of escalation from the tactical nuclear level). Second, there is the question of whether future SALT negotiations might involve such "gray area" issues as the U.S. forward-based systems (ground-based FB-111 and F-4 aircraft, carrier-based nuclear strike aircraft) and the Soviet Backfire bomber, mobile SS-20 MRBM, SU-19 strike bomber, and so forth.

Thus far, the Soviet systems that threaten America's allies in a strategic mode have been left out of the SALT negotiations, as have American forward-based systems that can reach the USSR from the European theater. There has been some negotiating, as yet not brought to fruition, over trading off a portion of the American nuclear forces in Western Europe for a withdrawal of some Soviet tank armies out of Central and Eastern Europe.

Spanning the domains of SALT, MBFR, and arms transfers is the question of whether the United States is to be allowed some transfer of cruise missile technology to its European allies. This matter remains ambiguous in light of the noncircumvention clause of the SALT II treaty. Also, near-term prohibitions on the range of United States-controlled ground-launched cruise missiles (GLCMs), if extended beyond the expiration of the treaty's three-year protocol, may preclude their relieving the more than 600 fighter-bombers now assigned to a nuclear strike role in Europe, which might have been freed for a nonnuclear phase of NATO defense.[26] Similarly, many nonnuclear precision attack roles will have been precluded by the restrictions on GLCM. All these matters and more may influence the kinds of force levels NATO might be able to accept as part of a future MBFR agreement. Otherwise, of course, to the extent an MBFR arrangement served to formalize Soviet conventional superiority in Central Europe, it would result in further NATO reliance on the U.S. strategic nuclear shield being negotiated over in SALT and/or on some of the theater nuclear weapons that might become the subject of future SALT negotiation. All these matters will, of course, affect future European decisions on their own strategic and tactical nuclear forces and on the still talked-about possibility of an all-European nuclear force. They could also affect decisions by France concerning the possible independent development of a neutron warhead.

Generally, all the problems involving linked trade-offs between the United States and USSR raise the dilemma of the impact of superpower accords on third-state behavior, that is, United States-Soviet actions on arms control may cause complications in the broader sense of global arms control. Talk of a French neutron bomb reminds us of past French (and Chinese) refusal to cooperate on NPT or CTB.

It is now commonly assumed that finalization of a CTBT awaits the completion of the SALT II negotiations and their ratification by the U.S. Senate. Here too, there are important linkages.[27] Both the United States and USSR will perceive an interest in conducting last-minute tests up to the point when all testing is prohibited (if it is), to allow for development of new weapons not precluded by SALT II. For the United States, this linkage may be important respecting the testing of new warheads for the M-X ICBMs, Trident SLBMs, and for a variety of emerging cruise missiles. Both superpowers will have an interest in combining the structure of SALT II and the timing of a CTB to allow for maximum future qualitative weapons developments. A CTB might also affect the central European balance to the extent it precluded modernization of tactical nuclear weapons for deployment in NATO. The preservation and maintenance of confidence in the existing U.S. nuclear stockpile is an additional issue involved in the CTB, which influences SALT. Finally, the still lingering questions about the verifiability of a CTBT, concerning low-yield Soviet tests, have obvious implications for the future of SALT and for the theater nuclear balance in Europe.

The Indian Ocean negotiations, on their face, appear a primarily bilateral measure intended to lower United States-Soviet tensions in one region and to produce a reciprocally bargained lowering of defense costs. Yet, if the United States ends up withdrawing from Diego Garcia (in exchange for a Soviet commitment not to replace its facilities lost at Berbera with new ones in Eritrea, Aden, or elsewhere), there may be implications extending into collateral arms control areas. Israel and Pakistan among others could suffer some loss of security, perhaps heightening nuclear ambitions. The arms requests of Kenya, Sudan, and perhaps others might escalate, as the modest yet at least potentially protective American presence was further withdrawn. For the future, again, the connection between arms transfers and bases, with possible implications for a variety of potential arms control arrangements, may bear watching.

The Bureaucratics of U.S. Arms Control Policy-Making: A Brief Note

Part of the reason for the seeming lack of attention in the United States to the corollary effects of discrete arms control measures may reside in the nature of the bureaucratic politics involved. Various arms control initiatives have been encouraged, and their negotiations pursued, by competing sub-bureaucracies (or by alliances between them along functional lines), which quite naturally tend to emphasize priorities in their own bailiwicks. The problem of compartmentalization has been compounded by the lack of simultaneity of issues coming to the forefront, and because initiatives may be difficult to reverse once they have picked up momentum, even if they may later be suspected as counterproductive from an overall arms control standpoint. Various arms control issues have become designated at various points as the "only game in town," which term was widely applied, for instance, to nonproliferation after the Indian nuclear test and the Brazil-West Germany deal.

It is not easy to describe the processes of interest articulation and interest aggregation as they apply to arms control, nor to determine how, as Luttwak has put it, "the new science of bureaucratic analysis teaches us that each bureaucracy is armed with a matrix of specific and collateral desiderata directly germane to its internal goals but ostensibly based on external goals."[28] And again here, arms control strategy is but a part of overall grand strategy, albeit a currently ascendant one.

For each arms control domain, there is some involvement by numerous agencies, for whom influence waxes and wanes with changes of key personnel, overall shifts in power between agencies, presidential preferences, changes of administration, and so forth. In each, the decision-making process is described by vertical layers of interdepartmental committees, ascending from the working level to the National Security Council (NSC), involving a diverse welter of vertical and horizontal bargaining. Arms control issues are hypothetically aggregated and coordinated at the levels of ACDA's director, the Assistant Secretary of State for Politico-Military Affairs (now a primary hub of arms control activity), and, of course, at the White House through the NSC. The reality, of course, may not be very ordered. Some observers, Luttwak for example, have wondered whether the collateral considerations bearing on nonproliferation have ever seriously been considered at the requisite levels of policy aggregation and claim the policy outputs lend themselves to a contrary inference.[29]

It would appear that, very often, a bureaucratic interest group pushing for policies in one domain will, either consciously or not, attempt to deny its impacts on others. The doves' dilemma has appeared a virtual bureaucratic heresy in the recent period. Likewise, there appears a considerable aversion to consideration of the political incentives to nonproliferation, which is compensated for by strictly technological solutions or, failing that, consideration of draconian sanctions that might well exacerbate the problem they were intended to solve. Throughout the U.S. national security bureaucracy, it is apparently an article of faith that SALT and CTB will have a measurable positive impact on nonproliferation, while the impact on it of the overall U.S. national security posture appears rarely if ever to be discussed, much less seriously taken into account.

The bureaucratics of arms control policies often involve specific sets of alliances within given issue areas, usually discernible along a spectrum running from "arms controllers" to those who concede lesser primacy to arms control considerations. The interagency alignments do, however, vary between issues. On bilateral or two-bloc issues such as SALT and MBFR, the traditional assumptions about a "hawkish" Pentagon set off against a more "dovish" State and ACDA are typically accurate, excepting for ACDA's brief shift to the right during the previous Republican administration. On proliferation, however, one recent period saw an alliance stretching across ACDA, State's Policy Planning Staff, and the Pentagon, faced off against interests aligned with the nuclear power industry in the former Energy Research and Development Administration (ERDA) and State's Bureau of Oceans, Environmental and Scientific Affairs (OES), which worried about American industry being competitively disadvantaged by unilateral restraints measures. The CTB has apparently pitted elements of the Department of Energy (notably its test laboratories) and the Pentagon against an opposing coalition in State and ACDA. In CATs, State's Politico-Military Affairs Bureau and ACDA have tilted with State's regional bureaus, while the Pentagon, once thought of as a wellspring of arms-selling fervor, has now become increasingly ambivalent in the light of new problems involving technology transfers and the competition for arms production between U.S. forces and some overseas clients.[30] Often cross-cutting these bureaucratic positions are interests on one or the other side of the Israel-Arab, Greece-Turkey, Iran-Saudi Arabia, and PRC-Taiwan pairings, which often resort to couching their arguments in the now legitimized language of arms control on behalf of respective clients.

The NSC, divided within itself along similar issue lines, attempts to orchestrate all this under the banner of a global issues approach. The product, however, in terms of overall arms control strategy, may still tend to evolve from an essentially short-term, ad hoc, country-by-country approach, wherein the long-range aggegation of arms control issues to a coherent strategy may be rendered very difficult.

Summary

The full-tilt pursuit of arms control in a variety of issue areas may involve some serious pitfalls and outright contradictions, providing the necessity for painful choices, improved coordination, and a more coherent, overall strategy. It is recognized, however, as one writer has lamented, that on the contrary, "theories on regime interaction can only be taken so far; action on many of them would otherwise be paralyzed."[31] Between paralysis, on the one hand, and confusion and contradiction, on the other, there may be a meeting ground where arms control priorities must be determined and acted on.

Amid this complexity, however, two crucial sets of questions seem paramount, involving primarily the critical relationships connecting SALT, CAT, and nonproliferation, as follows:

1. Whether the United States is, consciously or not, pursuing a virtual "counter-nonproliferation policy," in accepting nuclear parity with the USSR, reducing the credibility of its nuclear umbrella, and downgrading its global, conventional intervention capability and credibility. Related to that is the somewhat psychological, perhaps ethnocentric problem of being able to take seriously the real security concerns of some small states, as *they* perceive them.

2. Whether the present strenuous pursuit of CAT controls (including those on a unilateral basis) is worth the price in terms of its rather ambiguous ends and in the light of a host of possibly baneful collateral effects impacting on nonproliferation, SALT, and the overall U.S. national security posture.

These issues have not adequately been addressed as yet. They are not likely to disappear anytime soon.

Notes

1. The flavor of the earlier animus against arms control is rendered in Duncan Clarke, "Ups and Downs of Arms Control," *Bulletin of the Atomic Scientists*, September 1974, pp. 44-49. One former defense official is there quoted as worrying that the then brand-new ACDA was "going to be a Mecca for a wide variety of screwballs," and a "natural magnet for . . . the give-up groups."

2. "Towards a Comprehensive U.S. Arms Control Strategy," Derek Leebaert, Aspen Institute for Humanistic Studies, 1977. Reprinted with permission.

3. This terminology is drawn from Colin S. Gray, *The Geopolitics of the Nuclear Era* (New York: Crane, Russak, 1977), a National Strategy Information Center paper, p. 4.

4. See "U.N. Special Session on Disarmament," U.S. Department of State Bulletin Reprint (Washington, D.C.: U.S. Government Printing Office, August 1978); and William Epstein, "U.N. Special Session on Disarmament: How Much Progress?" *Survival* 20, no. 6 (November/December 1978):248-254.

5. A few exceptions are Leebaert, "Arms Control Strategy"; Edward Luttwak, *U.S. Foreign Policy in a Proliferating World* (Santa Monica, Calif.: 1975), California Seminar on Arms Control and Foreign Policy, Discussion Paper no. 68; and Harlan Cleveland, "The Future of Arms Control" (Paper delivered at Aspen Arms Control Workshop, Aspen, Colorado, August 8-12, 1977).

6. See, for example, Chalmers M. Roberts, *The Nuclear Years* (New York: Praeger, 1970); Trevor N. Dupuy and Gay M. Hammerman, eds., *A Documentary History of Arms Control and Disarmament* (New York: R. R. Bowker, 1973); John H. Barton and Lawrence Weiler, eds., *International Arms Control* (Stanford, Calif.: Stanford University Press, 1976); Bernard G. Bechhoefer, *Postwar Negotiations for Arms Control* (Washington, D.C.: Brookings Institution, 1961); and *Arms Control: Readings* from *Scientific American* (San Francisco: W.H. Freeman, 1973). Among the few works that have assayed some comprehensive ordering of—and theorizing on—arms control issues are David V. Edwards, *Arms Control in International Politics* (New York: Holt, Rinehart and Winston, 1969); and Walter C. Clemens, Jr., *The Superpowers and Arms Control* (Lexington, Mass.: D.C. Heath, 1973).

7. For one brief advocacy of increasing attention to unilateral arms control measures, see Franklin A. Long, "Arms Control from the Perspective of the Nineteen-Seventies," in F.A. Long and G.W. Rathjens, eds., *Arms, Defense Policy, and Arms Control* (New York: W.W. Norton, 1976), pp. 8-10.

8. See Bennett Ramberg, *The Seabed Arms Control Negotiations* (Denver: University of Denver Press, 1978), Monograph Series in World Affairs.

9. The primacy of the nuclear nonproliferation issue among arms control priorities is asserted by, for instance, Abram Chayes, as follows. "The control of superpower confrontation through nuclear arms-control measures has declined in relative importance as the confrontation has moderated in intensity. In the confused and still dangerous world to come, the main effort must be directed to the problems of nuclear weapons actually or potentially in hands other than those of the superpowers." See his "Nuclear Arms Control after the Cold War," in Long and Rathjens, *Arms, Defense Policy*, p. 32.

10. See Richart Burt, "Nuclear Proliferation and the Spread of New Conventional Weapons Technology," in Stephanie Neuman and Robert Harkavy, eds., *Arms Transfers in the Modern World* (New York: Praeger, 1979), pp. 89-108.

11. See Robert E. Harkavy, "The Pariah State Syndrome," *Orbis* 21, no. 3 (Fall 1977):623-649; and *The New York Times*, 17 April 1979, p. A3.

12. See Burt, "Nuclear Proliferation."

13. See Robert E. Harkavy, "The New Geopolitics: Arms Transfers

and the Major Powers' Competition for Overseas Bases," in Neuman and Harkavy, *Arms Transfers.*

14. *Arms Control: 1977* (Washington, D.C.: U.S. Government Printing Office, May 1978), annual report of U.S. Arms Control and Disarmament Agency, p. 14.

15. For an elaboration of this point, see Geoffrey Kemp, "The New Strategic Map: Geography, Arms Diffusion and the Southern Seas" (Paper delivered at Fletcher School's conference on the Implications of the Military Build-up in Non-industrial States, Boston, May 6-8, 1976).

16. See Luttwak, *U.S. Foreign Policy,* p. 10.

17. On possible nuclear chain effects, see Lewis A. Dunn and Herman Kahn, *Trends in Nuclear Proliferation, 1975-1995* (Croton-on-Hudson, N.Y.: Hudson Institute, 1975).

18. See Henry Scott-Stokes, "It's All Right to Talk Defense Again in Japan," *The New York Times Magazine,* 11 February 1979.

19. Luttwak, *U.S. Foreign Policy,* p. 14.

20. See chapter 6 by Jerome Slater.

21. John Newhouse, *Cold Dawn* (New York: Holt, Rinehart and Winston, 1973), pp. 103-104; and Barton and Weiler, *International Arms Control,* pp. 298-302.

22. See, for instance, Richard Garwin, "Declaratory Posture for the Second Nuclear Regime," in David C. Gompert et al., eds., *Nuclear Weapons and World Politics* (New York: McGraw-Hill, 1977), pp. 130-131.

23. William Beecher, "Egypt Developing Nerve Gas Weapons," *Boston Globe,* 6 June 1976, p. 1.

24. For a brief review of what is involved, see Drew Middleton, "Loss of Devices Watching Soviet a Serious Casualty of Iran Crisis," *The New York Times,* 18 January 1979, p. A14.

25. See, Joseph I. Coffey, *Arms Control and European Security* (New York: Praeger, 1977), especially chaps. 4, 5, 6, 8; and Ian Smart, Perspectives from Europe," in Mason Willrich and J.B. Rhinelander, eds., *SALT: The Moscow Agreements and Beyond* (New York: The Free Press, 1974), pp. 185-208.

26. John F. Lehman, "The Radical Change from Ford to Carter," *Commonsense* 1, no. 2 (Fall 1978):13-14.

27. See, Robert L. Pfaltzgraff, "The Proposed Comprehensive Test Ban Treaty," *Commonsense* 1, no. 2 (Fall 1978):44-56; and Samuel T. Cohen, *SALT and the Test Ban: Parallels and Prospects* (Santa Monica, Calif.: 1973), California Seminar on Arms Control and Foreign Policy, Discussion Paper.

28. Luttwak, *U.S. Foreign Policy,* p. 13.

29. Ibid., p. 14.

30. See Jo Husbands, "How the U.S. Makes Foreign Military Sales," in Neuman and Harkavy, *Arms Transfers.*

31. See Leebaert, p. 52.

The Arms Control Impact Statement: Program and Logic

Robert Lyle Butterworth

Since legislation requiring arms control impact statements (ACIS) for selected defense programs was passed in 1975, three sets of ACIS have been submitted to Congress. Virtually no one involved with national security policy considers the ACIS program to have been a resounding success, and a multitude of changes have been suggested.[1] But most of these suggestions, although well-intentioned, are ill-advised and potentially deleterious to national security policy. Implementing them might increase antagonistic frustration among executive and legislative branches and agencies to the extent that any progress made to date is reversed. Arms control might then be considered an impossible (hence undesirable) aim, and Congress might "simply abandon the whole impact statement process as hopelessly utopian."[2]

The weakness of most suggestions for legislative revision, and of the original program, lies in a failure to appreciate the bureaucratic politics and the objective problems involved in arms control issues. This chapter will begin with the first of these deficiencies, adopting a programmatic perspective to sketch elements in the implementation process that precluded fulfilling the goals of the legislative formulators. The results of this analysis cast doubt on the utility of further legislation to improve the ACIS process. The second part of this chapter addresses the ACIS program and the proposed remedies for it from a broader analytic perspective. This analysis shows that the program and the proposed modifications of it rest on neither a coherent conceptual rationale nor an effective consensus. The predictable result has been an evaluative chaos, in which competing goals, evaluation criteria, and proposals for change are jumbled together. This analytic assessment suggests modifying the program by changing legislative behavior rather than legislation.

Programmatic Assessment

To conduct a programmatic assessment, criteria for evaluating a program are drawn from its legislative history and the apparent motivations of its formulators. Space limitations prohibit carefully tracing the history of the ACIS program;[3] here I will merely summarize its three major goals:

—to make the executive branch formally and systematically consider the possible effects of proposed programs on arms control.

—to improve the quantity and quality of information submitted to the Congress on proposed defense programs, so it can better deliberate the merits of these programs.

—to enhance the role of the Arms Control and Disarmament Agency in the national security policy making process.[4]

Goal 1

To date, the ACIS program has exerted little influence on defense appropriation decisions by the executive branch or by Congress. A great deal of interagency wrangling and bloodletting has occurred, several confrontations between the Congress and the administration have been provoked, and tens of thousands of person-hours have been expended, but one is hard put to suggest that the outcome of defense decisions since the passing of the ACIS legislation would have been any different in its absence. There is no direct evidence that a weapon system that would earlier have been approved has been significantly altered or dropped owing to factors raised by the ACIS process. Indeed, there is only one case so far of a congressional decision in which an ACIS played a part: the August 1977 decision on funding for the enhanced radiation warhead (W-70 Mod 3) for the Lance missile. Senator Claiborne Pell noted that no ACIS had been submitted for this program, and Senator Hubert Humphrey convinced the administration that an ACIS was required prior to approval of the funding bill. A quickly prepared analysis from the Arms Control and Disarmament Agency (ACDA) was sanitized by the National Security Council (NSC) and provided to Humphrey. Presenting it to the Senate, he noted that "the statement is one that really fits the description of 'on the one hand' and 'on the other hand.' . . . The conclusion is one that does not give much of a conclusion."[5] The fact that the Senate then approved the bill, having in its possession this "marginally negative" set of assessments and without knowing whether the president would actually recommend continued development of the warhead, suggests that the ACIS was useful as a procedural device but not terribly important for its substantive content.[6] If this case provides an index of the health and vitality of the ACIS concept, the verdict must be cautious; at best it shows only a qualified fulfillment of the intentions underlying the original legislation.

Nor are there reliable indications that the program has made any other independent contributions to achieving the first goal. Generally speaking, the ACIS requirement has been viewed by all executive agencies involved as a problem to be solved in and of itself; any spillover effects in other decision-making processes have been diffuse. In past years, the Department of Energy (DOE) and the Department of Defense (DOD) have viewed the problem in damage-limiting terms—how to preserve maximum amounts of their jurisdictional integrity within the constraints set by the overall administration's willingness to avoid antagonizing Congress on this issue. ACDA and, to some extent, the State Department have viewed the problem in imperialist terms—how to increase access to weapons programs and strategic decisions, even those that are only remotely related to their agency or ACIS-related missions, within the constraints of minimizing threats to the degree of cooperation they already had achieved with other agencies. The NSC viewed the problem in conflict management terms—how to minimize interagency conflict and preserve the confidentiality of weapons planning, while minimizing frictions with Congress so as not to jeopardize budgetary requests. Furthermore, there are good reasons for the administration as a whole to view the ACIS as problems to be solved separately from weapons decision-making. As has often been noted, the program places the executive branch in a dilemma: "it will be difficult for the Executive to send to Congress a recommendation for a defense program and at the same time send an impact evaluation that the program would be detrimental to national arms control policy."[7]

Recommendations for legislatively improving program performance with respect to this goal generally run afoul of an intrinsic and serious measurement problem: the degree of goal achievement cannot be assessed very easily by Congress. The output of the program—the ACIS themselves—certainly cannot be used for this evaluation; as a Government Accounting Office (GAO) analysis noted, "It should be recognized that even improved arms control impact statements cannot be considered in and of themselves conclusive evidence as to Executive branch consideration of arms control aspects in its national security policymaking deliberations."[8] Nor will other programmatic "processual" criteria that are often used in similar cases serve as reliable indicators. Determining the interagency paper flow, determining whether basic drafts of the ACIS are "farmed out" to consulting groups and specially hired personnel or whether agency "regulars" are involved with them at the outset, and determining whether the ACIS are reviewed by high administration officials, all will not do the job. As a senior Congressional Research Service (CRS) analyst noted in connection with the first round of statements, the program aims at having the executive branch learn "to integrate defense and arms control policies at the genesis of weapons systems and defense programs," to "think through and resolve the conflicting policy considerations before it drafts a program to be proposed to Congress."[9] Probably the only procedure that would really indicate whether this goal was being met was suggested by the GAO, which involved having the executive branch make available to the Congress documentation that conclusively demonstrates its consideration of arms control problems in making decisions on U.S. national security, defense, and nuclear energy policy. These include interagency studies such as (1) Presidential Review Memoranda (formerly National Security Study Memoranda) and Presidential Directive Memoranda (formerly National Security Decision Memoranda) produced through the National Security Council, (2) transcripts of the Defense Systems Acquisition Review Council's meetings, and (3) Defense Concept Papers.[10]

As this report immediately noted, however, "the Executive branch might not be anxious to make available certain documents which have often been closely held."

Goal 2

At first blush, program achievement with respect to the second goal, enhancing the "quantity and quality of information submitted to the Congress on proposed defense programs," seems much easier to measure and to have been reasonably well fulfilled by the most recent round of ACIS. In addition to the submission of the executive branch, the program has generated as spin-offs information that Congress would otherwise not have had—reports from congressional support agencies. By this time, such additional information seems to be entrenched as part of the ACIS program; both the CRS and the GAO have established an ongoing concern with the ACIS.

Closer analysis, however, shows that there are problems with performance regarding this goal and that legislative remedies are not particularly well suited to correcting them. The ACIS are intended to make it possible for Congress "to better deliberate the merits" of proposed defense programs, but (as noted with goal 1) there is no direct evidence that this has occurred. In the past, this failing was due in part to timing and classification; the ACIS were submitted to Congress well after the budget proposals and, in the first two rounds, only in classified form. Recent legislation should correct these difficulties. But the deeper problem is lodged in the way in which Congress itself conducts its business. In other words, the informational content of ACIS is not quite as easy to measure as might initially seem to be the case, because the program goal is not interpreted in terms of the amount of crude data submitted. Instead, the program is aimed at acquiring information that can advance insights and understanding. Criticisms of earlier statements, for example, include the charges that they did not constitute an analysis, important arms control considerations were ignored, and weapons systems that could significantly affect arms control policy were ignored. Probably the best way to obtain an indicator of compliance with this program aim would be legislative specification of the content of ACIS, including more precision about what programs should be covered (because there is broad agreement that line-item budget figures are inadequate), what arms control considerations should be addressed, and what criteria should be used to evaluate a system's consistency with arms control policy. But doing so would require a level of detailed expertise that Congress has generally seemed unable or unwilling to develop regarding security issues.[11] A recent CRS study seems aimed at just this problem, although both the point just raised and the analytic assessment presented below cast doubt on the ability of Congress to make effective remedies.[12]

Goal 3

The third program goal, as quoted above, involves upgrading the role of the Arms Control and Disarmament Agency in the national security policymaking process, but it has already been noted that several participants felt by the conclusion of round two that ACDA's influence had been degraded or, at best, not strengthened. Here again, proposed legislative remedies are beset by serious problems of measuring program achievement. Certainly by the middle of the production process for round three many ACDA personnel felt that the Agency was in a stronger position with respect to the ACIS program, at least. But their comments seemed to be based entirely on the fact that the recent procedures provided ACDA with a definite role and task in the production process. Needless to say, there is often a large gap between activity and influence. Moreover, even if the Agency achieves more influence in this program, it would be in terms of the ACIS and not necessarily in terms of the broader scope of national security policymaking. The difficulty here is a direct corollary of the politics of the production process; ACDA's attempts to shape the product have cost it resources and goodwill, and its role has been used to circumscribe its access to other policy issues.

Some have proposed calling on ACDA to provide independent appraisals and testimony to Congress, but this procedure would not provide reliable indicators either, because it is inconceivable that an administration could tolerate an influential agency that was "blowing the whistle" on other influential agencies. This was a problem discussed extensively during congressional hearings on the original ACIS amendment, and most analysts agree that requiring such testimony from ACDA would either remove it from any meaningful policy role or produce highly suspect testimony. Probably the best course to achieve full implementation of this goal would be enactment of the proposals offered in the reports of two major governmental reviews, the Commission on the Organization of the Government for the

Conduct of Foreign Policy and the Farley study.[13] Obtaining indicators of achievement could probably best be achieved in the same way recommended to measure executive branch consideration of arms control issues, namely, access to crucial executive branch documents; but, again, such access is quite unlikely to be obtained.

Conclusions

The programmatic perspective used in this section evaluates a program's achievements in terms of its formulation goals, thereby viewing the implementation process in terms of compliance with congressional intent. This orientation leads to explaining programmatic success or failure in terms of the politics of compliance. Proposals for changing a program are then directed at obviating political obstacles to full compliance with congressional intent.

In the case of the ACIS program, popular explanations for program failure include the recalcitrance of the administration, bureaucratic rigidity, ignorance and stupidity on the part of various administrative leaders, aggressiveness or lack thereof on the part of some groups within administrative agencies, empire-building efforts on the part of certain congressional commitees, and the opposition of certain members of the Armed Services committees. Several supporters of the ACIS program note that there have been few incentives for DOD and DOE to comply fully with the law, because their budgetary authorizations are usually guaranteed by their comfortable relationship with the Armed Services committees, which care very little about the ACIS. The ambiguity in legislative requirements and the widely differing interpretations of what aims are really meant to be served by the ACIS program were interpreted by several executive branch personnel (and legislative as well) as raising questions about how seriously Congress would insist on very complete ACIS. On all sides one often encounters explanations for program failure based on uncertainty about what Congress was "after" and how the information would be used; the GAO report quotes one DOD official, for example, as complaining that "Congress asked us to shoot ourselves in the foot. Now Congress is complaining because we aren't doing it."[14] Another popular interpretation is that the program is still early on the "learning curve"; program formulators, implementors, and evaluators are still trying to determine what is wanted, what is possible to produce, and how it should be achieved and used.

Hence it seems plain that, congressional advocates to the contrary notwithstanding, the legislation creating the ACIS program is far from clear in terms of expressing congressional intent, the criteria by which programs are to be evaluated, the process that should be employed, the seriousness with which Congress would evaluate the resulting product, and the criteria by which Congress would do so. Predictably, in this context of ambiguity and confusion, subagency interests within the executive branch could attempt to shape the ACIS production process to serve their own particular policy aims. Hence several participants feel that the appropriate remedy is to specify precisely what is required. At the same time, several have recommended that Congress also specify the process that should be used in producing the ACIS; if ACDA is to play a stronger role, then that should be legislatively mandated.

As noted, however, it is difficult to conceive of possible legislative remedies that would remove political hindrances to full compliance with the ACIS goals. Congress would need to discover a means of mandating a stronger role for ACDA that would provide clear evidence if noncompliance should occur. In addition, Congress should structure its own processes to provide significant incentives for DOD and DOE to comply fully with the intent of the law. Insisting on satisfactory ACIS before a serious consideration of budgetary proposals begins would help, as would evidence of a real willingness to consider the ACIS in floor debate and not just in committee. But these are just the sort of changes that Congress finds very difficult to affect. In sum, the policy process in this issue area is not especially tractable for legislative manipulation. In part this limitation reflects institutional weaknesses and habits, but these factors are compounded by a deeper difficulty—the objective nature of the issues being addressed.

Analytic Assessment

Formulation

An analytic evaluation proceeds from analysts' perceptions of the objective problem addressed by the program and leads to assessment criteria based on the ways and degrees to which the program's formulation, implementation, and evaluation experiences can affect the issue area being considered, regardless of the intentions of the program's formulators. In this case there is no conflict between analytic and programmatic evaluations regarding problem definition; there are sound conceptual and historical grounds for the perceived need to take account of both defense and arms control considerations, which often are competing, in the making of national security policy. But if the justification of problem and need offered for the ACIS requirement is objectively defensible, the same is certainly not true for the program as formulated. The attempt to solve this problem by means of a document produced by the administration and submitted to Congress is seriously flawed in terms of both its coherence—consistency of the means with the goal—and its feasibility. It is particularly damning of the formulation process in this case that major problems in both respects were repeatedly identified during hearings on the proposal. Why, for example, should it be expected that Congress will be able to aggregate any conflicting arms control and defense merits of proposed weapons systems better than the executive branch? If the claim is not that Congress would do it better, but rather that the program provides a means for Congress to play more of a role and to increase pluralism in policy-making, why should it be expected that a document produced by the administration would enable Congress to do so? (The political problems with this approach have already been noted.) If Congress does want to play a more independent role, should it not reasonably expect to depend more on its own analyses?

The answers usually given to this line of questioning involve the merits of having the executive branch go through the exercise of considering the arms control implications of weapons proposals. But it has already been shown that Congress has not supplied itself (and may not be able to do so) with the means to assess whether the ACIS program actually has the "consciousness-raising" effects in the executive branch that were desired. Moreover, many participants insist that the ACIS exercise enters the decision-making process too late and that arms control factors are already considered earlier through existing administrative review procedures; thus only rarely, they suggest, could an ACIS be part of the presidential decision process. Even if arms control concerns did not play an important role in weapons decision-making prior to the ACIS program, there are sufficiently obvious problems with its timing to cast doubt on claims that it independently reversed that situation.

The program's most serious weakness, however, is in its unspecified call for a statement of the "arms control impacts" of selected weapons systems, as though what constituted such impacts were well understood and as though there were widely shared criteria for evaluating such impacts positively or negatively. In fact, this program crystallizes—but does not resolve—a host of contentious issues that are central to national security policy-making. Any attempt to implement this requirement leads one immediately to confronting profound and unresolved issues. What is the meaning of "national security" in the contemporary environment? How can deterrence best be obtained? Are there tradeoffs between national defense and arms control? If so, how much should be traded off for what in what context? The meaning of arms control implications in any particular context requires a view of the weapon's role in the overall national security posture and the threats being addressed. It may make little sense, therefore, to consider a particular weapon, or even a family of weapon systems, as having intrinsically significant arms control effects. In any event, evaluations of such effects are likely to reflect predispositions shaped by broader issues of security policy; there is neither a single compelling conceptual framework nor a broadly shared political consensus on such matters, and therefore analysts can legitimately differ over the arms control merits of a weapon.[15]

In these respects, the appropriateness of the program for the problem does not seem to have been considered very carefully by its formulators. The ACIS program is a case of what Charles O. Jones calls "analogous formulation," in which a program is created by "treating a new problem by relying on what was done in developing proposals for similar problems in the past—i.e., searching for analogies."[16] In this case, the analogy is found in the requirements of the National Environmental Protection Act for environmental impact statements. But this analogy is not at all good, for two major reasons. The nature of the arms control problem is itself a major difficulty; while one might reasonably expect to achieve agreement on what constitutes a polluted environment, it is far from easy to achieve agreement on what constitutes arms control or what contributes to it. Secondly, there was provided no clear procedure for resolving conflicts of interpretation; unlike the NEPA, the ACIS legislation explicitly denied the courts any role, while leaving unspecified both the criteria of satisfactory compliance and the remedy for unsatisfactory compliance. In consequence, there were serious grounds for questioning the degree of congressional commitment to the ACIS requirement, and the scope for bureaucratic infighting proved to be extremely broad when it came time to produce the ACIS.

Implementation

Even a poorly conceived program can in practice become a functional success if implementors can work with evaluators and formulators to achieve underlying program objectives, despite the formal wording of the legislation. The key to this possibility for the ACIS program lay in the questions that would be asked about a weapon system regarding its arms control implications; they comprise the operational core of the ACIS requirement, and deciding on them should focus attention on the objective problem to be solved—incorporating defense with arms control assessments in making national security policy. Several sets of questions have been proposed; some are suggested in the legislative history of the program; Representative John Seiberling provided a set prepared by Members of Congress for Peace through Law; ACDA had a preferred set when the program began; CRS provides another set; and the NSC prepared a set for round three.[17]

But to be useful, such questions must be derived from some overarching view of how arms control factors affect national security; otherwise the answers will not be interpretable in any coherent fashion. None of these lists of questions, however, included an explicit rationale that could be used as a conceptual map for understanding the answers. Consequently there was little if any conceptual counterweight to the ever-present incentives to resolve clashes over questions bureaucratically. By the beginning of round three, one of ACDA's staff members, deeply involved in the ACIS production process, made these remarks: "DOD always kicks about what 'arms control policy' is. Arms control policy is certainly not established; I am not sure what it involves. It is, in fact, whatever the President says it is. It depends entirely on the President's definition."[18] Not surprisingly, completed ACIS thus tend to embody the results of bureaucratic pluralism, fatigue, and attrition, and to be rather unenlightening (recall Humphrey's remarks concerning the W-70 Mod 3 statement).

Evaluation

Congressional evaluation of the ACIS submitted to it could have been expected to remedy many of the defects in the implementation process. In particular, one might have expected Congress to criticize the administration's product for failing to confront the objective problem squarely and thereby reorient the program in more useful directions. Even if such oversight had not led to a more satisfactory approach by the executive branch, the educational effects of congressional focusing on the objective problem, both for Congress and the broader political context, might have made important contributions to improving national security policy.

That these developments did not occur can be traced to the evaluative mechanism used by Congress. Several committee staff members and legislators themselves read and considered the statements submitted by the administration. But the major responsibility for reviewing, analyzing, and suggesting improvements was assigned to the CRS and the GAO. Whatever the merits of the agencies, this procedure means that an additional layer of bureaucracy is interposed between legislators who must exercise oversight and the actual analysis that informs their judgments. This is a failing, because the exercise of critiquing the ACIS and of trying to devise improvements in them has intrinsic educational merit apart from its eventual output.

This failing is compounded as the ACIS program stimulates an urge to expand congressional staff by adding technical expertise. It is very popular among personal and committee staff members (and those of CRS as well) to complain that Congress cannot do a satisfactory job of evaluating the ACIS until it has on hand the expertise to comprehend the advanced technology embodied in proposed weapons and verification mechanisms. The adherents of this opinion essentially argue that one can expect little from the ACIS program until enough personnel with both technical expertise and arms control sensitivities can be hired. There is some accuracy in this position, of course; Congress certainly needs to do better than it did during the early days of the Lance warhead debate when several thought that the W-70 Mod 3 was a chemical device, and certainly it needs to understand that a "neutron bomb" is not entirely devoid of heat and blast effects. But these misinterpretations are correctible by various means already available to Congress; the two erroneous perceptions cited here were corrected fairly readily, at any rate.

The call for further technical expertise thus seems, from an analytic perspective, an attempt to shirk responsibility. Technological information is important to evaluating the arms control impacts of weapons systems, but the evaluations hinge on difficult judgments about strategic and political matters. Of course it matters whether a weapon system can be detected under various meteorological conditions in different ways, but the significant implications of this technical question are political. What is required to evaluate and oversee the ACIS program, and what is currently lacking, are concepts and understandings dealing with the relationships among defense concerns, arms control considerations, and national security goals. Helping to determine these relationships is precisely the task that Congress claimed it was trying to achieve when it created the ACIS program to help assert its prerogatives in the national security arena. To try to reduce the matter to one of weapons technology is to belie the merit and seriousness of the original intent and to admit incompetence and/or otiosity in the face of significant problems of national security. Sufficient "hardware expertise" is already available to Congress; seriously lacking is expertise in the political implications of the hardware, understanding of what contributes to politically stable deterrence, and a conceptual grasp of the political technology of national security.

Conclusions

The analytic perspective used in this section evaluates a program in terms of its contributions to resolving an externally defined problem, thereby viewing formulation, implementation, and evaluation in terms of their conceptual coherence. This orientation leads one to explain programmatic success or failure in terms of problem understanding and focus. Proposals for changing a program are then directed at obviating diversions of effort and attention from objective problem-solving.

In the case of the ACIS program, this perspective leads to assessing the failure of the original legislation, and of most of its proposed legislative modifications, as being due to an inadequate appreciation of the objective problems involved in arms control issues. The legislative goals, although superficially clear, conceal a morass of complex issues requiring careful subjective assessments that are, for excellent reasons, very contentious. The legislative approach to these problems has had the effect of enforcing a separation between arms control considerations on the one hand and defense and national security concerns on the other. The effect of this separation has been to divert effort away from dealing with the objective problem and toward dealing with the ACIS requirements as a political problem. Most of the proposed legislative remedies would exacerbate this misdirection. It is futile to attempt to make sensible determinations of the arms control effects of weapons systems independently of some understanding of how such factors should be meshed with defense and national security concerns. If Congress insists on such futility by adopting measures intended to force the administration to produce documents that will achieve such a quixotic aim, frustration is likely to increase on all sides, and the program is likely to be viewed increasingly as the rope in a tug of war between branches of government fighting over balances of power and institutional prerogatives. In such a setting the possibility of dealing with the objective problem becomes even more remote. Arms control concerns will become highly politicized both within Congress, where they will become ammunition for those who know little and care less about the intricacies of contemporary security problems, and within the administration, where they will become vehicles for interagency power struggles. It is far from impossible that notions of arms control will become interpreted as ideological "code words" and denigrated by defense and security planners.

Recommendations

There are some improvements to the ACIS program that are suggested by an analytic perspective, that should also be desirable from a programmatic one, and that do not risk the dangers just noted. The aim of these changes is to redirect the policy system so that the objective problem is the focus of effort; specifically, they are intended to improve coordination between the ACIS program and national security concerns overall. They require no new legislation but call for changes in the behavior of the legislative branch; changes in these respects should be sufficient to ensure that behavior within the executive branch will also be appropriately altered.

Broader Concerns

The current program focuses congressional attention on a statement of arms control effects, but most congressional participants revealed in interviews that their primary concern is with national security effects. Congress should therefore change the way in which it evaluates the outputs of the ACIS program to reflect this broader concern. DOD and DOE budgetary requests should be evaluated in terms that include both defense and arms control considerations as well as an explicit rationale for the way in which the two were synthesized. This approach would help to clarify the logic of weapons proposals in terms of overall national security concerns. Some procedural modifications would be required to accomplish this change, but it should require no great additional burden simply to insert the ACIS already prepared into the budgetary justifications already prepared. In some cases, of course, writing an explicit synthesis of the two would require considerable additional effort—but that is precisely the aim of the program.[19]

Knowledge of Alternatives

The current program appears to be predicated on the assumption that there is a single approach to evaluating the arms control implications of any proposed weapons system. In fact, determination of the importance and existence of such effects, as well as whether they are positive or negative, depend on one's notions about broader questions of national security. The policy system would deal more directly with the objective problem, and there would be a higher likelihood of Congress helping to improve security policy if the ACIS program took account of this factor. Bearing in mind that any conceptual resolution of these broader issues can only be tentative, at present, Congress would do well to have a checklist of arms control issues and problems against which to compare various analyses. Several ACIS could then be produced for salient weapons systems, each couched in terms of alternative outlooks on major issues of national security policy and showing explicitly how evaluations of arms control effects can be derived from these broader concerns. Congress has a variety of resources available to generate such checklists and evaluations; its support agencies, staffs, outside consultants, and the administration would all play appropriate roles. It should not be expected that a right answer will emerge from these conflicting views; this recommendation is based on a recognition that right answers are very hard to come by in this policy area. By making comparative evaluations of the same weapon system from alternative perspectives on security policy, Congress will at least have information directly available about the broader issues involved and the broader consequences of the choices it approves.

Direct Involvement in Analysis

This proposal is based on the critique of Congress' evaluation mechanisms presented earlier; the concern is to limit the additional layers of bureaucracy that insulate legislators from the analytic process involved in evaluating products of the ACIS program, on the grounds that useful benefits flow from the process of trying to understand the issues involved. It is probably too much to expect legislators themselves to engage systematically in such activity, but it would be helpful at least to have their personal and committee staffs do so. If the CRS and other analysts were also kept involved, ideally legislators would then have several products to compare, together with immediately available information about the underlying sources of differences among the various statements.

These proposals for change are quite different from the more sweeping recommendations for additional legislation that flow from programmatic perspectives, but they are more likely to accomplish useful goals and to satisfy congressional concerns than are the programmatic ones. The difficulty lies in making the ACIS program meaningfully related to the substance of national security decisions. This difficulty arises because the content of these decisions frustrates efforts to separate constituent aspects of these policy problems and to make choices in segmented fashion. Without an overarching perspective on these issues, it is nearly impossible to determine the appropriate questions to ask and to interpret technical information. In consequence, choices about these matters cannot be usefully preprogrammed; the policy system dealing with them must incorporate high degrees of flexibility, not only to accommodate changes in prevailing outlooks on the major issues involved but also to recognize the uncertainties involved—any resolution of these issues can only be provisional. Hence these proposals are aimed not at achieving a particular content to security policy decisions, nor at having policy options generated in particular ways. Instead, the goal is a better understanding of the issues involved and the consequences of alternative decisions. The result of implementing these proposals might well be that decisions will continue to be made as they have in the past but with better arguments in favor of them.

Notes

1. Most of the suggested improvements discussed in interviews can be found in the following reports: Foreign Affairs and National Defense Division, Congressional Research Service, Library of Congress, *Analysis of Arms Control Impact Statements Submitted in Connection with the Fiscal Year 1978 Budget Request* (Washington, D.C.: GPO, April 1977), hereinafter cited as CRS *Report*; Comptroller General of the United States, *Statements that Analyze Effects of Proposed Programs on Arms Control Need Improvement* (Washington, D.C.: GPO, 20 October 1977), hereinafter cited as GAO *Report*; and Comptroller General of the United

States, *Improved Procedures Needed for Identifying Programs Requiring Arms Control Impact Statements* (Washington, D.C.: GPO, 27 September 1978).

2. Philip M. Boffey, "Arms Control Impact Statements Again Have Little Impact," *Science* 196:4295 (10 June 1977):1181.

3. Fuller information about the program's history is provided in Butterworth, "The Arms Control Impact Statement: A Programmatic Assessment," *Policy Studies Journal* 8:1 (Autumn 1979):76-84; and Butterworth, "The Arms Control Impact Statement: Gauging the Effects," *Occasional Papers*, Center for Arms Control and International Security Studies, University of Pittsburgh, (forthcoming, 1980).

4. Interviewing and analysis of the legislative history confirm this summary of the program's goals provided in the GAO *Report*, p. 18.

5. U.S., Congress, Senate, Senator Humphrey speaking for the ACIS, 95th Cong., 1st sess., 13 July 1977, *Congressional Record*, S 11764.

6. The public text of the arms control impact statement submitted in conjunction with the request for funding for the Lance warhead is printed in U.S., Congress, Senate, 95th Cong., 1st sess., 13 July 1977, *Congressional Record*, S 11763-S 11764.

7. Memo from Charles Gellner to Senate Foreign Relations Committee, 20 August 1976, reprinted in CRS *Report*, p. 371.

8. GAO *Report*, p. 28.

9. Gellner, memo reprinted in CRS *Report*, p. 371.

10. GAO *Report*, p. 25.

11. See Les Aspin, "The Defense Budget and Foreign Policy: The Role of Congress," in F.A. Long and R.W. Rathjens, eds., *Arms, Defense Policy, and Arms Control* (New York: W.W. Norton, 1976), pp. 155-174.

12. Foreign Affairs and National Defense Division, Congressional Research Service, Library of Congress, *Evaluation of Fiscal Year 1979 Arms Control Impact Statements: Toward More Informed Congressional Participation in National Security Policymaking* (Washington, D.C.: GPO, 3 January 1979).

13. Commission on the Organization of the Government for the Conduct of Foreign Policy, Robert D. Murphy, chairman, *Report: Appendix K: Adequacy of Current Organization: Defense and Arms Control* (Washington, D.C.: GPO, June 1975); and U.S., Congress, House, Committee on Foreign Affairs, *Arms Control and Disarmament Agency, Hearings*, before the Subcommittee on National Security Policy and Scientific Developments, House of Representatives, 93d Cong., 2d sess., 1974.

14. GAO *Report*, p. 20.

15. Representative Les Aspin's remarks during the Lance warhead controversy illustrate the problem. "Basically the neutron bomb is not really a good issue, and it points up the problems that liberals have in arms control.

The real issue is whether you want to have tactical nuclear weapons or not. . . . Liberals haven't got any set of criteria to judge what is a good weapon, what is a necessary weapon, and what is a bad weapon." Quoted in Bernard Weinraub, "What Role for Neutron Bomb?" *New York Times*, 17 July 1977, sec. 4, p. 4.

16. Charles O. Jones, *An Introduction to the Study of Public Policy*, 2nd ed. (North Scituate, Mass.,: Duxbury Press, 1977), p. 56.

17. U.S., Congress, House, Representative John Seiberling speaking for ACIS evaluation criteria, 94th Cong., 2d sess., September 15, 1976, *Congressional Record*, H 10166-H 10168.

18. Interview data.

19. Parts of this recommendation are similar to a suggestion made in the report of the Farley study concerning the desirability of "requiring broader and fuller analytic justification of defense budget and policy proposals." (Quoted earlier and cited in n. 13.)

10 Military Research and Development: Institutions, Output, and Arms Control

Judith Reppy

Introduction

Military research and development (R&D) has long been recognized as an important element in our national security. First, and most obviously, today's research and development projects are tomorrow's deployed weapons in the field. Military R&D supports the replacement of current weapons with improved versions; this is the outcome of the bulk of R&D activity. It may also yield innovations causing substantial shifts in military capability and entailing changes in doctrine, tactics, and the organization of forces. The introduction of nuclear weapons touched off one such revolution; less profound, but still important, shifts in military organization may be expected from the introduction of miniature guidance systems into conventional weapons and from the enhanced reconnaissance capabilities of satellites. Finally, incremental changes in a number of technologies may accumulate, resulting in a "revolutionary" shift in capability with doctrinal implications, as in the cruise missile and the greatly increased accuracy of intercontinental ballistic missiles (ICBMs).[1]

Since World War II the United States has pursued a policy of technological superiority across the board. For example, Secretary of Defense Melvin Laird stated in 1970, "There is one thing we do know, we cannot settle for anything short of technological leadership in R&D related to national security," and many similar statements over the years could be cited.[2] American officials have argued that the Soviet Union's superiority in numbers of men and deployed weapons, especially on the European front, can only be countered by a qualitative edge on our side. Other hoped-for outcomes from our military R&D program are the identification of potential technological advances by the enemy (the hedge against technological surprise), new capabilities in verification that may support arms control measures, and enhanced standing in the eyes of the world—friend and foe alike—as a result of a perception of U.S. technological superiority.

Technological superiority by itself does not translate directly into military superiority: weapons designed to exploit a lower level of technology may be as effective as more sophisticated weapons when produced in quantity and integrated with an appropriate military doctrine.[3] The traditional reliance of the United States on high technology thus does not guarantee military superiority. The military user's demand for weapons is typically for both "more" and "better," but the supply of new developments is constrained by the state of technology and the budget. Consequently, the question of the proper degree of emphasis on high technology has been seen very much as a trade-off between quality and quantity.[4]

Driving this concern is the fact that U.S. weapons have become ever more expensive as their level of technology has increased (even though the new weapons may not offer any greater relative capability, given that Soviet systems are also improving). In principle, advanced technology need not mean higher unit costs: there are, for example, process innovations that reduce production costs and new technologies, like integrated circuits, that totally dominate the technology they replace in capability and lower cost. In practice, however, higher technology has been associated with higher real per unit costs and the number of units procured has, in general, declined.

Investment in military R&D also involves an intertemporal trade-off. Spending on additional already-developed equipment, more divisions, or training exercises will increase military strength in the short run more than development of new, technologically sophisticated weapons. Thus, the allocation of resources to R&D should bear some relationship to a judgment about the national security needs of the present versus those of the future, and should balance the numbers of systems funded for development with the projected capability to procure and deploy those systems in the future. If the number of systems in full-scale development or their degree of technical sophistication greatly exceed the budgetary capacity for ultimate procurement, then money is being wasted.[5]

In addition to the opportunity costs of the resources devoted to military R&D, a large R&D program may entail other, more significant costs as a result of the dynamic interactions between our weapons developments and those of the Soviet Union. The deployment of a major new weapons system by one power typically evokes a response from the other side. If, however, the reaction takes place in response to R&D programs rather than actually deployed systems, then the reaction time is shortened, accelerating the arms race. We may face a real threat stimulated by the USSR's knowledge of a development of our own, a development that may never reach production. For example, the Russian fighter plane, MIG 25 (Foxbat), was a response to our development program for the B-70 bomber, a plane we never procured. And Russian tests, not deployments, were the source of the alleged missile gap of the early sixties that led us to accelerate our own missile programs. Moreover, to the extent that we succeed in our policy of maintaining broad technological superiority, we will be engaged not so much in a reciprocating, action-reaction pattern as in a situation that is constantly perturbed by our own technological advances, with the USSR engaged in a persistent effort to erase the technological gap.

Characteristics of the U.S. Military R&D Program

The largest part of the U.S. program for military R&D is funded through the Department of Defense's (DOD) Research, Development, Test and Engineering (RDT&E) budget category, which currently runs about $12 billion per year, or about 10 percent of the total DOD budget. Other significant programs of military R&D are the nuclear weapons development of the Department of Energy (DOE) and the inhouse R&D programs of defense contractors, each running about $1 billion dollars per year.

A thriving establishment for the performance of military R&D has evolved in the United States since World War II in response to continued high levels of federal funding. For many years military R&D accounted for over half the total R&D performed in the United States, and it is still roughly half of federally funded R&D. Private industry performs the bulk of our military R&D; RDT&E contracts are eagerly sought as a means to maintain technological competence and to win a preferred position in the competition for subsequent procurement contracts. Government-sponsored military laboratories play an important role in certain highly specialized technologies and as a source of technical expertise for DOD program managers.

Table 10-1 displays the dollar amounts for the RDT&E budget and its ratio to total DOD spending and to DOD investment in equipment (RDT&E

Table 10-1
DOD Budget, Selected Categories, FY 1962-1978, Outlay Basis
(millions of current dollars)

				RDT&E as Percentage	
Year	Total DOD	Procurement	RDT&E	Total DOD	RDT&E Plus Procurement
1965	45973	11839	6236	13.6	34.5
1966	54178	14339	6259	11.6	30.4
1967	67457	19012	7160	10.6	27.4
1968	77373	23283	7747	10.1	25.0
1969	77872	23988	7457	9.6	23.7
1970	77150	21584	7166	9.3	24.9
1971	74546	18858	7303	9.8	27.9
1972	75151	17131	7881	10.5	31.5
1973	73297	15654	8157	11.1	34.3
1974	77625	15241	8582	10.1	36.0
1975	85020	16042	8866	10.4	35.6
1976	88036	15964	8923	10.1	39.9
TQ	21925	3766	2206	10.1	36.9
1977	92521	18178	9795	10.6	35.0
1978	102086	21552	10714	10.5	33.2

Sources: 1962-76: Office of Management and Budget, "Federal Government Finances," February 1977, (mimeo); 1977-78: Department of Defense (Comptroller), "National Defense Budget Estimates for FY 1979."

plus procurement) from 1965 to 1978. The apparent doubling of DOD spending over the period is a result of inflation; in constant dollars the 1965 and 1978 figures are virtually identical.[6] Because we are interested in the allocative decisions made by DOD, percentage breakdowns of the budget are more relevant. Since the mid-sixties the fraction of the DOD budget allocated to RDT&E has been quite stable at about 10 percent. R&D as a percentage of investment spending, however, has varied widely as a consequence of changes in spending on procurement. In the drawdown in procurement spending after Vietnam, RDT&E as a percentage of total DOD investment rose to the truly amazing figure of nearly 40 percent.

The stability of RDT&E's share of the overall DOD budget suggests that the RDT&E budget is set by a rule-of-thumb. Such stability can be defended as good policy, since projects with long gestation periods need protection from fluctuating levels of support. The uncertainty inherent in new developments argues for steady funding for the early stages of R&D. But the case for stable funding depends on that stability being reflected in individual programs. Table 10-2 gives the percentage breakdown of the RDT&E budget by program for FY 1965-77. Close examination reveals substantial shifts; particularly noteworthy is the decline in dollars allocated to military astronautics. Even this level of disaggregation conceals important shifts in program direction.[7] Just as the overall RDT&E budget has apparently been subject to percentage guidelines, the major budget breakdowns tend also to acquire a certain stability based on the fact that each year's budget is dominated by program starts of previous years—new starts are only a small percentage of total spending. Within program categories, individual programs do not enjoy security of funding. Internal DOD decisions or congressional cuts may impose a costly "stop-go" pattern, and, indeed, the degree of fluctuation in funding is a major criticism of the management of the RDT&E program.[8]

Traditional budget categories may also obscure substantial changes in the technological content of programs. The most obvious current example is the importance of sophisticated electronics and microcomputers in many systems under development; the DOD now spends over a third of its procurement dollars for electronics of one kind or another, but this important insight into the nature of the RDT&E program is nowhere evident in the budget.

Another way to analyze program content is to group the individual projects by mission. Table 10-3 shows this breakout for FY 1972-79, the years for which these data are available. The strategic mission has provided the most challenging technical task for military R&D. Reconnaissance satellites, the achievement of high accuracy for missiles after thousands of miles of transit, and the manufacture of large nuclear submarines have consistently pushed the state of the art in a number of technologies. But, although strategic systems have provided the "big-ticket" items in the

Table 10-2
Percentage Allocation of RDT&E Funds, FY 1965-1977, by Program

Program	1965	1966	1967	1968	1969	1970	1971	1972	1973	1974	1975	1976	1977
Military sciences	9.7	9.2	8.0	7.2	7.8	7.2	7.1	6.8	5.8	5.4	4.7	4.7	4.8
Aircraft and related equipment	17.1	16.7	17.2	16.2	14.3	20.9	24.1	26.0	23.5	20.7	19.2	20.5	21.0
Missiles and related equipment	30.6	29.9	32.6	33.6	32.9	31.3	28.6	23.8	26.8	25.9	25.2	24.1	23.2
Military astronautics and related equipment	14.0	14.8	15.0	14.4	14.4	8.8	6.3	5.1	5.3	7.3	6.1	6.2	5.5
Ships and small craft	4.0	4.5	4.1	3.5	4.5	4.5	4.0	6.5	7.9	8.1	7.4	6.4	6.8
Ordinance, combat vehicles and related equipment	5.4	6.1	4.7	4.3	4.8	4.5	4.2	4.8	4.8	5.2	5.5	5.9	7.0
Other equipment	12.1	12.8	13.0	15.1	15.4	15.9	19.0	19.2	19.1	20.1	21.5	22.2	21.9
Management and support	7.0	6.1	5.5	5.6	5.7	6.8	6.6	7.5	6.8	7.3	10.3	10.1	9.8

Source: Joy Jepson, "Financial Obligations by DOD for Military Research and Development," Center for Naval Analyses, 1971; for 1969-1977, see National Science Foundation, "An Analysis of Federal R&D Funding, FY 1969-1977," (Washington, D.C.), mimeo.

Table 10-3
Percentage Allocation of RDT&E Budget by Mission, FY 1972-1979

Mission	1972	1973	1974	1975	1976	1977	1978 (Estimates)	1979 (Estimates)
Technology base	18.4	17.2	16.9	16.0	16.1	16.0	15.9	16.1
Advanced technology development	3.0	2.0	2.5	3.5	6.0	5.1	4.3	4.8
Strategic programs	19.9	23.7	23.5	25.0	24.1	22.2	22.2	17.9
Tactical programs	38.0	36.7	35.1	34.1	31.4	36.6	38.8	41.0
Intelligence and communications	6.2	6.6	8.3	7.5	9.6	7.9	7.4	8.9
Programwide management and support	14.5	13.8	13.7	13.9	12.6	12.3	11.3	11.3

Source: National Science Foundation, "An Analysis of Federal R&D Funding by Function: Fiscal Years 1969-78 (Washington, D.C.)."

budget, the total number of strategic systems is relatively small, and spending on the strategic mission is currently only about 18 percent of the RDT&E budget. This figure will no doubt shift up again if a major modernization of our strategic arsenal is undertaken. The largest part of the budget (40 percent) is spent in the tactical category; the growth in this mission area has mirrored the increased emphasis on NATO defense in the overall DOD program. The category contains a multitude of programs whose smaller average size reflects the less demanding technological problems and the lower priority of any single project. The technology base program, which supports basic and applied research across the whole spectrum of military-related technology, is also characterized by numerous small projects.

More than one pattern can be discerned in the RDT&E program. The common public image of military R&D is of a high-risk enterprise, exhibiting dramatic breakthroughs and rapid advances in capability. This description reflects the high level of technical performance demanded by military systems compared to their civilian counterparts, plus the very large scale of our investment in military R&D. Although the total impact is indeed impressive, the actual increase in capability from individual projects within this large R&D effort is most often the result of an incremental approach to improving existing weapons associated with traditional missions.[9] There are dramatic exceptions to this rule, mostly associated with the strategic mission, but they remain exceptions when compared to the bulk of the effort funded by the RDT&E budget.

Initiation and Management of R&D Programs

The military services are responsible for initiating and managing the thousands of R&D projects that make up the total R&D program. This single fact goes far in explaining the outputs of the RDT&E program, the organizational structure for conducting the program, and the network of contacts that has developed between R&D performers (mainly industry) and R&D users. Formal DOD procedures call for approval of a statement of military requirement before a project enters exploratory development. The military requirement stating the capability desired, as tempered by the knowledge of what is technologically feasible, links the military user to the developer in the R&D community. Sometimes the requirement may originate in the demonstration of a new technological capability, but formally it will come from the operational command.

The military requirements reflect the missions assigned to each service, and, in many cases, the standard method for performing that mission, for example, carrier-based airplanes with specific capabilities. Thus, new weapons originating in the services tend to perpetuate existing missions and genealogies of hardware. For example, the cancellation of the B-1 was followed immediately by the formation of an Air Force task force to draw up requirements for a future manned penetrating bomber.

This stability of weapon type, even while technical sophistication is increasing, can be viewed as a result of the stability of basic doctrine—for example, the Air Force flies—or, more fundamentally, as an expression of bureaucratic essence and resistance to change. In any case only a small fraction of each year's RDT&E budget is devoted to new departures. The resistance of the services to the introduction of new missions or different technical approaches for established missions is well illustrated by the case of the Navy's initial reluctance to develop the fleet ballistic missile; more recent examples are the low priority assigned to remotely piloted vehicles by the Air Force and the argument over large versus small aircraft carriers for the Navy.[10]

New programs must compete with other developments for funding within the service's RDT&E budget allotment. The formal budget cycle has been well described elsewhere.[11] To maintain a place in the budget throughout its lengthy development cycle a program needs to enjoy technical success; it needs even more the backing of a strong advocacy group well placed in the Pentagon hierarchy.[12] The bias again is to follow-on developments for well-established missions, since these systems will already enjoy broad support within the service and the Office of the Secretary of Defense.[13] To take advantage of this base of support new technology tends to cluster around major systems developments; for example, radar developments are funded as part of aircraft programs. This tendency in turn is responsible in part for the "gold-plating" phenomenon—the tendency for a weapons system to become more and more technically sophisticated as it moves through the development cycle.

Placing the R&D function within the military services helps to maximize contact between users and developers. It leads, however, to persistent problems with funding and sponsorship for programs that do not fall in a traditional mission area or that cut across service boundaries. The Office of the Secretary of Defense (OSD) is able to some extent to overcome this tendency to parochialism through its participation in the annual budget cycle, its authority to designate joint programs, and its sponsorship of certain high-risk programs by the Advanced Research Projects Agency (ARPA). Overall, however, OSD's role is largely one of review and coordination of service-initiated and -managed programs. For each major program the Defense System Acquisition Review Council (DSARC) meets to make formal recommendations to the Secretary of Defense at decision milestones. The DSARC is chaired by the Undersecretary for Defense Research Engineering and Acquisition, whose office oversees the technology base as well as major systems development and acquisition. The staff of this office becomes involved in substantial detail in the individual programs of the services during program and budget review. Other important elements in OSD's centralized direction of the RDT&E program are the Office of the Assistant Secretary for Program Analysis and Evaluation (the successors to McNamara's whiz kids) and the Comptroller's Office.

The overall influence of the OSD staff on R&D programs is not easily defined. The services clearly dominate the implementation of policy through their budgeting procedures and program decisions, even though ultimate responsibility to approve or disapprove rests with the Secretary of Defense. The OSD staff has considerable informal power, however, and uses it, particularly during the informal consultations and bargaining that precede formal program review by the DSARC. OSD's influence is more likely to take the form of nay-saying, if only because the budgeting process almost inevitably involves cutting program size. New programs rarely originate in OSD; not surprisingly, suggestions from above to initiate or accelerate specific programs are likely to be resisted within the services unless accompanied by budget dollars.

Direction and Control of Military R&D

The arguments for seeking better control over military R&D were touched on in the introduction. Our RDT&E effort is large, absorbing a sizeable fraction of the resources available for investment in military hardware each year. The output from the program has been criticized by some as being too little, too late, and too expensive; conversely, the arms control community has tended to view the rate of advance in military technology as too rapid. These disparate views correspond to different beliefs about the nature of national security and the proper role for military technology in enhancing it. For the first group, a more capable or cost-effective weapon is, by definition, to be desired, while the second group would add consideration of the effect of the weapon on international stability to the list of criteria.

Thus, success in directing and controlling military R&D must be evaluated in relation to a definite perspective or level of analysis. If the chief problem for the R&D program is to maintain technological superiority, then the task of direction and control of the program becomes one of optimal allocation of resources: How large should the RDT&E budget be? Within this budget which programs should be emphasized? How rapidly should development of a weapons system proceed, given the trade-offs between technological risk and the cost of delay? It is safe to say that this is the light in which the military R&D program is viewed by the majority of the defense establishment, not least those concerned directly with the management of the RDT&E program.

There has been considerable debate over the proper degree of central control of the RDT&E program, with a general presumption that decentralized management is most appropriate for R&D activities.[14] The trade-off is between the greater flexibility and responsiveness to user needs associated with decentralization and the desire to impose systemwide priorities and to avoid duplication of programs between the services. The current DOD system leaves program initiation and management to the services, while the extensive formal procedures within DOD, such as the DSARC, offer a mechanism for centralized direction of the overall program. Much of the apparatus for review at decision milestones and in the budget cycle is explicitly designed to insure that projects address a valid military requirement and that the proposed solutions are cost effective. These procedures for enforcing rationality—defined in terms of military utility, however—carry their own penalties. The managerial tendency is to subdivide the large and complex task of evaluating R&D programs to reap the benefits of specialized expertise, but the resulting organizational structure provides access points for pressure from various interest groups, ranging from the defense contractors through the program's proponents within the military services and in Congress. The large number of participants and the diversity of interests represented suggest that bureaucratic politics will dominate the decision process, particularly the sensitive process of setting budget priorities.

The formal decision process in itself affects program output. The lengthy review process allows time for a program to be attacked repeatedly in the budget cycle, for expensive design changes to be introduced, for costs to escalate, and for the character of the threat to alter. Congress may add to the delay by its actions, which, increasingly in recent years, concern the details of individual programs. The end result may be a weapon that made sense when initiated but has become vulnerable to criticism as too costly, technically obsolescent, and possibly irrelevant to the threat by the time it is ready for production.[15] Our tolerance for such outcomes depends on our perception of how urgently the weapon's capability is needed. In peacetime there is a temptation to postpone production and deployment of a newly developed weapon to take advantage of a greater technical advance in a more distant future. The review procedures for the RDT&E program are not the source of this tendency to defer production, but they allow ample opportunities for it to be expressed.

If immediate needs are pressing, or if the need is for greater numbers of weapons rather than for advanced technology, then the current procedures, which are conducive to delays and technological embellishment, may diminish the military effectiveness of the R&D product. It should not be forgotten, however, that these procedures were introduced in the first place to deal with serious problems in the RDT&E program, problems that had arisen in the absence of regular broad-ranging review of major programs. The problems associated with the review procedures must be weighed against the benefits they confer: on balance, the DSARC and related procedures seem to have improved the management of weapons development.

Procedures for rational decision-making within the context of a large and complex agency like the DOD have proved to involve intrinsic costs of delay and opportunities for intervention by special-interest groups; similarly the policy of seeking superiority across the whole spectrum of military-related technology has resulted in an inherent conflict between the resources devoted to maintaining the constantly expanding technology base and the fiscal constraints on ultimate production of the new weapons. Having calculated a large technology base, the DOD faces the problem of selecting which of its products to push forward into full-scale development and production. But the very size of the R&D establishment—the military labs, the hundreds of defense contractors, the service personnel involved in program management, and the ultimate users of the R&D products—produces multiple pressures to carry forward in development more programs than can eventually be bought.

Bureaucratic pressures to maintain programs, joined with the very large number of programs supported in the technology base, create a situation in which selective control is difficult. The budget is the ultimate discipline, but even budget constraints have an elastic quality because of the opportunities to preserve programs by stretching them out over a longer period with reduced annual funding. Failure to impose more sharply department-wide priorities on the services' R&D programs ends in creating additional delays for those programs that are crowding the budget in the costly stage of full-scale development.

There is an element of logic to the apparent inefficiency of stretching out programs, since military requirements, once stated, do not go away simply because the current technology does not prove capable or affordable. The phoenixlike quality of many development programs—for example, the neutron bomb, or the manned penetrating bomber—can be the result of persistent military interest in these weapons as well as the push from the technological community. But, given that the task of the RDT&E

program is the development of cost-effective weapons leading to timely production and deployment, increased unit costs and delay from program stretchouts imposed for budgetary reasons are a signal that the total program is out of balance and resources are being misallocated.

The RDT&E Program and Arms Control

From a broader arms control perspective, the problem of directing and controlling the military R&D process is not one of maximizing military effectiveness while minimizing development time or costs. Rather it is the problem posed by the inability of institutions to adjust to the flow of new weapons that the R&D program has produced. This can be glimpsed in the difficulty that the military have sometimes had in absorbing a new technical capability—for example, the experience of the Army in adapting computers for battlefield use.[16] It extends to the apparent failure of top-ranking DOD officials to consider the long-term consequences of introducing a new weapon, including its adoption by other countries—what has been called the "fallacy of the last move."[17] The classic example is our development of multiple independently targeted reentry vehicles (MIRV), a technology that, deployed also by the Russians, now threatens our land-based missile force. The consequences of possible proliferation of cruise missile technology to third countries provides a more current case: cruise missiles may in the future provide a more accessible and less expensive technology for nuclear weapons delivery for small nuclear and near-nuclear states.

Congress has also been slow to undertake effective oversight of the RDT&E program and even slower to integrate that oversight into a general view of national security. In this respect the requirement for arms control impact statements for major weapons developments is an innovation of considerable promise. After a disappointing start, the quality of the impact statements appears to be improving. Whether Congress and other agencies in the government will give much weight to the issues raised in the improved impact statements is, of course, yet to be determined.[18]

Most seriously, perhaps, the slow and painstaking negotiation of strategic arms limitation treaties with the Soviet Union has lagged behind the introduction of new military technology. While SALT I negotiations were going on, the technology for MIRV went from development to deployment by the United States; the protocol on offensive weapons negotiated at SALT I was, in a sense, obsolescent before it was signed. Similarly, cruise missiles have emerged as a major U.S. strategic program during the SALT II negotiations, posing difficulties for those negotiations and raising the question of whether the negotiating process can ever deal effectively with the problems posed by rapidly evolving weapons.[19]

In general, any specific arms control agreement between two contending nations will shift the locus of competition to a different, noncontrolled arena. Thus, quantitative limits in SALT I spurred investment in new technologies that were not limited by the treaty. Limits on strategic arms tend to redirect the military competition to general purpose forces. Recognizing this effect, and in the absence of any proposal for lessening the underlying hostility of the two opposing states, it could be argued that competition in the sphere of technology favors the United States and that we should not attempt to shift the arena of conflict. But against this argument lies the realization that advances in military technology may be so uniquely powerful and unpredictable, that, even if we succeed in preserving technological superiority, we may create a world still more dangerous for ourselves than the one we now inhabit.

For many reasons arms control negotiations aimed at military R&D, rather than deployed weapons, seem almost certain to fail; even the frequent suggestion of indirect control via a ban on weapons tests has serious drawbacks as an arms control technique.[20] Therefore, it seems only prudent to evaluate constantly our military R&D program in the context of our own national security, looking for ways to enhance our security through our own decisions, without relying on any mutual restraint on the part of the Soviet Union, however welcome that would be.

We have invested in new military technology on the basis of military requirements and as an end in itself; the actual effect on our national security has been problematic. At best it is a mixed record. On the strategic side, new developments in missile accuracy and antisubmarine warfare have been pursued with little regard for their potential destabilizing effects. Technology used in reconnaissance satellites, which were decisive in removing the verification problems blocking formal arms control agreements, also contributes to accurate targeting of missile sites and potential first-strike capability. The SALT agreements have not regulated new military technologies; instead, the quantitative limits have been an incentive to qualitative changes. Nor is the effect of new technology for conventional weapons on international stability well understood, partly because the very large number of systems and the multiplicity of ways in which they can be deployed make any analysis of deterrence very complicated. Nevertheless, we continue the development of these new weapons across the board.

These problems argue for a slowing of the pace of technical change to allow perceptions and analysis to catch up with evolving capabilities. More selectivity in the RDT&E program, to redress the problems of program balance discussed in the last section, would be even more desirable if coupled to a sensitivity to the arms control implications of proposed developments. An obvious brake for technological change is reductions in the RDT&E budget; denial of funds to a program is perhaps the surest way of eliminating it. A further advantage of budget constraints is that they tend to restrain the demand for new technology as well as the supply, as military requirements are scrubbed to match the fiscal realities. The disadvantage, of course, is the tendency already noted for budget constraints to lead to programs being funded at lower levels over more years, rather than cancelled. And while a tighter budget might produce a more cost-effective RDT&E program, it would not necessarily produce a program with fewer weapons developments with destabilizing characteristics. Nevertheless, when money is scarce, there is a wholesome reluctance in the services to propose programs that might be vulnerable to elimination later in the budget process. Therefore, one could expect that more attention in the executive branch and on the part of Congress to the potential dangers of the volume and pace of new military technology would create natural incentives in the services to reduce allocation of their resources to weapons that appear provocative.

With hard decisions on the budget there must also come the discipline to carry the selective policy back into the development cycle to reduce the number of systems entering advanced development. The connection between a policy of maintaining broad technological superiority and the difficulty of managing the bureaucratic interest groups that that policy nurtures should be explicitly recognized.

There are doubtless some weapons with obviously destabilizing characteristics that will nevertheless appear desirable or even necessary for national security reasons. The case for restraint must be based on evaluation of the situation in a long-run perspective—and, of course, most weapons take many years to develop and deploy in militarily significant numbers—and on the realization that there are usually several alternative combinations of forces, weapons, and tactics that can yield equivalent results. The neutron bomb, for example, is one way to destroy tanks but there are many others. Even so, there may be times when development of a new, but potentially destabilizing, technology may still be preferable to foregoing that capability; the argument here is that the decision process should fully weigh the long-run consequences and the feasibility of different solutions.

Clearly, however, such a policy rests on a perception that is far from universal: namely, that the risks of doing less military R&D are more manageable than the potential instabilities promised by a continuance of the present pace of technological change in weapons. Dampening the rate of technological change in the interest of arms control would require not only the political muscle to deny funds to important interest groups, but also a willingness to accept a degree of risk by foregoing some technological opportunities. It is probable, however, that a selective strategy for military R&D could reduce the size and cost of the RDT&E program, freeing funds for other uses such as increased procurement or training, without a net negative impact on the military balance. Under a properly broad perspective of national security, the choice of weapons developments would include a careful look at their probable impact on international stability as well as their military usefulness in a narrower sense. It is not really sensible to expect the Department of Defense to perform this kind of scrutiny with sufficient objectivity, even under the discipline of a reduced RDT&E budget. Therefore, some further outside influence on the process is needed. An expanded role for the National Security Council in weapons decisions is one possibility. At the minimum there should be an increase in the influence of the Arms Control and Disarmament Agency on the arms control impact statements and in the use of the impact statements and other such analyses by Congress to question the rationale for new weapons.

Notes

1. See the articles by Deborah Shapley on "Technological Creep and the Arms Race" in *Science* 201 (22 September 1978):1102-1105; 201 (29 September 1978):1192-1196; 202 (20 October 1978):289-292.

2. U.S. Congress, Senate, Committee on Appropriations, *Department of Defense Appropriations for Fiscal Year 1971, Hearings Before the Subcommittee of the Senate Committee on Appropriations*, 91st Congress, 2d Session, 1970, p. 46.

3. See David Holloway, "Military Technology" in Ronald Amman et al., eds., *The Technological Level of Soviet Industry* (New Haven, Conn.: Yale University Press, 1977), pp. 412-414.

4. For example, Elmo Zumwalt, Jr., *On Watch* (New York: Quadrangle/The New York Times Book Co., 1976), chap. 4.

5. For example, the future procurement costs implied by the Army's current programs in full-scale development would require a 64 percent increase in its funds for procurement by fiscal year 1984. See "New Systems Post Huge 'Bow Wave' for Army Budget," *Armed Forces Journal International* 115, no. 10 (June 1978):10-12.

6. DOD (Comptroller), "National Defense Budget Estimates for FY 1979" (mimeo, n.d.), p. 8. In constant 1972 dollars, DOD outlays were $67.1 billion in FY 1965 and $68.8 billion in FY 1979.

7. Cf. Peter B. Natchez and Irwin C. Bupp, "Policy and Priority in the Budgetary Process," *American Political Science Review* 67 (September 1973):951-963.

8. See, for example, Defense Science Board, "Report of the Acquisition Task Force," March 1978, p. 84.

9. See Alexander H. Flax, "R&D Balance," *Foreign Affairs* 57 (Fall 1978):211-213. For a contrasting view of the U.S. style of military R&D see Bruno Augenstein, "Military RDT&E: Raison d'Etre and Policy

Background," in William Schneider, Jr., and Francis P. Hoeber, eds., *Arms, Men and Military Budgets: Issues for FY77* (New York: Crane, Russak & Co., 1976), pp. 215-253.

10. See Vincent Davis, *The Politics of Innovation Patterns in Navy Cases*, The Social Science Foundation and Graduate School of International Studies Monograph Series, vol. 4, no. 3. (Denver: The University of Denver, 1966-1967), p. 24; Samuel L. Hall, "Weapons Choices and Advanced Technology: The RPV," Peace Studies Program Occasional Paper no. 10 (Ithaca, New York: Cornell University, September 1978), pp. 34-45; and R. James Woolsey, "Planning a Navy: The Risks of Conventional Wisdom," *International Security* 3 (Summer 1978):17-29.

11. Lawrence J. Korb, "The Budget Process in the Department of Defense: 1947-1977: The Strengths and Weaknesses of Three Systems," *Public Administration Review* 37 (July/August 1977):334-346.

12. Davis, *Innovation Patterns*.

13. Recent changes in response to the requirements of Circular A-109 of the Office of Management and Budget are designed to broaden the range of alternatives considered. DOD has introduced a "Milestone O" for major programs at which the Secretary of Defense must approve the service's statement of mission need. Alternative technological approaches, including upgrading existing weapons, are explored between Milestone O and Milestone I. (Major programs are defined as those involving anticipated costs of more than $75 million in RDT&E or $300 million in production.)

14. See, for example, *U.S. Military R&D Management*, The Center for Strategic and International Studies, Special Report Series no. 14, (Washington, D.C.: Georgetown University, 1973), pp. 15-24; 68-69.

15. For a vigorous elaboration of these ideas, see Defense Science Board, "Acquisition Task Force."

26. Kenneth H. Bacon, "Army Believes Its Battlefield Computer Is Perfected after Delays, Cost Overruns," *The Wall Street Journal*, 3 October 1977, p. 16.

17. Herbert F. York, "Military Technology and the National Security," *Scientific American*, August 1969, reprinted in *Arms Control: Readings from Scientific American*, Herbert F. York, comp. (San Francisco: W.H. Freeman and Co., 1973), p. 197.

18. See chapter 9 of this book.

19. Christoph Bertram has suggested arms control agreements focused on missions rather than weapons; such an agreement could absorb new technology without requiring renegotiation, providing the proscribed mission was not affected. See his "The Future of Arms Control: Part II, Arms Control and Technological Change: Elements of a New Approach," Adelphi Papers no. 146 (London: International Institute for Strategic Studies, 1978). The disadvantage of this approach is that most weapons are

multimission. Given the relatively short time needed for redeployment (as compared to development and production) the warning time for rupture of the agreement would be short, lessening the stability of the arms control regime.

20. Ibid., pp. 11-13.

11 The Process and Problems of Linking Policy and Force Structure through the Defense Budget Process

Lawrence J. Korb

Introduction

The outcome of the defense budget process should be a force posture or structure that supports or carries out the national security policy of the nation. The first part of this essay will discuss how the Department of Defense (DOD) attempts, within the annual budgetary process, to marry its force structure to policy, and the second part will focus on the impediments to linking perfectly those two elements.

The Process

The current budgetary process within DOD is outlined in figure 11-1. As indicated, the Pentagon presently uses two separate but complementary and interrelated control systems to formulate its annual budget: planning, programming and budgeting (PPBS) and zero-based budgeting (ZBB).[1] PPBS was first brought to the Pentagon in 1961, and ZBB was grafted onto PPBS in 1977. The purpose of these two systems is to ensure that, within the funding level allocated to DOD, the decision-makers will choose that set of programs that supports best the prescribed policy.

The planning phase of the budget process commences in the fall of each year, that is, about 15 months before the budget must be presented to Congress, and lasts until the following spring. During this phase the Secretary of Defense reviews inputs from the uniformed heads of the military services, the Joint Chiefs of Staff (JCS),[2] on the nature of the military threat facing the nation and on our commitments, and from the National Security Council System (NSC) on our present policy. The JCS input comes in the form of an analysis known as the Joint Strategic Planning Document (JSPD), and the NSC inputs are called presidential decisions (PD). The current national security policy of this nation was promulgated in August 1977 in PD-18.

The Secretary integrates these documents with a budgetary target received from the Office of Management and Budget (OMB) into a comprehensive

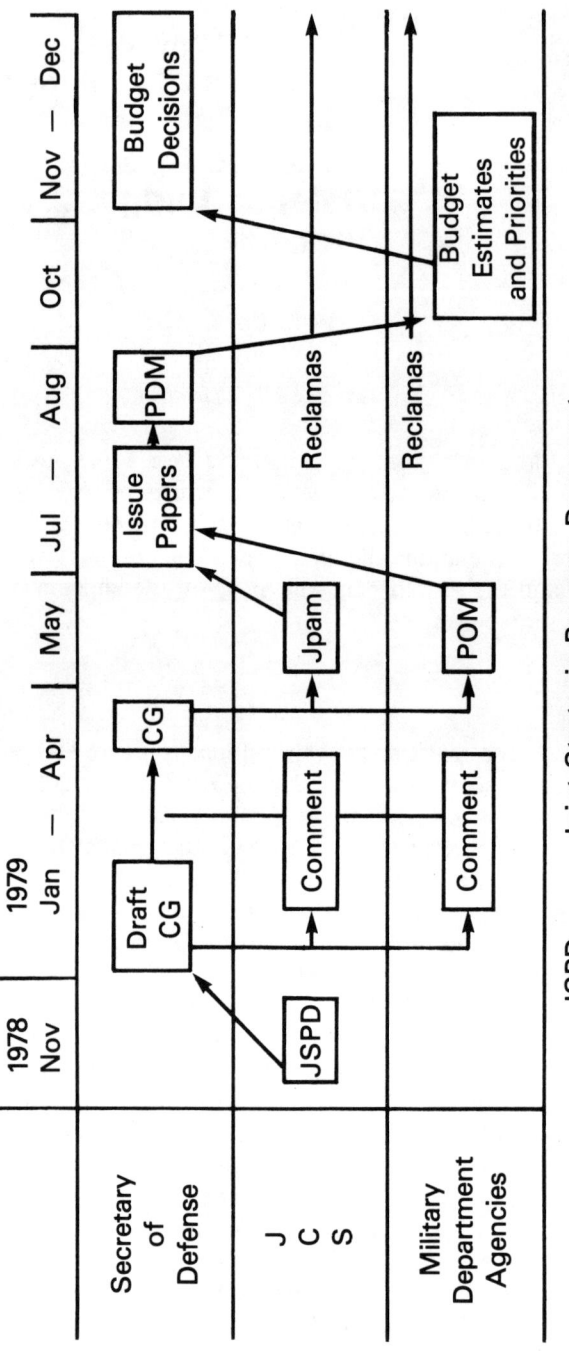

Figure 11-1. FY 1981 DOD Management System.

Defense Budget Process

planning document known as the consolidated guidance (CG). The CG provides subunits within DOD with the rationale underlying our defense policy and offers them specific guidance on how best to structure their programs to carry out that policy. For example, the CG tells the Army how many sets of unit equipment it must preposition in Europe and provides a timetable for meeting the objective. In the early spring, the planning process is completed when the president, the Secretary of Defense, and the JCS meet to ensure that the force structure laid down by the CG is responding to the established policy and provides reasonable assurance of meeting the threat.

The programming phase lasts through the summer and into the fall. During this phase the three military departments and the ten defense agencies submit their program objective memoranda (POM).[3] In the POMs, these organizations request the men and material that they feel are necessary to support the CG. The POMs are reviewed for consistency and cost effectiveness by both the military and civilian hierarchy within DOD. The JCS analyze the service and agency POMs in the Joint Strategic Assessment Memoranda (JSAM). This analysis provides their corporate military judgment on whether the sum of the programs in the individual POMs will add up to a balanced and effective military force. The staff of the Secretary of Defense, which is known as the Office of the Secretary of Defense (OSD), reviews the POMs to see if they conform to the letter and spirit of the CG. On the basis of this review, OSD prepares a set of issue papers, which point out areas where deviations from the CG have occurred. These papers also provide some options for the Secretary on more cost-effective ways to marry the program to the policy. The Secretary concludes the programming cycle in late summer by deciding these issues.

The budgetary cycle commences on October 1st of each year, when the military departments and the defense agencies submit their requests for funds to implement the approved programs at three funding levels: basic, minimum, and enhanced, along with an explicit description of the benefits gained and lost at each level. The basic level is the one contained in the CG, and the enhanced level is about 5 percent above and the minimum level 5 percent below. For the next 3 months these budgets are scrutinized by members of the Comptroller's office in DOD and by personnel from OMB. In their analysis, these individuals not only analyze the cost data, but through the use of ZBB, develop a priority listing of programs at different budgetary levels; that is, they rank order the programs in accordance with their contribution to achieving defense objectives. When the president makes his final decision on the defense total, all those programs ranked below that level are eliminated from the budget, which is forwarded to Congress.

The Problems

In theory the PPBS and ZBB processes just discussed should provide for a force structure closely related to the national security policy of the nation. However, in practice, the fit between policy and force structure is quite loose. This lack of symmetry between the budget and policy is caused by eight interrelated economic and political factors. The second part of this chapter will focus on these factors.

First, in spite of our great wealth, this nation simply does not have the resources to support fully our present military policy. Our current policy, as enunciated in PD-18, is based on the assumption that our armed forces should be equipped to fight a major conventional war with the Soviet Bloc in Europe while handling a minor contingency elsewhere in the world, for example, the Persian Gulf. To support this "one-and-a-half-war" policy, the JCS estimate that our general purpose or conventional forces need a minimum of 750 ships, 30 Army and Marine Corps ground divisions, and 35 Air Force tactical air wings.[4] The annual cost of such a force structure would be about $250 billion. The FY 1980 budget level of approximately $125 billion can support a force of "only" 475 ships, 19 ground divisions, and 26 tactical air wings. Some analysts argue that with its present force level this nation would have a difficult time just handling a major conventional war in Europe with the Warsaw Pact nations, let alone a simultaneous contingency somewhere else in the world.[5]

The gap between policy and budget caused by resource constraints has existed all through the post-World War II period. Its existence was vividly illustrated by the events that took place during the decade of the 1960s. At that time the force structure supported by our defense budget supposedly was capable of handling simultaneously a major war with the Soviets in Europe and with the Chinese in Asia and another contingency elsewhere (two-and-half-war doctrine). Yet to handle just the "half" war or minor contingency in Southeast Asia, DOD had to decrease its force structure in Europe. Moreover, in 1968, when the North Koreans seized the Pueblo, our lack of a military response was attributable primarily to the inability of the armed forces to fight a war in Korea while deeply enmeshed in Vietnam.[6]

Similarly in October 1973, the only way in which DOD could resupply the beleaguered Israelis was to deplete its own equipment in Europe. Moreover, because of resource constraints, these stocks were not fully restored to their pre-October, 1973 levels until 1978.

Second, the responsible political leaders are rarely able to provide concrete guidance to our military leaders on how this country will respond to specific situations. This situation occurs for two reasons. First, our elected officials usually do not know in their own minds how they will react to certain contingencies. People succeed in political life by keeping their options open. Politicians usually do not like to tie themselves down to specific courses of action in advance. Second, it is very difficult to provide such guidance in the abstract. There is so much uncertainty and room for misperception in international politics that any guidance that might be offered can easily prove to be erroneous. However, when the military planner in the Pentagon is developing his force structure, he should have the answers to such questions as: Will the United States become militarily involved if the Peoples Republic of China takes offensive action against the Republic of China on Taiwan? How much territory in Western Europe will the NATO forces have to yield before the United States will resort to the use of tactical nuclear weapons? Will this nation intervene militarily in the Middle East if there is another Arab oil embargo? The answers to questions such as these can have a significant impact on the forces that are bought. Usually the defense planner must be content with only the vaguest of guidance and is forced to guess about our intentions and those of our adversaries. Often he guesses wrong, and then the armed forces are not adequately equipped to carry out the actual policy.

The ambiguity of the guidance currently being offered to military planners by political leaders can be illustrated by analyzing some sections of PD-18.[7] According to this document, DOD will not allow the present military balance with the Soviet Union to deteriorate. However, PD-18 does not provide defense officials with any way to measure or operationalize the balance. Similarly, one part of PD-18 instructs the military planner to shape his conventional forces primarily to wage a short intensive war on the central front in Europe. However, elsewhere the document proclaims that this nation will fulfill all its military commitments in the Pacific and will continue to protect the flanks of NATO. Since the war-fighting environment of the Pacific and the NATO flanks is so radically different from that of the central front in Europe, and since he does not have sufficient forces to accomplish all these missions, the defense planner is thus left to his own devices on how to structure his forces.

Third, the length of time involved in the production of the defense budget can make outmoded or irrelevant any policy guidance which may have been given. The budget process within the executive branch takes 20 months from beginning to end. It then takes the Congress another 9 months to authorize and appropriate funds for DOD. Consider, for example, that President Carter took office 3 months into FY 1977. Work on the FY 1977 defense budget, which was supposed to support his military policy, began in May 1974, when Richard Nixon was still president. The executive phase of that process was concluded in December 1975 by Gerald Ford who, at that time, was uncertain that his own party would given him its presidential nomination. Congress completed action on the FY 1977 budget in late September 1976, as Gerald Ford appeared to be overtaking Jimmy Carter in the race for the presidency.

Fourth, because of its enormous size, the defense budget can have a dramatic impact on the economic health of the nation. Expenditures for defense in FY 1980 represent about 25 percent of the entire federal budget and approximately 5 percent of our gross national product (GNP). Of the fifteen functions for which the federal government spends money, the national defense function absorbs the second largest amount of funds. Only the income security function, which provides direct financial assistance to individuals, consumes more money. Similarly, of the twelve major agencies in the federal government, DOD is the second most expensive. Only the Department of Health, Education and Welfare (HEW) has a larger budget than DOD.

At the present time, about 80 percent of the people employed by the federal government work for DOD. In addition, it is estimated that approximately 1.2 million jobs in the private sector are dependent directly on defense spending.[8] Since 1976, when the size of the defense budget began to rise by about 4 percent per year in real terms, about 240,000 military-related jobs have been created. For many areas of the nation, employment generated by defense spending is crucial. Cities like Los Angeles, Seattle, Wichita, Kansas, and Lynn, Massachusetts, and states like Texas and Connecticut are almost totally dependent on defense contracts for their economic well-being. Moreover, changes in the size of the defense budget can severely distort the economy of the nation as a whole. According to Michael Evans of Chase Econometrics Associates, real GNP would fall by twice the amount of a Defense Department budget cut if there were no compensating tax cut or government expenditures.[9] Similarly, increases in defense spending tend to exacerbate the inflation rate because military spending puts money into the hands of workers without expanding the supply of goods that they can buy. Thus, political leaders can be loathe to make drastic changes in the size or shape of the defense budget, even if these changes are deemed necessary to support policy.

In addition to its size, the defense budget is more controllable than any of the other departmental budgets, that is, DOD's funding level can be changed without changing substantive law. This is in stark contrast to the situation that prevails in most areas of the federal bureaucracy. The budgets of agencies like HEW or the Veterans Administration (VA) are basically uncontrollable. If people meet the criteria established for programs like social security, medicare, or the G.I. bill, by current law, the government has no choice but to pay them. This is not the case with defense. For example, in the FY 1979 defense budget, which totaled $115 billion, almost $74 billion was controllable. The defense budget thus represented 57 percent of all the controllable or discretionary funds within the entire federal budget.

Therefore, if a chief executive needs to vary the size of the total federal budget to achieve a particular economic or monetary goal, he usually alters the defense total somewhat. Generally this means reducing the size of the defense budget, but on occasion presidents have increased the defense total. Throughout the entire post-World War II period, every administration has used the defense budget to achieve domestic economic goals without making corresponding policy changes.

President Truman cut defense spending for FY 1951 below the level of the previous year despite the fact that in the interim the Communists had taken over China and the Soviets had exploded an atomic bomb.[10] The former president took this action because of the importance he placed on the need to achieve a balanced budget. In 1957, President Eisenhower refused to raise defense spending to speed up our missile program in spite of the fact that the Sputnik launch had shown the Soviets to be far ahead of the United States in intercontinental missile capability. The former general argued that allocating more than 10 percent of the GNP to defense would ruin this nation's economy.[11]

In his first 6 months in office President Kennedy increased defense spending by 12 percent, because in his opinion that was the quickest and most politically acceptable way of pumping money into the economy. According to his press secretary, Kenneth O'Donnell, his own inclination was to spend more in the social areas.[12] In 1971, President Nixon added $6 billion to the expected level of the defense budget to stimulate the economy during the 1972 election year.[13] Four years later President Ford cut $7 billion from DOD to keep his election year budget below $400 billion.[14] Finally, in 1978, President Carter was forced to reduce defense spending for FY 1980 by some $3 billion below projected levels to keep the federal deficit for FY 1980 from going above $30 billion.[15] In taking these steps none of these six chief executives modified his military policy to conform to the altered size of the defense budget.

Fifth, there exists no purely scientific way of allocating the limited resources to support a particular policy. Theoretically, PPBS, which views outputs, costs, and goals together, and the techniques of ZBB and systems analysis provide the framework and tools for making such decisions in the defense budget process. While PPBS, ZBB, and systems analysis can help in making budgetary decisions, they are only a partial aid. Many of the crucial variables that affect such decisions are not quantifiable. For example, how does one decide what percentage of the Soviet population and industrial base this nation must have the capability to destroy to support our policy of deterring the Soviet Union from launching a nuclear strike against the United States or our allies? Moreover, even when one is dealing with variables, which can be reduced to numbers, there may be no mathematical function that can express the desired relationship. For example, how does the decision-maker compare the damage potential and cost of a ship with that of a plane or a tank? Thus, many of the decisions in the defense budget must be the product of judgment and intuition. Such kinds of budgetary decisions do not necessarily provide the best support to the established policy.

Sixth, even if all the right decision-making tools were available, the scope of the defense budget is simply too vast for any one central authority to administer in a coherent manner. Presently, the defense budget has approximately 1,700 program elements, over 5,000 line items, and 137 different accounting systems. Each of the services and the ten defense agenies prepares its own separate budgetary input. Moreover, none of those units shares a common view of strategy and force structure. For example, because of interservice rivalries, each of the military services tries to buy a force structure that will permit it to carry out its functions independently and that emphasizes its glamorous missions. Theoretically, it is the function of the Secretary of Defense and the JCS to ensure that all of the separate inputs are molded into a coherent, balanced, and responsive force structure. However, the Secretary has neither the time nor the staff to accomplish such a herculean task. All the defense secretary can hope to do is catch some of the more glaring inconsistencies. The JCS are similarly encumbered. Congressional resistance to the concept of a general staff limits the size of the joint staff to 400. This number is hardly sufficient to perform the task of integrating the budgets of individual services and agencies let alone carry out the planning and operational responsibilities of the JCS.[16] In addition, it is impossible to expect a service chief, acting in his corporate capacity, to analyze objectively the inputs of his own service, which he, acting in his own service capacity, had just formulated.

The case of the neutron bomb provides an excellent example of how an individual program, which is at variance with administration policy, can end up in the defense budget. In August 1976, the Energy Research and Development Administration (ERDA) requested a small amount of funds for FY 1978 to begin production of a neutron warhead for the Army's Lance missile. In late 1976, the outgoing Ford administration approved that request and included information on the new weapon in the large number of briefing books prepared for the incoming Carter administration. However, neither the new president nor any of his advisors noticed that there was a few million dollars for this weapon in the $120 billion FY 1978 defense budget, which they submitted to Congress in February 1977. The existence of this weapon in their budget was first brought to their attention in June 1977 by an article in the *Washington Post*. This discovery brought great embarrassment to a president who in his Inaugural Address had spoken of "ridding the earth of nuclear weapons."[17]

The Secretary of Defense's difficulties in formulating a coherent and consistent budget are also compounded by the fact that before his budget goes into effect, it must be reviewed and acted upon by no less than ten

Defense Budget Process

separate committees within the Congress. The Secretary attempts to control and coordinate the inputs of the various subunits of his department by using ten program categories, for example, strategic, general purpose, research and development. This device enables him to eliminate much of the unnecessary duplication and glaring gaps in the force structure proposals of the separate subgroups in DOD. However, Congress authorizes and appropriates funds to DOD's subunits by line item, for example, procurement Navy. Thus, when changing a particular line item, the Congress can and often does distort a carefully balanced program designed to support a particular policy. For example, in 1975 Congress nearly wrecked DOD's ship maintenance program by putting a ceiling on the number of civilian employees for the Navy Department.

Seventh, the output of the defense budget process is severely constrained by political realities. In the final analysis, the size and distribution of the defense budget are affected strongly by the positions and relative influence of the players involved in the process. For example, in the 1969-1975 period Congress responded to the anti-defense mood in the nation by slashing some $50 billion from the defense budget requests of presidents Nixon and Ford. This led to a real decline of 40 percent in the size of the defense budget and a diminution of U.S. capabilities at the same time that the size of Soviet expenditures and their military capabilities were increasing markedly. Approximately 300 unnecessary bases are now kept open because they happen to be in areas represented by influential members of Congress. Marginally useful weapon systems, like the F-18 aircraft, are built because of the influence of certain sectors of business and labor. Outmoded weapon systems programs, like the A-7 aircraft, are continued in production because they are built in the districts of powerful legislators. Duplication of effort in our tactical air programs exists because the separate services seek to preserve their own identities and have sufficient influence within the political system to maintain their separateness.

The impact of politics forces the Department of Defense not only to modify the size of the budget but also to allocate resources to areas that do not necessarily support our military policy. These resources are then unavailable for developing the required force structure. For example, about 5 percent of the defense budget is consumed by the unnecessary bases. These funds could be better utilized to cure the shortage of equipment for our forces in the European theater.

Political considerations also prevent DOD from implementing specific policies even when resources are available. For example, to protect our ICBM force from increasingly accurate and powerful Soviet missiles, DOD wishes to make some of its land-based missiles mobile either by placing them in trenches or by digging additional silos and rotating the missiles among them. However, elected officials from the likely sites in Iowa,

Nebraska, Colorado, and Kansas are already putting pressure on the Carter administration not to dig the trenches or the decoy silos in their states.[18] In the late 1960s and the early 1970s, DOD ran into a similar problem when it tried to find a suitable location for its low-frequency transmitting facility for communicating with its fleet ballistic missile submarines (FBM). Intense pressure from elected officials from proposed locations in Wisconsin, Michigan, and Texas made it impossible for DOD to build Project Seafarer in any of these locations. Lack of a reliable facility for communicating with our FBMs has prevented DOD from increasing its reliance on this most survivable retaliatory system.

Eighth, present policy options are often constrained by past budgetary decisions. A weapon system funded in a particular budget takes about 6 years before it becomes operational and then can last up to 30 years. Thus, the bulk of the force structure on which the policy-maker must now rely to support his policy was initially procured a decade ago. Some of the weapon systems, like the B-52 bomber, were developed as far back as World War II. Moreover, if a policy-maker wishes to alter the present force structure, it will take him at least a decade to change it substantially. Since no policy-maker ever comes into office without a force that is already in being, he often is in the paradoxical position of having force structure determine his policy rather than vice versa.

The impact of past decisions on current policy is vividly illustrated by the attempt of the Carter administration to alter our maritime policy. The president and his advisors wish the Navy to be configured primarily for sea control rather than power projection, that is, they want the Navy to provide protection for critical waterways, rather than exerting sea-based military force against objectives on the shore. However, because of decisions made in the 1950s and the 1960s, the Navy is configured primarily for power projection, that is, it now possesses twelve aircraft carriers. Moreover, these twelve carriers will last until the next century. Providing funds for merely maintaining and protecting these carriers and their aircraft will leave limited funds for buying very many forces for sea control.

Conclusion

Despite these problems, the policy and supporting force structure (which is developed through the defense budget process) normally are not completely out of phase. Many of the impediments discussed affect defense policy on the margin. For example, economic policy considerations may result in a change as high as 10 percent in the level of defense expenditures without a policy change. But, it is hard to envision a 50 percent change without a policy alteration. Nonetheless, the existence of these limiting factors should make the policy-maker and the scholar cautious about expecting to achieve or implement the desired military policy.

Defense Budget Process

Notes

1. The steps in the current budgetary process are outlined in an October 26, 1977 memorandum from the Secretary of Defense to the Service Secretaries and the chairman of the Joint Chiefs of Staff.

2. The JCS is composed of the chiefs of the four military services and a chairman who can be a member of any of the military services. The chiefs begin work on their input about 6 months before it is sent to the Secretary of Defense.

3. The Navy Department includes both the Navy and Marine Corps.

4. The best source on the National Security Policy of the Carter administration is a speech by Secretary of Defense Harold Brown to the Thirty-fourth Annual Dinner of the National Security Industrial Association, Washington, D.C., September 15, 1977.

5. See, for example, International Institute for Strategic Studies, *The Military Balance, 1978-1979* (London: 1978), pp. 108-119.

6. Lyndon Johnson, *The Vantage Point* (New York: Holt, Rinehart and Winston, 1971), p. 536.

7. PD-18 is a classified document. However, its contents are summarized in Brown's speech to the National Security Industrial Association; Harold Brown, *Annual Defense Department Report, FY 1979*, 2 February 1978, pp. 1-10; Bernard Weinraub, "Brown Seeks to Cut Involvement of the Navy in Nonnuclear War," *New York Times*, 26 January 1978, p. 1; and George Wilson, "New U.S. Military Plan: European, Persian Focus," *Washington Post*, 27 January 1978, p. A-1.

8. For two excellent summaries of the analyses of the impact of defense spending on the economy see Ann Crittenden, "Economy Geared to Military Will Cut Jobs, Fuel Inflation," *New York Times*, 19 November 1978, p. 17; and Donald Rumsfeld, *Annual Defense Report, FY 1978*, 17 January 1977, pp. 323-24.

9. Crittenden, "Economy Geared to Military."

10. Walter Millis, *The Forrestal Diaries* (New York: Viking, 1951), p. 415.

11. U.S. Congress, House Committee on Appropriations, *Hearings on the FY 1959 Defense Budget*, p. 353.

12. Kenneth O'Donnell and Dave Powers, *Johnny We Hardly Knew Ye* (New York: Viking, 1972), p. 167.

13. Interviews with officials in the Office of Management and Budget, July 1972.

14. Richard Levine, "The Pentagon Loses a Talented Leader." *The Wall Street Journal*, 3 November 1975, p. 3.

15. "Defense Cuts Eyed by Boss of Budget," *New York Times*, 19 November 1978, p. 3.

16. The service staffs each have over 2,000 people.

17. The neutron bomb snafu is well summarized in Walter Pincus, "Neutron Warhead Wouldn't be Deployed Until '79, Hill Told," *Washington Post*, 8 July 1977, p. A-3.

18. See, for example, Mary Kay Quinlan, "Decoy Missile Silos Worry Bedell, Others," *Omaha World Herald*, 20 September 1978, p. 4.

Part III
Approaches to the Use and Control of Force

12

Defining Strategic Issues: How to Avoid Isometric Exercises

George H. Quester

The argument in this chapter is not by any means that the strategic arms race between the United States and Soviet Union is unreal, or that there is no need for concern and vigilance about the maintenance of adequate deterrent forces to make sure that the other side does not one day find the launching of a World War III attractive. Such concerns are indeed very real.

Rather the argument is that we at times risk adding a worsening of our problem by acting as if the possibilities and scenarios we had conjured up were already proven. Skeptics about the arms race sometimes impute this to the deliberate machinations of a military-industrial complex that has a vested interest in keeping alive the arms race, but the argument here will not attach much significance to such accusations. Rather the kinds of problems to be discussed hinge on logical tricks we play on ourselves, the results of certain kinds of simplifications and abstractions that make the strategic arms balance look logically neater, but at a price of making World War III look more threatening than it actually is.

The Nature of the Problem

What indeed should be our list of worries about strategic nuclear weapons? Without a doubt, our first concern must indeed be that World War III be prevented. There are several kinds of such a war outbreak to be concerned about. One would be the deliberate launching of such a war, because one side had worked itself into a position where it would suffer very little retaliation against its population centers and thus could at a bearable cost conquer the world by a nuclear first-strike. Another kind of World War III to fear is the preemptive stampede into such a war, wherein each side suspects that the other is about to launch a first-strike of the type described, wherein each side then feels that it will at least have less to lose for having beaten the other to the punch. This would be a "war nobody wanted," as each side truly would have preferred to remain at peace.

No one denies, to repeat, that this is a serious concern, the most serious concern. By investing in assured second-strike forces of our own, while perhaps forswearing any great accumulation of first-strike counterforce capabilities on our side, we can greatly reduce the likelihood of such an actual outbreak of a World War III, and much of this indeed has been done all along.

Someone concerned about a Soviet buildup in missile totals would however note that this cannot be the end of our list of concerns. A second important concern is that the fear of a Soviet-launched World War III not be allowed to weaken U.S. resolve in defense of our allies and our principles around the globe. Spokesmen for greater investments in strategic forces, in the wake of Soviet acquisitions of new missiles, will thus sometimes concede that they do not ever expect World War III to happen, but they will nonetheless express the fear that the mere prospect that it might happen would inhibit future presidents from pursuing the ordinary policies that are appropriate to American values.

A third concern will be quite parallel, namely that the peoples and governments of Western Europe and Japan not be similarly intimidated, as a consequence of either of the two factors already noted. Europeans could be "Finlandized" because they saw some possibility of a thermonuclear war or because they saw a possibility of the United States being inhibited by such a prospect. They might accede to Soviet demands concerning the political or economic practices of their societies, concessions that we would all like to forestall.

"Finlandization" is possibly an imprecise phrase. It projects a pattern widely imputed to Finland, that the mere threat of military action by the USSR suffices to impose various unpalatable choices on Helsinki. Skeptics might note that life in Finland is indeed far different from life in Poland or Bulgaria or the USSR; countervailing forces must be at work to bolster the Finnish position. It may be that Moscow thus gets its way on the things that matter less to Finns, that is, their statements about foreign policy, while the Finns get their way on things that matter more, the nature of their domestic life-style. Yet there is also no gainsaying the fact that Moscow does get its way in Finland more than it does in Belgium or France. One of our goals is to preserve the degree of independence that obtains in Bruxelles and Paris and Bonn and Tokyo.

Antidotes to Problems

What then, are the antidotes to our problems? For the actual risk of World War III, we need to maintain the kind of nuclear forces that can very assuredly destroy the cities of the USSR, should Moscow ever elect to begin such a war. At the same time we will wish to keep Moscow from fearing that we are about to start such a war ourselves; an avoidance of an excessive counterforce capability would serve to reduce such fears.

Open and clear analysis has been important in developing our understanding of what is needed here, and in assuring that it is indeed put into place. But what then of our second and third problems, the avoiding of a show of fear of Soviet power? Here we are much more in the realm of the psychological than the physical. Here it may even be true that there is no problem unless one is aware of a problem. The problem is not quite as self-generating and self-sustaining as a financial panic, to which President Roosevelt could respond that "the only thing we have to fear is fear itself." There is a reality to nuclear deterrence problems, such that we have other things to fear besides fear. Yet excessive fear, or excessive tidiness in abstracting and clarifying our fears, can still be something to fear in its own right, something we would do much better to avoid.

Those who argue that Soviet missile growth is alarming do so in good faith, just as those who dismiss the threat are similarly analysts speaking their honest feelings. Yet if one presses the spokesmen for the alarmed position, it is interesting that their lengthier discussions often concede that the second and third problems we have listed in fact dominate the first, that it is not truly the risk of World War III that they are concerned about, but rather the possibility that Americans and Europeans in the future may tend to be intimidated by the prospect of World War III.

For example, Colin Gray:

> This discussion could be misleading, in that it has dwelt upon the foreign policy relevance of actual strategic nuclear employment, or of crises that threaten such employment. In practice, while acute confrontations arise only rarely, the strategic posture "works" day by day pervasively in diplomacy. Americans' perceptions of their country's relative standing, perceptions by others, and the American sense of what risks are involved in particular possible enterprises—all rest, in part, though in ways that are incalculable, upon assessments of the state of the strategic nuclear balance. Nobody knows, with any confidence, how a World War III would terminate. Would there be a victor? Does such a concept make sense? But everybody knows which way the balance is tending, and this knowledge contributes to a constricting of American freedom of foreign policy action.[1]

Or Edward Luttwak:

> Nuclear weapons of intercontinental range are no doubt overrated as constituents of overall national power by political leaders all over the world, but unfortunately it is their own beliefs, however misguided, which determine the authority of the military strength of the superpowers in their counsels. Any competent analysis of the actual capabilities of the Soviet and American intercontinental nuclear forces deployed at the time of the 1972 Moscow accords, revealed that the latter were far superior by every relevant measurement. But it is not the recondite calculations of technical experts that count in the world political arena, but rather the untaught perceptions of political leaders in which simple numerical indices loom large.[2]

Citing this line of argument might strike a reader as a resumption of an old debate about worst-case analysis. The military is usually accused of basing its budget proposals on the worst that could happen. An enemy's capabilities become the yardstick, since his intentions can never be trusted. But the old debate was concerned mostly with monetary extravagance, whereas the new issues are more complicated.

Where the avoidance of World War III is truly the problem, we may not want to move very far away from worst-case analysis. One indeed wants overkill, and redundancy, and probably at least a triad of delivery capabilities in order to retaliate after any first-strike by Moscow. Yet one cannot be concerned only for preparing against the worst. If we systematically exaggerate the worst the other side can do, we in effect give him political returns as a free gift. These political returns may be much more serious a loss than any waste of our resources.

A Salient Example: Missile Accuracy

The most important current disturbant to equanimity about the strategic balance comes on the topic of missile accuracy. The submarine-based component of strategic forces does not (for the moment) seem in jeopardy, and the bomber portion of the strategic weapons triad may indeed be winning a new lease on life by the addition of air-launched cruise missiles. But accuracies on intercontinental land-based nuclear missiles are seen to be improving continually. When this trend is combined with multiple warheads, it begins to suggest preemptive counterforce first-strikes against an adversary's land-based missile forces, hardly a welcome development.

As noted, this new counterforce accuracy will not be at all relevant to submarine-based missile forces, which will remain the "ace in the hole" of deterrent power on each side. Yet many analysts see the combination of multiple warheads and improved accuracy as offering Moscow an option of destroying all the land-based missiles of the United States during some future crisis, as part of a deliberate Soviet move to demonstrate superior position and resolve. The new counterforce accuracy might thus mindlessly convert the ICBMs in North Dakota (or, for the United States, ones in Siberia) into an attractive nuisance, whetting a targeter's appetite for a "limited strategic war" during a crisis, simply because "we do better if we shoot first than if they shoot first."

Perhaps it is already too late to head off the very accurate multiple-warhead missile by some kind of missile test-ban. As each improvement in accuracy is accomplished, significant arms control becomes more difficult, for it is hard to prove that one has forgotten technology already under test. The arguments for spending additional billions on weapons systems are thus

Defining Strategic Issues 199

strengthened in each of the superpowers, with greater economic sacrifice and political irritation.

Concern about the survivability of Minuteman missiles based in underground silos on the North American continent is always appropriate, but could it be that we have played a logical trick on ourselves here? Without anyone intending that it happen, have we consistently underestimated the difficulties of a Soviet counterforce strike against these silos, thus passing up some real opportunities that might still be available in a ban on the testing of the more accurate missiles?

The standard index of missile accuracy is the circular error probable (CEP), a circle around an intended target such that half of the warheads will fall within it. If the circle is large, the missile is obviously inaccurate; if the radius of the circle is small, one begins to have the accuracies needed for counterforce strikes, even against "hardened" missile silos. The CEP for the German V-2 rocket in World War II was a dismal 25 miles; half the rockets landed more than 25 miles from their designated target.[3] By contrast, figures are now being bandied about for attainable CEPs of 300 feet or less in the latest missiles, even as the distance they travel has increased many-fold.

Such an index of accuracy lends itself to calculations of destructiveness or "kill probability," once one knows the explosive power of the nuclear warhead and the probable thickness of the concrete fortifications protecting the target. It is an easy index to refer to at seminars, at congressional hearings, at strategy planning sessions, and at cocktail parties. Proponents of new missiles can employ it, and so can proponents of arms control. It can provide an index of measurement so that persons with very different political values can still communicate with each other.

Yet can it be that we have all been internalizing a definition of CEP that leads us to assume more threatening developments than indeed exist? There is at least some lack of clarity as to what is counted in, to settle the "half of all warheads" that fall within the circle. One can cite three well-informed discussions of the subject here to illustrate the possibility of confusion. First, the definition from the *SIPRI* (Stockholm International Peace Research Institute) *Yearbook*: "Circular Error Probability (CEP) is the radius of a circle, centred on the target, within which 50 per cent of the weapons or munitions aimed at the target will fall."[4] Or, as defined in a recent book by Laurence Martin, which well illustrates the kinds of optimistic (that is, pessimistic in terms of peace) predictions we have been discussing:

> The accuracy of a missile is expressed as "circular error probable" (CEP); that is, the radius of a circle within which a re-entry vehicle has a 50 percent chance of falling. The CEP of early, prototype long-range missiles of the mid-fifties was about five miles at intercontinental ranges. A decade later, missiles like Minuteman were expected to have a CEP of less than half a mile and it was confidently predicted that this error could, if desired, be reduced to tens of feet by the late seventies.[5]

But, alternatively, as defined in an Institute for Strategic Studies *Adelphi Paper* by Ian Smart:

> The accuracy with which offensive missiles deliver their warheads against a target on the ground is measured in terms of the circular error probable (CEP). This is the radius of a circle centred on the target within which 50 percent of the warheads can be expected to fall. . . . A missile system with an accuracy of 0.5 n.m. CEP is therefore one which can be expected to deliver 50 percent of its warheads within a radius of half a nautical mile around the target.[6]

Are we thus counting all the warheads of a missile system (Smart) or just "incoming warheads" (SIPRI and Martin) in computing the batting average for such systems' accuracy? The figures circulated for accuracies of 700 feet, or 70, or 7 feet, are indeed sometimes obtained only by leaving out all cases where missiles fail to fire in the first place, or where they go drastically off course immediately after launching, or where the multiple-warhead separation system fails. This may all be a little like the gasoline-mileage figures for automobiles that are calculated by driving all day at a constant speed of 48 miles an hour, figures that could turn out twice as bad. More realistic stop-and-go driving yields far less favorable results.

What would we discover if CEP were defined more meaningfully, based on half of all warheads that were fired with the intention of hitting the specified target? Could it even be that a CEP thus defined might sometimes be growing, rather than shrinking, which would be good news indeed for arms control?

The professional strategic planners of the United States as well as our academic strategic analysts, are of course aware of these complications and subtleties when they make assessments of the most effective possible Soviet first-strike (and, one supposes, of the most effective possible American first-strike). Considerations of likely missile failure and guidance system breakdowns, and of fratricide, and so forth, are all taken into account in the calculations of the SIOP (the single integrated operations plan), which guides American targeting for a World War III. One assumes that Soviet war planners are similarly sophisticated in their calculations.

The cost of the shorthand of CEP and World War III does not thus come so much in possibly erroneous war-planning, but rather more inadvertently as we wander into the public discussion. Because of a seductively appealing shorthand, we may inflict the very damage on ourselves that we wish to avoid. We convince ourselves that we are doomed to lack resolve in the future, and/or that our allies are bound to lack resolve.

On the real side of the missile accuracy problem, we convince ourselves that it is already too late to head off any of its worse ramifications. We are not arguing here that missile accuracies will not sooner or later be a problem.

Defining Strategic Issues

Such improved accuracies can indeed be destabilizing and may be bad for arms control. Yet all the problem may not yet be upon us, and some of it therefore may still be capable of being contained. Accurate missiles may not be quite as "technologically sweet" as some of their proponents would contend. They are based on a precarious and deliberate technology; we subliminally mislead ourselves, no matter what side we are on, if we let our technological shorthand seem to show us something that is not yet there.

If the CEP is the variable that professionals will call to the attention of citizens, let it thus at least be of real relevance to the citizen. How missiles are discussed can often be as important as how they will be used.

If the additional black box guidance system of any new missile increases the failure rate of the missile, this should thus be included in the CEP discussion if we are to have anything serious to work with. One does not have to have read too much by Ralph Nader to develop a healthy skepticism in the seventies about the reliability of complicated gadgets. A society that has become used to bringing appliances back for repairs might now discover that it is losing, rather than gaining, accuracies in the moves for multiple independently targeted reentry vehicles (MIRV) to maneuverable reentry vehicles (MARV), once account is taken of the greater risk of malfunction in the more complicated terminal guidance system. One similarly could lose reliability in the move from Polaris to Poseidon. Such losses in no way threaten the basic countervalue retaliatory role of nuclear missile forces. But they suggest that cryptic references to CEP, defined as dubiously as it has been, can prematurely alarm us, or tempt us, about a counterforce mission.

Old gadgets often work better than new; anyone who has ridden the Long Island Railroad (LIRR) or the Bay Area Rapid Transit (BART) knows this. Unlike the LIRR or BART, however, the U.S. Air Force will have little in the way of daily routine to get the bugs out by ordinary operational shakedown. A terminal guidance system that depends on Russian terrain features to achieve its last increment of accuracy will never undergo a field test. A different definition of CEP might indeed thus give us a paradoxical suggestion that deployed missiles could be less accurate in 1982 than in 1978. At least it might tell us that we have until 1982, rather than until 1980, to clamp some kind of lid on missile accuracies, to preclude scenarios of counterforce attack.

The simplifications we have been discussing pose the possibility not only of our exaggerating the Soviet threat, but also of exaggerating possibilities of a U.S. counterforce capability against Soviet missile sites. It would be a significant cost if we became intent about such options at a time when the facts of the matter did not really warrant them, or if our concern were to encourage the Russians to expand their own capabilities in compensation for our improved CEPs.

An extreme of such excessive abstraction is thus illustrated with the

American speculation cited that the Russians might in some future crisis elect to teach us a lesson by using their high-accuracy missiles in a counterforce strike at American land-based missiles. This conjectured attack would be carefully orchestrated to avoid American population, so that we would not lash back with our submarine-based missiles but would instead perhaps back out of West Berlin.

Worrying about the best possible assumptions for the Soviet side, American estimates have emerged that no more than 800,000 Americans might be killed in such a "surgically clean" Soviet counterforce missile attack. The premises for this "low" figure include several that are extraordinarily questionable in their neatness: for example that the United States will have cooperated by acquiring substantial civil-defense fall-out shelters and that the Soviet attacks will come when the winds are optimal for avoiding dispersion of radioactive fallout, specifically in August.

When these special assumptions are relaxed, the numbers of Americans killed as "collateral damage" in such a Soviet "demonstration strike" climbs quickly into the tens of millions, perhaps to 25 or 30 million, and the chance of U.S. submarine-based missiles not being fired against Russian population centers starts to look slim indeed. The idea that the Russians would somehow be able to challenge us in this very peculiar game of "chicken," but only in one very predictable month of the year, serves again as an example of neat and clean abstraction taking on a life of its own and, indeed, running wild.

Some Other Examples

One could say a few words now about another kind of analytical simplification or verbal trap that causes us similar difficulty. This amounts almost to a reprise of the introduction to our argument, for it refers to the number of times when the phrases "Soviet strike" or "World War III" are used in discussions of the subject as a shorthand for "prospect of a Soviet strike" or "fear of World War III."

The use of the shorthand is quite innocent. Congressmen and newspapers editors would become altogether bored and fatigued if they had to listen again and again to references to "fear of a Soviet first strike" or "fear of fear of a Soviet first strike." As a result, the phrase "Soviet first-strike" gets substituted, as an easy-to-listen-to substitute for the longer and more involuted phrase. When secretaries of defense Melvin Laird, James Schlesinger, or Harold Brown thus presented testimony arguing that a Soviet missile attack was plausible for the late 1980s (unless recommended American force expansions were funded), their honest intent may have been to warn that their successors would have to worry about this possibility, rather than that the attack was actually going to happen. Looking ahead, any patriotic American may wish to take steps now so that his president and cabinet will not be intimidated in the future. But we exaggerate and exacerbate the problem when we use references to the real nuclear disaster as a shorthand for fears of that disaster.

What is the net impact then of the use of this shorthand? The result is that we systematically increase in our own minds the likelihood that such a thermonuclear war would ever be launched, because the shorthand for simplicity's sake paraphrases fear of war, or fear of intimidation, into war. Although this may be necessary for the processes of our internal discussions, it serves nonetheless to give the USSR some more of a free ride in terms of the political impact that the Politburo must be presumed to have been seeking.

There is something entirely scientific and commendable in the various American efforts to distill the essence of necessary U.S. strategic power for our confrontation with the Russians, as we develop very tangible measures of CEPs or numbers of warheads, or throwweights, or equivalent megatonnage. Yet along with the science of this, we also display a craving for a simple and tangible reassurance, for a "bean-counting" measure that will leave us immune to Soviet attack. As we press too hard for the tangibility of this reassurance, we may lose points in the political contests that really matter the most.

Looking into the future, one might anticipate similar tendencies to oversimplify and overrate the Soviet capacity in antisubmarine warfare (ASW), then casting doubt on another critical part of the triad. Similarly premature pronouncements of success may come forward about Soviet defenses against the cruise missiles to be fired from American-manned bombers, and about the effectiveness of Soviet civil defense systems. (Indeed, this last example has already come to life).[7]

Parallel examples away from the context of a nuclear World War III will show up in the western discussions of the power of Soviet tank forces and in the great importance and significance assigned to the new Soviet navy. The use of "ship-days" as a measure of comparative naval presence in bodies of water like the Mediterranean Sea and the Indian Ocean may seem logical and simple, but it can mask important weaknesses in the Soviet deployments.[8]

The skeptic will charge that the vested interests in defense preparations are deliberately exaggerating Soviet military potential. Yet what we may have to fear even more are the exaggerations that are not at all deliberate but rather the result of the analytical simplifications intended to make manageable the problem of comparing military forces, simplifications that in the process, however, exact a price because Soviet capabilities are exaggerated.

The Asymmetry of Idea Development

The Soviet-American strategic arms confrontation is not symmetrical. This elementary fact would have been cited very quickly, by those who fear the USSR, amid suggestions that the Moscow leadership can be very callous about accepting the retaliation we impose on the Russian population in a World War III and thus can make the threats of a thermonuclear war much more real. Yet there are other asymmetries.

It is a remarkable fact that the overwhelming bulk of discussions of the essential nature of the strategic arms race, and of growing Soviet relative power, and of possible Soviet threats, comes from the West. The asymmetry here was bizarrely illustrated in the Strategic Arms Limitation Talks (SALT), where the Soviet delegations typically cited western publications as their sources of numbers on their own missile inventories, even using western nomenclature.

If this is extreme, the fact remains that most of the conceptualization of what is important or menacing about the arms race has been left in western hands. If there are logical traps, they are of our own making. Goering may have intimidated Britain and France in 1938 by showing Charles Lindbergh what the Luftwaffe was allegedly developing in air power, but the USSR has not been playing that game, or has not needed to. The Russians do acquire the weapons, but we are the ones who compose the prose describing them.

We are indeed an open society, with a free press, and with an enormous appetite for news and curiosity about the world. If there is in fact a distinguishing characteristic about the free world, and about the United States in particular, it comes in the extent to which the "right to know" is pursued. This pursuit imposes some burdens on the United States, as compared with the Soviet Union's totally managed press, but it also conveys some advantages. The western press is seen throughout the world as the only one worth reading, the only one that in its reports conveys some important evidence about the true state of affairs.

Let it then be made clear that we are not proposing any American move closer to Soviet practice, any form of state control or censorship of the press to preclude the reporting of the possibilities of Soviet weapons breakthroughs. If such moves were to come, they would lower the quality of life far more than the gains could possibly be worth. The result, moreover, would simply be that the credibility of what was printed in the West would diminish.

The U.S. government has no right to manage the news; it can be expected to present its own position on what is happening, and why, a position that then has an impact on any overall assessment the public reaches. It would be uncharacteristic and impossible for the government of the United

States to have no influence here, anymore than any other government, or any other important actor, could express opinions that did not somehow affect the consensus.

The U.S. government should not try to expand or to shed such influence, therefore, but might direct it in ways that were more appropriate to the purposes it indeed wants to serve. At the least, we might not have our government arguing positions in public that serve exactly the opposite purposes from what it intends.

If there were a real risk of a Soviet first-strike capability, it would thus be altogether appropriate for defense officials and others to sound the alarm. If the real threat is rather that we may only come to fear such a capacity in the future, and thus may be inhibited by Soviet bluster, then we do much better to consider carefully whether the Soviet objective accomplishment has not often been overstated.

But surely the Russians will notice if the public and semipublic statements of Americans on defense cease discussing the CEP in such precise and didactic terms, cease crediting Moscow with ever growing missile accuracies. Will not the Russians simply respond by picking up this discussion themselves, beginning to publish their own version of *Aviation Week*, holding their own congressional hearings?

If they were to try to do so, all well and good. The Soviets, to begin, would have difficulty in adjusting to this kind of publicity generation, used to a much cruder form of propaganda and very comfortably accustomed now to having the western media do their more subtle work for them. At the least, we would then force Moscow to begin supplying some hard data, with the risks that the Russians would begin telling us something we did not already know (rather than having us always tell them what we know about them).

As things stand, moreover, the USSR has the best of both worlds, cashing in on a reputation around the world for having ever-more-accurate missiles, ever-more-powerful military forces, while (in the SALT negotiations and elsewhere) choosing to deny having such capabilities, forcing the United States to accept the burden of proof that the West has a need for matching weapons on its side. A greater western reticence about attributing such capabilities to the Russians would thus force Moscow to give up one, or the other, of these advantages. If the Russians kept silent, then the input to "Finlandization" would not be restored. If they began proclaiming their own missile accuracies and MIRV tests and missile totals, and civil defense programs, then the case for writing matching U.S. capabilities into a final SALT agreement would have been conceded.

We have already mentioned the ludicrousness of letting the Russians use western citations of their own missile strengths as the basic bargaining data for the SALT talks since 1969. At the extreme, this apparently saw Russian military officers on the SALT delegation urging American negotiators not to discuss such "military secrets" in front of Russian civilians.

This is hardly to suggest that there would be some great kind of liberalization or destabilization of Soviet society if the Kremlin were forced to publicize its own military forces, rather than having the West touting its alleged strengths. If some Soviet civilians have lacked details on the military luxuries their government has been purchasing, they might now become disgruntled upon getting the news, but this is a disgruntlement that the KGB is surely capable of handling. Rather, the point is simply that the Russians are not good at taking on this kind of task, that they would not be good at splitting the differences between power propaganda and SALT negotiating positions, so that we would induce them to make mistakes in forcing them into playing a new position.

Past Experiences

Are there models in history of how one would like the U.S. government to handle this problem? We are not suggesting moving into some awful new world of thought control, but rather the more familiar world of a government that has control over its own tone, while addressing a public which on its own has already become a little more distrustful of scientific predictions and analytical abstractions.

On the political side, our examplar might indeed be the administration of President Eisenhower. Beset by critics who argued that bomber gaps and missile gaps were emerging favorable to the Russians, Eisenhower managed again and again to obscure the issues in a way that muted the discussion that thus kept defense expenditures lower, and that also reduced the political capital Moscow could draw from such advantages. Eisenhower's Secretary of Defense, Charles E. Wilson, at one point summed it up simply in opining that "the Russians are not ten feet tall."

On the technological side, our model, as suggested in the specific discussion of the missile accuracy problem, is also readily at hand. We simply need to internalize and digest the contemporary ecologists' distrust of technological calculations and forecasts. Nothing ever works right anymore, nothing ever works exactly as predicted, and this needs to be taken into account when considering the power of the Soviet military. In many ways, this also was a part of the folk-wisdom of the Eisenhower years, replaced then by the very different rational activism of the Kennedy administration.

It may be, as Charles E. Wilson argued, that we have all along had too excessive a respect for the Soviet Union. Whether or not this is the case, we quite possibly have too much respect for technology, assuming that things are going to work merely because the prototypes have been tested, merely because the plans look good. America in many ways has been a more success-oriented and success-accustomed place, as compared, for example, with Europe. At times our foreign policy has been criticized as expecting too much continued success for American ventures. Here it is being criticized for anticipating too much success in others' ventures.

Notes

1. Reprinted by permission from *Foreign Affairs*, July 1978. Copyright 1978 by Council on Foreign Relations, Inc.

2. Edward N. Luttwak, "SALT and the Meaning of Strategy," *The Washington Review of Strategic and International Studies* 1, no. 2 (April 1978):25.

3. Neville Brown, *Nuclear War* (London: Pall Mall Press, 1964), p. 70.

4. Stockholm International Peace Research Institute, *SIPRI Yearbook of World Armaments and Disarmament, 1978* (London: Taylor and Francis, 1978), pp. 4, 446.

5. Laurence Martin, *Arms and Strategy* (New York: David McKay Company, 1973), p. 22.

6. Ian Smart, "Advanced Strategic Missiles: A Short Guide," *Adelphi Papers*, no. 63 (London: International Institute for Strategic Studies, 1969), p. 3. Reprinted with permission.

7. On civil defense and alleged Soviet investments therein, see the analysis by T.K. Jones, *Civil Defense Review, Hearings before the Committee on Armed Services,* House of Representatives, 94th Congress, 2d Session (Washington, D.C.: 1976), pp. 206-267.

8. For an example of an alarmed survey of Soviet naval presence around the globe, see Norman Polmar, *Soviet Naval Power: Challenge for the 1970's* (New York: Crane and Russak, 1974).

13 Arms Control: A Theoretical Perspective

Patrick M. Morgan

Despite our intense interest in arms control, we have little or no theoretical grasp of the subject. We lack precision in our conceptions of arms control, can offer nothing systematic to explain the conditions under which it is likely to be attempted or to succeed, and disagree about the nature of the negotiations involved. We still do not have a framework for evaluating the prospects for arms control today and in the near or distant future. It is a venerable approach to the problem of violent conflict, one we are now into in a big way, yet we do not know all that much about it.

Like many concepts, arms control is seldom carefully defined. Most popular is Schelling's view that arms control seeks to reduce the likelihood of war, the damage if one occurs, and the costs of the arms race. Enlarging on this, it is useful to think of arms control as a strategy for deriving security in a heavily armed world, a strategy that accepts the existence of military forces and tries to limit their harmful consequences. In other words, arms control consists of unilateral and multilateral steps with respect to military forces designed to contain the harmful consequences associated with nations continuing to have arms. If we categorize those harmful consequences we have a typology of arms control objectives.[1] Armed forces cost money—some arms control measures cut expenditures. Weapons may impose environmental costs—arms control can reduce or eliminate them. Weapons can incite horizontal or vertical proliferation with attendant costs—arms control may attempt to prevent this. The existence and dispositions of armed forces can encourage attacks and war, that is, be destabilizing—arms control may limit these effects. Weapons may be stolen, accidentally explode, be used contrary to orders—arms control may try to limit uncontrolled use or the harmful results of such use. Armed forces do great damage in war—arms control can limit the incidence of war and contain its ravages.

In practicing arms control, governments anticipate the continuing utility of military forces for national security and other goals. Thus arms control embraces the traditional solution to the national security problem (have arms and be prepared to fight), a solution that a strategy of disarmament rejects. Disarmament and arms control are not stages on a continuum but largely contradictory, something papered over by arms controllers' talk about one-step-at-a-time remedies for the arms race.[2] As arms controllers, governments have timetables for eliminating arms that put this just about in time for the second coming.

As arms play a major role in the international system and can have quite unacceptable costs, arms control is needed to keep those costs within tolerable limits. This means that arms control plays a significant role in any sustained interstate system, supplementing other arrangements that contribute to stability. Although the term "arms control" is recent, the practice may be as old as violent conflicts between societies. Primitive societies developed many arms control practices, presumably far back in the Stone Age, for use domestically and with outsiders. These included keeping the size of bands small to reduce the incidence of member conflicts, curbing arrogance via "put-downs" (to use a modern term) or share-the-wealth measures, and quite elaborate forms of ritual combat.[3] Arms control is almost certainly older than disarmament because arms were once necessary for food. Weapons for the hunt were also the weapons of war, so disarmament was impossible. It was the coming of agriculture as an alternative source of food that made disarmament conceivable, and it is no coincidence that Isaiah speaks of converting "swords into plowshares."

Linked to an ongoing international system, arms control will readily reflect the distribution of power in that system and competitive struggles among the members. This makes it difficult both to reach agreements (tacit or explicit) and to sustain them—the search for a competitive advantage being constant. It is also why arms control is often disappointing. Arms control advocates are sometimes really after disarmament. As arms control is the handmaiden of a continuing reliance on arms, these people are bound to be disappointed. Others want arms control to confer greater competitive advantages in international politics. Many critics of SALT, for example, demand that it secure or enhance American advantages while reducing or eliminating those of the Russians. Few negotiable agreements are apt to please them.

Arms control is old, but its importance today is historically unique. We have abandoned hopes of disarmament, seeing it as incompatible with contemporary international politics, and have explored arms control in more depth than past eras. Our preoccupation with arms control also stems from the destructive nature of modern weapons. We cannot bring ourselves to disarm but dare not employ much of the military power we possess. We are made arms controllers by necessity, by our dependence on weapons beyond bearing if used. This shifts arms control from a peripheral to a central role in national security policy.

The primary expression of this is our overwhelming reliance on strategic deterrence. Throughout history arms were created to be used; some opponents might be coerced without fighting, but it was always expected that sooner or later arms would be used and they were designed accordingly.

Many contemporary weapons are to work by never having to be used. Their point is to contain others' use of arms. A more arm-control-like function is hard to imagine. Given our preoccupation with avoiding central war, nuclear deterrence is a particulary important kind of arms control, using weapons to forestall the most awful consequences associated with weapons. Since deterrence is the primary objective of our strategic forces, arms control conceived in this way is the central feature of national security policy.

This is not a widely appreciated point. It is customary to relate arms control to deterrence only in steps to stabilize the strategic balance and eliminate incentives to attack first. If such measures specifically seek to strengthen deterrence, why reserve the term "arms control" for them and not that which they are supposed to enhance? The essence of arms control is restraint on military forces within and via the framework supplied by those forces, which certainly would encompass deterrence. That is why our foremost arms control negotiations are intended to sustain deterrence by stabilizing the strategic balance, why debate about our deterrence postures is largely conducted in arms control terms—whether various weapons, strategies, and prospective deployments are stabilizing or destabilizing in their effects, controllable in a crisis or war, likely to invite escalation, likely to encourage proliferation, and so on. In our earlier typology, deterrence clearly falls under avoiding the destructive effects of arms by curbing their deliberate use.

Preconditions for Arms Control

Part of a theory of arms control would be a list of prerequisites for it or conditions under which it can occur. The ones discussed later must, I think, all exist simultaneously if arms control is to take place. They are set forth in relatively comprehensive terms; other conditions that might be cited can be subsumed under these as helpful but not necessary.

First Condition: Available Technology
Makes It Possible

Technology can condition the likelihood of arms control in both physical and psychological ways. In simple physical terms, available technology dictates verification possibilities, on which the chances for meaningful agreements often rest. Nuclear weapons lend themselves to proliferation controls because it is difficult to develop and test them secretly—the specialized installations required are not easily hidden (as the South Africans found out), and the tests measurably disturb the environment.

Available technology also dictates the feasibility of certain controls over one's own forces, to prevent inadvertent or unauthorized use.

However, technological change may reduce or eliminate vulnerability to observation or susceptibility to constraint, thereby frustrating arms control. Restrictions on one weapon may be evaded by development of an alternate system. Large, readily detected weapons may be replaced by versions more compact and difficult to spot. Multiple independently-targeted reentry vehicles (MIRV) made it impossible to count deployed warheads with precision. The cruise missile will do the same for delivery vehicles and will erase the visible distinctions between deployed conventional and strategic missiles. Mininukes and enhanced radiation weapons could reduce some of the most visible aspects of the threshold between conventional and nuclear weapons. Improvements in accuracy are now eliminating the distinction between first- and second-strike weapons.[4]

Technology also affects the psychological climate for arms control. Impulses to arms control have often sprung from the appearance of new arms so awful as to arouse widespread dread. The trouble is that people can get used to almost anything, including weapons once deemed despicable. A grim side of human history is the ready adaptation of our sensibilities to our military technology. Weapons have often aroused opposition as unmanly (the longbow), inhuman or unchivalrous (gunpowder), or immoral (submarine warfare, strategic bombing), but in the end such scruples were overcome. However, in this century we have devised weapons not readily gotten used to. Their use in war has, if anything, increased the repugnance they arouse—witness the effect of poison gas in World War I and the atomic bomb in World War II. Biological warfare weapons seem equally distasteful. In the race between new weapons and old sensibilities, we have reached the point where certain weapons are incompatible with what most of us will ever accept as being human. Under these circumstances, technology forces recourse to arms control. It is just such weapons that we count on to make deterrence work. The idea of deterrence is very old, but the reality of weapons of mass destruction deliverable over great distances makes it psychologically much more plausible and thus more effective.

Finally, technological changes associated with warfare have made it increasingly possible to achieve an overwhelming victory via strategic surprise or lightning war. This invites living amid hair triggers and constant alerts or with huge standing forces that are fiscally and politically unpalatable. Many states have chosen the latter course, but unhappily. In this context arms control has an undeniable appeal, as a way to stabilize deterrence at a less burdensome level of preparation by containing opportunities for strategic surprise.

Second Condition: A Favorable International Political Situation

Here we are talking about specific political conditions that at any one time affect the chances for arms control. It is frequently asserted that the political situation must be just right for arms control. Hedley Bull ascribes the Washington naval agreements to the participants' temporary satisfaction with the status quo and eagerness to avoid unprofitable rivalries. William Epstein finds that the nonproliferation treaty emerged because the time was ripe in terms of global politics. The favorable conditions may pertain to the general state of the international system or to certain elements in relations among key states. To illustrate the latter, emphasis has been put on the importance of parity as a prerequisite for superpower agreements. Paul Warnke has asserted in connection with SALT that "it's only the fact that strategic parity exists that makes it possible to negotiate."[5]

Arms control is mostly for dealing with competitors and antagonists. (Among friends, disarmament can be more suitable.) But the antagonism must be within limits. Numerous historical examples suggest that deterrence works best against governments not particularly inclined to attack, and it is far less effective against those determined to alter the status quo by force if necessary. The postwar era has been one in which two blocs worried greatly about attack and accordingly worked hard at deterrence, a deterrence sustained by the fact that neither was fundamentally inclined to challenge the other militarily.

The degree of antagonism among the parties involved appears directly relevant to arms control in other ways as well. As Hans Morgenthau pointed out, the coming of total war among deeply committed antagonists eliminated many traditional restraints on war. Hefty antagonisms short of war have the same effect; many kinds of arms control were beyond reach in the depths of the Cold War. After all, arms control involves recognizing certain mutual interests, and one measure of the gravity of a conflict is the degree to which the parties see nothing in common. Along these lines, other things being equal, an old rivalry should be better suited to arms control than a new one. The antagonist is familiar, the costs more obvious, the conflict more boring and, in the way of the world, the combatants more cynical and pragmatic. This could be why Samuel Huntington once found that the chances an arms race will lead to war decline as the race lengthens.

Of course, antagonisms can vary considerably in the short run, affecting the timing of initiatives and the immediate responsiveness of the parties involved. The SALT talks were delayed by the invasion of Czechoslovakia, for instance, and the Vietnam War made progress on seemingly unrelated arms control problems a good deal more difficult.

*Third Condition: Significant Parallels in the
Arms Cultures Involved*

Arms control cannot be achieved without communication, leading to a degree of cooperation and based on shared or interlocking perceptions. Deterrence theory has long accepted the necessity of this among antagonists. Literature on other forms of arms control makes a similar point. Thus it seems vital that the elites involved have sufficiently overlapping arms-and-security cultures. This can be true in several ways. States may have similar sorts of regimes, which define national security in common terms. The French Revolution and nationalism devastated previously successful limits on European wars born of the common view of the world held by the monarchs and aristocracies involved.

Where governments rely on the same kinds of weapons, hold parallel views about how wars should be fought, and use similar indexes of national military strength, this facilitates communication about restrictions on arms, particularly efforts at tacit cooperation. For instance, it takes a common perspective of some sort to develop a mutual escalation ladder for limiting a war.

The importance of this is most evident in a war where the two sides have different battlefield "etiquettes" growing out of differing weapons and military structures. Like any implement, arms are a part of a larger culture, designed to meet needs as perceived from its perspective and, in turn, helping shape behavior in it. Different battlefield etiquettes can lead each party to regard the other as brutal, treacherous, and inhumane. Colonial wars are rich in examples, as were American Indian wars. The Vietnamese used ambush, assassination, random terror, hit-and-run raids—reflecting the kinds of weapons they had, their strategies and objectives, their view of the war. The Americans used massive bombing, massive shelling, defoliation, search-and-destroy missions—an extension of American culture, military resources, and military structures. Given this, neither thought the other a very honorable enemy, which made it difficult to contain the war.

Common views on arms and national security among antagonists may be encouraged by a long rivalry and an extended arms race. Some Americans, and apparently some Russians, now hold that the superpowers share a unique perspective shaped by their competition, their arsenals, and their special responsibilities, and that this perspective facilitates arms control. But major critics of SALT (for allegedly giving the Russians too much) believe the Russians do not share our arms culture, that they seek war-winning not deterrence, strategic superiority not parity, and that detente and arms control negotiations are to them a continuation of the struggle, not its diminution. Therefore they are held to be unsuitable partners for true arms control.

A final point is that many perceived barriers to arms control also fall into this category. Analysts have pointed out the difficulties posed by asymmetries in nations' strategic postures. Different geographical locations, kinds of weapons, strategic doctrines, and military needs can make it very difficult for states to agree to equivalent restraints. All such difficulties are part of the general importance of "cultural" elements as the term is used here.[6]

Fourth Condition: Officials Perceive Arms Control Possibilities and Are Receptive

It is not enough that conditions make arms control possible. Someone must perceive this, and it must be someone in power. And that someone must be favorably disposed toward the kind of arms control that is possible. What factors condition the likelihood that this will happen?

One obstacle would be a leader's belief that military power and international political leverage are directly related, or an intellectual and emotional preference for war. I would guess that Sparta was not a hospitable environment for arms control ideas. Nazi Germany definitely was not. At the peak of the Cold War, both the United States and USSR were not. Arms control does not flourish when international relationships are viewed in black and white, where force and violence are revered, where a subtle appreciation of mutual interests among antagonists has not taken hold. The expectation that military strength directly creates power is traditional, often easy to sell in domestic politics, and not always very far from the truth. But it is not true. Deterrence is not necessarily enhanced by making the nation militarily less vulnerable and increasing its offensive potential. As "spiral theorists" fear, expanding military power invites either a corresponding buildup elsewhere or offsetting diplomatic combinations, as the Russians can testify. Alas, this notion, while false, is terribly tempting. A government infected by it will be interested only in arms control that ensures its ascendance. The idea takes its most appealing form as "negotiating from strength" via accumulation of sufficient "bargaining chips," for then departures from arms control are justified as contributing to it.

Another obstacle is a reluctance to accept external restraints on weapons decisions. Governmental antipathy toward outside control on anything is intensified when it comes to arms. One analyst has pointed out that "like state leaders elsewhere, Soviet leaders have been very conservative in preferring to rely on unilateral, non-negotiated decisions on armed forces rather than to accept the kind of arms control agreements that could be negotiated with rivals."[7] States must look to their own security and cannot ignore the fact that security has always been grounded on military power. To accept negotiated external restraints will seem to risk national security on a poor substitute for outright military strength.

Also relevant is that freedom to dispose of military might as one sees fit is the ultimate expression of independence for sovereign states. This is why deterrence is the most acceptable form of arms control. Its restraints on military power are derived from each government's military expression of its autonomy and without sacrificing the sinews of war in case war comes.

As a general rule, then, the less disturbing to continued reliance on arms an arms control idea is, the more likely it is to be implemented. The perfect arms control proposal, in terms of getting it accepted, would be one each party believed handed it a military advantage. More plausible but still unlikely would be a proposal that inhibits arms but which no party, despite exhaustive scrutiny, finds disadvantageous. Most plausible are proposals that carry no apparent disadvantages to the parties because they barely inhibit arms at all—test ban treaties that allow all necessary testing, SALT agreements that ban weapons the signers did not want to produce, treaties that bar nuclear weapons from spots where no one wishes to put them. In short, the chances national leaders will be receptive to arms control possibilities other than deterrence normally decline in proportion to the degree of meaningful arms constraints involved, and even with deterrence governments chafe under the restraints necessary to keep it stable.

Underlying all this is a still more important factor, the nature of the decision-makers involved. I have argued elsewhere that standard models of rationality are deficient for explaining how deterrence works.[8] Also inadequate are approaches to decision-making that refer mainly to unconscious factors—psychological features or organizational inertia, for instance. I have suggested a model that, for want of a better term, I label "sensible decision-making." Here the decision-maker is conscious and somewhat rational. He is, however, sensitive to his own and others' limitations, in that he realizes how psychological and organizational factors can be important, how impossible it is to calculate the probable consequences of actions with any precision, how chance can play a part, how information is often insufficient or incorrect. Although he is not paralyzed, he is sorely tempted to delay decisions in hopes of containing mistakes and is given to incremental modes of decision and action.

Where an official is not, by personality and experience, inclined to this sort of decision-making, circumstances often force him to be so. Partly it is the nature of the problems he faces. But is is also the dynamics of leader-selection processes and the press of bureaucratic, legislative, and electoral considerations that impose this kind of decision-making. Such decision-making is the norm, and it is within normal patterns of decision-making that deterrence is most likely to work. Departures from the norm, as in certain kinds of hostile confrontations or in the appearance of leaders not given to a cautious prudence, create much poorer conditions in which to attempt deterrence.

This analysis can be extended to other types of arms control. Arms control is far better suited to sensible decision-makers than the far more radical step of disarmament, and is therefore far more appealing. Arms control proposals can be designed so as to involve decisions and actions that are: (1) moderate in nature and immediate effects; (2) incremental in the nature of the changes involved; (3) unlikely to foreclose any important options; (4) not dependent on elaborate and precise cost-benefit calculations; and (5) rich in hedges against uncertain, possibly dangerous, consequences.

Any significant disarmament proposal will not be able to offer all these features—one or more will be missing. This makes disarmament a radical step, a sharp departure from normal practice. Such a venture into the unknown inevitably appears ill-advised in comparison with arms control.

Deterrence works, to a considerable extent, because the right sort of government is the target of the retaliatory threat. If we extend this view, arms control measures as a whole are favorably received primarily, maybe only, when "sensible" governments are involved. Governments interested in radical steps to adjust the world will hardly be intrigued by arms control possibilities; the Washington and London naval agreements were tossed overboard precisely when such governments appeared in Tokyo and Berlin. Conversely a government seriously interested in the radical departure of meaningful disarmament would view arms control efforts with distaste, as pap designed to make tolerable a fundamentally intolerable situation.

Fifth Condition: The Domestic Political Situation Is Favorable

Obviously, no government can undertake arms control without an adequate base of political support. It also helps if leaders perceive arms control as offering a variety of payoffs—a place in history, improved reelection chances, and the like. An additional requirement of some importance is that officials who favor arms control efforts contain and outmaneuver those who do not. Primarily a bureaucratic struggle in any political system, this spills over into electoral politics in democratic societies.

The most formidable obstacle here is that military professionals are unavoidably influential on national security matters, and many arms control measures are not consonant with their professional outlook or bureaucratic self interest. Even when it comes to deterrence, military officials are strongly inclined to seek such large forces as to undermine other arms control possibilities and to prefer war-winning postures to simpler (and cheaper) deterrence policies.

If arms control efforts are to succeed, ways around the difficulty must be found. High officials must endorse arms control for a start, but then a strategy to neutralize opposition must be devised. Some possibilities are illustrated by recent history. One tactic is to generate alternative expertise on national security matters. This is the rationale for having an ACDA, giving arms control proponents a bureaucratic base. The existence of an alternate perspective can give decision-makers more room to maneuver on arms control issues (although ACDA is not necessarily always opposed to the Pentagon on these matters). A sizable community of civilian experts who regularly think in arms control terms about national security matters can have a similar effect. One persistent concern about Soviet amenability to arms control arises from the evidence that strategic policy analysis in the USSR is dominated by the military, who also tightly control access to relevant information.

Another maneuver is to strike a deal with the opponents. The price for JCS support of the Test Ban Treaty in the Kennedy administration was a very vigorous underground nuclear testing program, speeding the development of MIRV. In exchange for DOD and JCS support for the SALT I agreements, the president agreed to vigorously pursue Trident, the B-1, and the cruise missile. A similar strategy emerged for SALT II, with money pumped into M-X and Trident, and ACDA openly stating that SALT II will be accompanied by substantial military expenditures to upgrade our forces. Although it is difficult to be certain, something similar seems to regularly occur in the USSR. Brezhnev has supported very high military spending in the midst of SALT efforts, and brought the minister of defense into the Politburo on the eve of Nixon's visit to Moscow.

This tactic is never more than partially successful, for such deals run counter to most kinds of arms control. They bring more weapons, or newer and better weapons, or the technological flexibility to devise many new weapons. Such results are used by opponents of arms control in other governments to heighten suspicion about it.

Next there is the tactic of isolating the opponents from the negotiations, to prepare a fait accompli. This was Kissinger's most notable device, implemented in various ways: develop multiple positions (building blocks) so that the Pentagon is forced into numerous positions instead of fixing on one; use the Dobrynin "back channel" to settle key issues; let the president personally negotiate key force levels. This only works under certain circumstances and then only once. The Carter administration has been plagued by numerous leaks on SALT II precisely because opponents did not want to get boxed in and leave the initiative with the president.

Sixth Condition: A Specific Occasion that Permits an Arms Control Decision

Wars, arms races, and weapons programs derive from complex decision processes, the flow of which is not readily manipulated. Yet arms control attempts just such manipulation and thus faces bureaucratic and political inertia. Powerful officials with arms control proclivities must seize on or contrive to create appropriate opportunities to bring arms control considerations to bear. Quite a few kinds of occasions lend themselves to arms control efforts, some political, others organizational, still others psychological in nature. Each has its limitations, which we can briefly explore.

One occasion is a change in the government. New leaders are entitled to try new policies and see things a bit differently; the inertia behind old policies is temporarily reduced. Of course, a new government may settle on policies less supportive of arms control. The Kennedy administration took a much tougher view of the military forces necessary for security than its predecessor, and Khrushchev's downfall saw the same outlook triumph in the Soviet Union.

A psychologically derived occasion is a major failure or near failure in arms control. Deterrence nearly collapsed in October 1962, which helped greatly in producing the test ban treaty the following year. India's "peaceful" nuclear explosion galvanized creation of the "suppliers' club." An accidental explosion of a nuclear weapon in a very public way would do wonders for arms control efforts. This is akin to having to wait until a dam bursts before it is possible to seriously inspect and repair dams.

Yet another occasion is the point of decision on developing a new weapons system, particularly when it represents a major generational shift or quantum leap. Relatively infrequent is the prospective system that will revolutionize military capacities, such as the atomic bomb. More common is a major system becoming obsolete, when a decision looms as to whether to replace it and if so with what. In either case it is possible to argue that a new system should not be developed. Oppenheimer took this course on the hydrogen bomb. The increasing vulnerability of Minuteman has been accompanied by proposals to abandon the triad by eliminating land-based ICBMs.

However, not developing certain weapons (in hopes others will not) is seldom attractive and often impossible. Research and development can be difficult to monitor, posing a serious verification problem. In addition, avoiding research and development forecloses unknown options as well as the one supposed to be eliminated. Also, it is politically easier to put off the hard decision about whether a weapon is worth having, leaving one able to say "this is not a decision to buy, just giving us an honest opportunity to see if we want to buy."

What really makes arms control at this point difficult is that there is seldom a clear decision to develop a weapon. As Herbert York has pointed out, weapons are extensions of knowledge and technology devised for other purposes. Others note that weapons development involves a stream of constantly adjusted decisions so that the resulting system bears little resemblance to what officials thought was authorized in the first place. Weapons systems are not made—they grow.[9]

Well then, what about at the point of a decision to deploy? Obviously, the more consequential the weapon the larger the arms control opportunity in most cases. Facing vast costs and an uncertain outcome, a government may well question the utility of going ahead. Examples are the B-1 and the ABM. With biological weapons it even proved possible to reverse prior decisions to deploy.

Still, it is hard to be optimistic. An arms race serves multiple purposes and is itself a political, not just a military, competition. This makes deployments just that much harder to contain. In addition, as development and testing draw to a close sunk costs are substantial, and (normally) the system works. It has the sweet glow of being on the frontiers of the state of the art. Many people now stand to benefit substantially from deployment. Thus a decision not to deploy is unlikely, which is why some analysts urge constraints on research and development establishments as the key to arms control.

That leaves the point of decision on using a weapon. We are brought almost by default to seek restraint on the use of weapons. Hence we have our reliance on deterrence and our efforts to stabilize it, plus the attention lavished on the control of escalation after hostilities have broken out. We now appreciate more fully the possible breaks in events, the thresholds and plateaus, around which to organize restraint amid crisis or war.

Despite the fact that a decision to actually use a weapon can offer a clear opportunity for arms control, the case of the atomic bomb in 1945 is not comforting. That was a decision made without full and careful consideration of possible consequences; it mainly flowed from what had gone before and from initial assumptions never reexamined.

The gravest difficulty associated with finding a suitable occasion is that usually the occasion must arise for several political systems at roughly the same time. Otherwise, the complications and drawbacks are multiplied. For instance, to lag in development, deployment, or use of a weapon and then get an offer to freeze the situation is to be invited to accept a permanent inferiority, obviously unattractive and not very saleable politically. It is particularly unattractive given the possibilities that an opponent may cheat or that the agreement may not last. On the other hand, the party ahead may find little virtue in an agreement that allows a rival to catch up, something also difficult to sell politically.

SALT agreements illustrate one way this problem can be managed. Judging from the impending agreements, the quantitative leader in delivery systems (the USSR) has conceded its lead in exchange for a chance to erase the qualitative lead of the United States (and, via MIRV, match our force-loadings figure). A similar trade-off, of quantitative leads, has formed the basis of NATO offers in the Mutual Force Reduction talks in Europe (trading U.S. nuclear weapons for Soviet ground forces). Those negotiations are, alas, rich in illustrations of the difficulties involved in arranging such deals.

Arms Control Prospects

Reviewing the six conditions necessary for arms control, we can find grounds for both optimism and pessimism about its prospects. The impact of technology is probably favorable on balance. Many contemporary weapons reinforce incentives for deterrence, because their use is feared and because they sustain the continuous technical possibility of a devastating surprise attack. The technology and the effects associated with nuclear weapons have facilitated certain kinds of controls and the verification of numerous agreements. While research and development constantly threaten to undermine the containment of weapons, progress in the technology of monitoring and verification has thus far more than kept pace.[10] Many advanced systems remain sufficiently complex and expensive to discourage governments from developing them.

The international political situation was favorable, but it is now becoming far less so. The superpowers reached rough strategic parity some time ago, and their rivalry lasted long enough to take the sharp edges off their hostility. Over the years they extended their protection to other states in a credible way, and their considerable control over many states allowed some containment of weapons and wars. However, this relatively favorable era for many kinds of arms control is slipping away. As an adjunct to the status quo, arms control is undermined when existing international arrangements begin to come apart.[11] Contemporary arms control structures and the thinking behind them are largely the product of a mature superpower competition in a fairly bipolar world. Where that bipolarity continues—in strategic arsenals—we see some successful negotiations, eliminating uncertainties that would otherwise gravely complicate strategic planning. But other arms control efforts look more like attempts to retain bipolarity or to limit the effects of its passing, attempts temporarily successful at best.

For too long it has been anticipated that proliferation would erode bipolarity, when it is the passing of bipolarity that breeds proliferation. A less structured, less superpower-dominated world is one of greater uncertainty and insecurity, particularly when the credibility of extended deterrence by the superpowers has declined. More interest in arms, including nuclear weapons, is inevitable as states seek arms control via enhanced national capacities for deterrence. For much of the world arms are multiplying, growing in expense, and increasing in potential destructiveness. Efforts at deterrence flourish at the expense of other types of arms control. The question is, can a relatively stable system ultimately emerge out of this?

In terms of the third, fourth, and fifth conditions, the possibilities for arms control appear better. The United States and USSR now have more compatible arms and security cultures, with mutual understanding facilitated by negotiations and agreements. There seem both to be a broader appreciation in many capitals that international influence does not simply grow out of the barrel of a gun and a reluctant acceptance of interdependence even on some sensitive arms decisions. Very significant is the fact that officials in many governments have a sophisticated awareness of the possibilities for arms control. Contributing to this has been the emergence of arms control as a vigorous analytical field. Both have helped create a climate of broad public support in various countries. Since Khrushchev there has been no superpower government strongly inclined to radical departures and highly risky maneuvers, that is, these governments have been "sensible." With regard to developing countries, however, Cuban adventures and revolutionary turmoil in such places as Iran make for less confidence that this is the case.

A series of opportunities for arms control decisions have appeared, many at roughly the same time, for the parties involved. The superpowers have been on a plateau with respect to the nature of major weapons for the past 30 years—simply refining their nuclear and thermonuclear weapons, bombers, fighters, tanks and small arms. The one great change, the development of missiles, was foreshadowed by the V-2 and occurred so long ago that it has become integrated and understood. Thus, opportunities for arms limitation have not been associated with preventing quantum leaps but rather with curtailing limited advances and modest proliferations. These are inherently small opportunities for small achievements, not a bad way to describe the arms restraints we have had.

Should the relevant factors permit further success in arms control, there is still the larger question of whether it can ever be a reliable solution to the problem of arms and war. The answer would seem to be that it cannot. It is like a tourniquet for a bad wound—at best it limits the damage and may facilitate treatment, and if not used correctly it makes things worse.

In its defense, we must note the possibility that sustained arms control efforts and successes could move us a long way toward security communities in which the resort to force is abandoned. However, it has offsetting flaws. One is the friction between deterrence and other arms control measures. Deterrence is enormously expensive, at the nuclear or the conventional level. It is not easily implemented without setting off spirals of suspicion, insecurity, and conflict. Hence it is likely to encourage proliferation, vertical and, eventually, horizontal. It often magnifies the problem of accidental or inadvertent use of weapons. Finally, by encouraging proliferation, deterrence markedly increases the potential costs of its failures. A world relying heavily on deterrence is an inhospitable one for other sorts of

Arms Control: A Theoretical Perspective

arms control. Thus, we are entitled to be pessimistic about the chances for nuclear nonproliferation or the slowing of arms sales. And arms limitations are too often circumvented by clever maneuvering within the restraints—producing "pocket" battleships in an earlier day, or a more potent missile in the same size package and silo today.

Hence more reservations are in order about continuing to rely for security in the international system on the superpowers' enlarging capabilities for destruction. Arms cut-backs could help, and in strategic weapons there could be substantial cuts with no resulting first-strike incentives. This might take us toward a broad security community that would permit further cuts. But arms control often conflicts directly with such a course, most obviously in deterrence. It largely rests on the notion that weapons and conflicts can be sufficiently contained almost indefinitely. As Fred Iklé has said, we assume nuclear immortality, which helps sustain the will to retain arms. There are parallels at the level of conventional forces. Arms control touches on only the peripheral features of an arms competition.

Finally, in an era preoccupied with arms control, meaningful arms cuts get ruled out as a large step into unknown territory. They would mean taking risks and foreclosing some military options for limiting those risks. This is not the behavior of "sensible" governments. Leaders both willing and able to gamble do not often appear, and when they do the gambles may be for war rather than for peace. For the cautious decision-maker, "it is one thing to say that we have far more than enough weapons for deterrence, but who is to say—and to persuade others—how far that number can reasonably drop before deterrence is in fact diminished? Who wants to rock the boat?"[12]

In a way we are trapped. A single government willing to gamble, by ordinary standards, can create a war, but it would take several such governments to bring serious arms reduction. Hence the paradox of arms control in our time. It manages arms while sensible governments exist, but it facilitates (or fails to prevent) the stockpiling of arms for use in war generated by the eventual government that is not sensible. The security it offers is temporary at best.

Notes

1. Left off this list is arms control as a political barometer. See Thomas Larson, *Disarmament and Soviet Policy, 1964-1968* (Englewood Cliffs, N.J. Prentice-Hall, 1969), p. 3; Morton Halperin and Dwight Perkins, *Communist China and Arms Control* (New York: Praeger, 1965), p. 136. Also left out are domestic political uses of arms control.

2. As in William Ansberry, *Arms Control and Disarmament: Success or Failure?* (Berkeley, Calif.: McCutchan Publishing, 1969), pp. 2, 7.

3. See John Pfeiffer, *The Emergence of Society* (New York: McGraw-Hill, 1977), pp. 31-34, 61-63, 86-94.

4. On parallels in conventional weapons, see James Foster, "The Future of Conventional Arms Control," in John Endicott and Roy Stafford, eds., *American Defense Policy* (Baltimore: Johns Hopkins University Press, 1977), pp. 127-137.

5. Hedley Bull, *The Control of the Arms Race* (New York: Praeger, 1965), pp. 10-11; William Epstein, *The Last Chance* (New York: The Free Press, 1976), pp. 120-124; Paul Warnke, "SALT II: Toward A More Secure World," speech before the Overseas Writers Club, Washington, January 6, 1978, distributed by ACDA.

6. See Dennis Ross, "Rethinking Soviet Strategic Policy: Inputs and Implications," ACIS Working Paper no. 5 (UCLA Center For Arms Control and International Security, June 1977); also Paul Doty et al., "The Race to Control Nuclear Arms," *Foreign Affairs,* October 1976, pp. 123-126.

7. Larson, *Disarmament*, p. 97.

8. Patrick Morgan, *Deterrence, A Conceptual Analysis* (Beverly Hills, Calif.: Sage Publications, 1977).

9. See Herbert York, *Race to Oblivion* (New York: Simon and Schuster, 1970); Herbert York and G. Allen Greb, "Strategic Reconnaissance," *Bulletin of the Atomic Scientists,* April 1977, p. 41; J.A. Stockfish, *Plowshares into Swords* (New York: Mason and Lipscomb, 1973); Graham Allison and Frederic Morris, "Armaments and Arms Control: Exploring the Determinants of Military Weapons," in Franklin Long and George Rathjens, *Arms, Defense Policy, and Arms Control* (New York: W.W. Norton, 1976), pp. 99-129.

10. For the view that research often contributes to arms control see John Steinbruner, "Beyond Rational Deterrence," *World Politics*, 29, no. 2 (January 1976):242-243; or Albert Wohlstetter, "Racing Forward? Or Ambling Back?" *Survey* 22, no. 3/4 (Summer/Autumn 1976):211-217.

11. See Hedley Bull, "Arms Control and World Order," *International Security* 1, no. 1 (Summer 1976):3-16.

12. Bernard Brodie, "On the Objectives of Arms Control," *International Security* 1, no. 1 (Summer 1976):28.

14. American Approaches to Military Strategy, Arms Control, and Disarmament: A Critique of the Postwar Experience

Lincoln P. Bloomfield

Preface

Whatever else the United States has in common with other states, three singular qualities make its arms and arms control policies close to unique:

1. The United States of 1945 abandoned a century-and-a-half dream of isolation to assume primary responsibility for organizing a coalition against what many regarded as an emergent menace to international peace and stability. The confrontation was magnified by the fact that the USSR was the only other country in the world possessing, not only great power, but also a self-image as not just another state, but (like the United States) a universally valid idea in action.

2. For 20 years after World War II the United States had preeminence in a new weapon whose astronomical destructive power altered the very idea of military strategy, but that preeminence declined.

3. The American "way of war" (as Earl Ravenal christened it) has traditionally preached military victory as the only legitimate object of war, fastidiously rejecting the classic view of Carl von Clausewitz that "war is nothing but a continuation of political intercourse by other means."[1]

The American "Way of War"

The United States historically was spared the subculture of a military aristocracy based on a unified general staff. American thinking remained happily immune from the romanticizing of violence of some nineteenth-century forerunners of twentieth-century German pathology. Historically, few Americans shared the spirit of Field Marshal Helmuth von Moltke's declaration that "war is an integral part of God's ordering of the universe," or Friederich Nietzsche's even more egregious machismo: "Freedom means

---

This chapter was written while the author was professor of political science at the Massachusetts Institute of Technology and in no way reflects the policies of the U.S. government.

that the manly instincts which delight in war and victory dominate over other instincts, for example, over those of "pleasure." . . . The free man is a *warrior*."[2]

Americans typically spread a moralistic gloss over war, as when the influential early American strategist Captain (later Admiral) Alfred Thayer Mahan allowed that "the purpose of military power is to provide time for moral ideas to take root."

In the same spirit Woodrow Wilson in World War I and Franklin Roosevelt in World War II—even Harry Truman in Korea and Lyndon Johnson in Vietnam—explained U.S. military involvement in what Hans Morgenthau and George Kennan would call "legalistic-moralistic" terms.[3]

War was seen not as acquisitive, but as punitive and reformist, although the United States in fact fought British, Mexicans, Spaniards, and Indians for the unvarnished acquisition of territory. By World War I, American leaders felt that military strategy should be focused on "pure military objectives." This meant defeating enemy forces in the field and destroying or crippling the opponent's industrial war-making power. Thus President Wilson in World War I could insist on self-determination for captured lands as a basic war aim. Thus Franklin Roosevelt could insist that "political" questions wait till the war was over, usually to the despair of his British ally Churchill (and doubtless to the amazement of his Soviet ally Stalin). The U.S. posture was not without moral merit, placing as it did the lives of soldiers above postwar strategic advantage, even while others did not. United States experiences in Korea and Vietnam bear out the conclusions of a former Defense Department official:

> The entire American mode of defense is not that of a steadily committed global imperial power, continuously maintaining its magnetic field of force over the whole strategic universe. Geography, and the circumstances of the founding and building of this nation, have—for better or worse—endowed us with a "fortress" mentality. We give battle if necessary and when provoked. We are likely to use "leverage" on our ally, to secure certain reforms that will make our temporary alliance with him more palatable to our sensibilities. We will pursue the battle to an unconditional—sometimes unnecessary—outcome; or we will abandon the field when it suits our purposes—when we think we have done "enough."[4]

The Global Context

The development of U.S. strategic thinking since World War II has taken place against three elements that combined to ensure ambiguity in policy. First was the stark reality of a powerful adversary state. Against the USSR's

A Critique of the Postwar Experience

perceived menace the United States reacted, at least in Europe, in historically familiar ways for the leader of a status quo coalition.

Second, the mounting confrontation took place against a backdrop of global turbulence, including interstate and civil war. Many parties to conflict became linked to the superpowers by networks of treaty relationships. Others played the superpowers against one another for support. Temptation incessantly arose for great power intervention.

But the third reality was equally compelling. Nuclear weapons were not just new points along the familiar continuum of explosive power. The ability to annihilate entire centers of population and industry, followed by lethal radioactive fallout, was unlike anything known before by humankind. The details are so well known that one example suffices: a single U.S. nuclear-powered missile-firing submarine can deliver more destructive power on to a range of targets than that used by all sides in all of World War II.

From 1945 to 1949 the United States had a monopoly of nuclear weaponry, although the numbers were small, and the stockpiles, we now know, astonishingly vulnerable. From 1949, when the Soviets shocked the West by exploding a nuclear device years before it was predicted by most observers, both sides began to be visibly deterred. From 1954 or so a general war would have involved thermonuclear weapons 10 to 20 times more powerful than fission bombs. From the mid-1950s on, nuclear strategy became complicated by the entry of Britain, then France, then China into the lists of nuclear weapons powers.

The virtually total damage done to Hiroshima and Nagasaki, dwarfed by successor weapons, meant that while the threat of nuclear weapons might be useful for blackmail (although there was little evidence for this), their actual use was hard to relate to any rational political purpose. This is doubtless why, in a period of unprecedented global tension over fundamental issues, World War III has not taken place, and why early predictions of a linear increase in the number of nuclear weapons states have proven false.

Some Americans today fear that the Soviet Union, despite the disproportionality of nuclear weapons, contemplates fighting and "winning" a nuclear war. Soviet military journals fuel this fear by expounding detailed doctrines of the winnability of such a war, doctrines seemingly convergent with observed deployments and posturings of Soviet forces on the ground.[5]

Offsetting this is evidence that Soviet rulers are almost paranoidally defense-minded, traumatized by previous invasions, and obsessed by the China threat to the East. Nevertheless, Soviet policy still runs high risks in the nuclear era. Expansion of its influence-seeking, backed by increasingly "projectable" power, makes conflicts in the Middle East and southern Africa potentially explosive.

Living with Doctrinal Ambiguity

American strategic doctrines from 1945 to the present reflect the triple reality of unusable nuclear arsenals, superpower competition and tension, and global turbulence. Not surprisingly therefore, each iteration of American doctrine concerning strategic weapons systems and military deployments has embodied concepts that were at root contradictory. Every effort to restate military doctrine has had to take into account both the possibility of war with the Soviet Union, and the likelihood that such a war would entail destruction of a magnitude that removed it from any recognizable calculus of costs and benefits.

Three events empirically confirmed the contradiction. First, when a proxy superpower war did break out, in Korea in 1950, President Truman inquired as to the size and location of Soviet nuclear stockpiles—and then ordered U.S. air and ground forces into action in a war that at times resembled not World War II but World War I. President Eisenhower, on the other hand, is widely believed to have implied a nuclear threat to push armistice negotiations off dead center in 1953. But on the one occasion during the war itself when the White House even mentioned the word "nuclear," British Prime Minister Clement Attlee rushed to Washington to secure assurances that the United States had no intention of using nuclear weapons. In fact, given the Korean terrain and form of warfare, it made no military sense whatever, apart from the worldwide moral revulsion that was certain to follow. (It might also be recalled that Eisenhower consistently argued for a generalized "nonrecourse-to-force" doctrine).

Second was the formulation by U.S. Secretary of State John Foster Dulles in 1954 of the so-called massive retaliation doctrine. The concept was entirely consistent with the view that great power war was synonymous with Armageddon; Dulles simply put that truth into words with his customary gracelessness. But he soon had to deny that he meant to imply that any outbreak of hostilities, however trivial or ambiguous, would launch the U.S. Strategic Air Command bombers on Soviet targets. The whole episode gave deterrence a bad name, although it clearly represented the dominant strain of both military and civilian thinking in the first years of the nuclear age.

A third clue was to be found in the white paper issued in 1955 by the British Defense Minister, Churchill's son-in-law, Duncan Sandys. In an historically unique official pronunciamento by a great power, he acknowledged flatly that, faced with thermonuclear weapons, Her Majesty's government could no longer give the British people the traditional assurance that they would survive a major war.

The 1962 Cuban missile crisis, it is generally agreed, was the closest the superpowers have come to a nuclear holocaust. It is widely believed that U.S. nuclear (and local conventional) superiority was what enabled President

Kennedy to face down Soviet Premier Khrushchev. But President Kennedy's chief security adviser McGeorge Bundy, in full recollection of that and other hair-raising crises in the 1960s, later spelled out in some detail the gulf that persists between those who "game out" nuclear exchanges, on the one hand, and real-world American (and Soviet) leaders who on the evidence have no intention of being led to the use of even one nuclear weapon:

> There is an enormous gulf between what political leaders really think about nuclear weapons and what is assumed in complex calculations of relative "advantage" in simulated strategic warfare. . . . In sane politics . . . there is no level of superiority which will make a strategic first strike between the two great states anything but an act of utter folly.[6]

Indeed all postwar presidents, and all Soviet political leaders starting with Malenkov in 1953, shortly after Stalin died, have publicly reiterated their conviction that nuclear war would spell mutual suicide. How can one square that with Eisenhower's and Kennedy's implied threat of the use of nuclear weapons in the midst of acute crisis? Or with Khrushchev's public invocation forty-odd times of Soviet nuclear might between 1954 and 1964? The answer is two-fold. First, so long as there are crises and deliverable nuclear arsenals, there is a finite possibility of a fateful decision to launch, however irrational that decision both in prospect and retrospect. This finite possibility has furnished the most compelling argument for strategic nuclear arms control and, to the extent possible, disarmament.

The second reason is that Clausewitz and Mao were right: some strategically inclined leaders still do consider war and politics, force and policy, to be flip sides of the same coin. In that sense nuclear weapons are theoretically "usable," but not for their explosive effect, which is insanely disproportionate to any recognizable political objective. They are arguably usable for the "explosion" they create, as it were, inside the heads of people who are threatened.

Many strategists, rather than drawing revolutionary or utopian conclusions from the ineluctable facts of nuclear power, have struggled to adapt to the stark reality of nuclear weaponry the traditional categories of strategy. A notable example was Henry Kissinger, who in 1956 sought to update Clausewitzian principles of proportional rationality to accommodate the new reality of disproportionate nuclear weaponry;

> The doctrinal challenge of the nuclear age is therefore the ability to use force with discrimination and to establish political goals in which the question of national survival is not involved in every issue.
>
> The goal of war can no longer be military victory as we have known it. Rather it should be the attainment of certain specific political conditions which are fully understood by the opponent.[7]

The implication was that nuclear war could be limited, although Kissinger subsequently had to amend his views of limited nuclear war to take account of the obvious irrationality of actual use (and Korea showed that the nuclear age would feature limited nonnuclear wars).

In the early 1960s the Kennedy administration adopted a strategy it christened "flexible response." This was intended to equip the United States to be able to respond to Soviet (or Chinese) provocation without going directly to Armageddon à la Dulles. It rested on the assumption that there were possible thresholds between conventional tank and infantry warfare on the one hand, and Neville Shute's scenario of global human annihilation in his book *On the Beach*.[8]

Alongside this conceptual shift was another at the strategic level. Secretary of Defense Robert S. McNamara, in a famous speech at Ann Arbor, Michigan, in June 1962, enunciated a new twist on the massive retaliation theme. The superpowers had hitherto targeted their bombs (and increasingly, missiles) on population centers, chiefly because accuracies involving, say, a .5-mile error ruled out "surgical" strikes on smaller industrial or military targets. McNamara argued that military targeting should be approached as "in the past," that is, strategic weapons should be targeted on the enemy forces rather than on its civilian population. In this way nuclear warfare, should it happen, could be made to look much more like old-fashioned warfare in which armies went after armies and spared the civilians.

The conceptual struggle among defense intellectuals to adapt continues to the present day. During the Ford administration, Defense Secretary James Schlesinger brought into the open the continuing in-house discussion of the whole range of options, including what came to be christened "war-fighting strategies." The theme continued into the Carter administration with debate about using enhanced radiation weapons—the so-called neutron bombs—to stop Soviet tank attacks.

In both cases, as in the previous decades, the issue was how to make it seem plausible that the United States would resort to nuclear weapons to rebuff an attack by militarily-stronger conventional forces in Europe. "Plausible" implied that it was possible to reduce the probability that use of small tactical nuclear weapons would inevitably lead to intercontinental strikes on each other's homelands.

The Deep Paradox of Deterrence

The latter point is crucial to an understanding of the problems of U.S. strategic concepts in the nuclear age. Nuclear weapons are suicidal; but to keep anyone from initiating mutual suicide, you must appear seriously willing to commit suicide yourself.

Military strategy has for 30 years been based on this conceptual dilemma. Deterrence rests on a theory derived from principles of human psychology. At its essence, if you want to deter or dissuade someone from taking an action inimical to you or your allies, you must make him believe that you will retaliate in return, inflicting intolerable damage on him even if it kills you in the process.

From this near-metaphysical equation came the whole succession of alternate strategies for the United States between 1954 and the present. Deterrence theory lies at the heart of all the other principles shaping U.S. nuclear strategy. It provides the doctrinal basis for all military programs aimed at maintaining a "secure retaliatory second-strike capability" that will function regardless of a first-strike a mad enemy might launch against us. This logic undergirds the late 1950s argument for hardened underground ICBM firing sites, the 1960s argument for keeping some bombers in the air at all times, the 1970s argument for building new mobile/hidden missiles and cruise missiles, and the case throughout for going to sea where (at least so far) U.S. nuclear-powered missile-firing submarines can lie mostly undetected, able to launch a retaliatory blow regardless of what the other side does first.

Many in the peace movement deplore the strategy of deterrence, along with containment and high defense budgets. But the concept has much to commend it, so long as nuclear weapons are going to be around. I have already suggested that fear of the consequences of nuclear warfare has several times prevented World War III. The weakness of the deterrence idea lies not in its immorality, but in its inner logic. For deterrence rests on a subjective belief, conviction, or perception regarding the likelihood of the other side doing something harmful to you even if it kills him. This special logic requires that each side believe that no matter how irrational, even suicidal, there is a finite probability that the other, if sufficiently pressed, may actually try to fight a nuclear war. Both sides may know in their bones that there can be no winners (regardless of the fretful attempts by military theologians on both sides to redefine "victory" as survival of a few socialists or capitalists who can "take over"). Nevertheless, to deter you must look and sound as if you are prepared to go through with an irrational and inhumane response to a genocidal attack. Your threat must be plausible and credible, although, given the inherent illogic, it is unclear if anyone is wholly committed. But the trick is not to make your opponent certain this will happen. It is to leave him uncertain that it will not.

The flexible response debates in the 1960s concerning the European theater exemplified the dilemma. United States strategy became governed by a concept of warfare in which the stationing of several thousand tactical nuclear weapons would convince Moscow that the United States might respond with nuclear warfare if they invaded Western Europe. But NATO had also to plan a conventional response to reinforce the hope that a theater war would not escalate. Conceptually and verbally, it was the best of both worlds. The Soviets would be deterred if not by increased conventional forces, then, as a last resort, by U.S. "tacnukes" and would not attack. But if they did, and deterrence had failed, the war could somehow be contained. Left even more uncertain—and thus equally deterring—was the possibility that in a high crisis the "firebreak" between theater and intercontinental nuclear weapons could not be preserved.

United States strategy was not made in a vacuum. The Soviet Union by the mid-1960s had a respectable deliverable ICBM force and increasing numbers of missile-firing submarines. Soviet leaders were talking proudly of the "changed correlation of forces" in the world. This meant that Washington's ability to deter attacks on allies became markedly less credible. French President Charles de Gaulle worried publicly about erosion of the hitherto unquestioned willingness of the United States to respond to a Soviet conventional military thrust with nuclear weapons. In addition, weapons we called "tactical" were accurately perceived by our West German allies as strategic so far as their own homeland was concerned.

But doctrine alone does not drive strategy. The other driving force is that not-so-silent third party to the strategic arms race: mutual technological advance. By the start of the 1980s, the inexorable pace of technological change left the parties continuously lagging behind in their political and diplomatic efforts to cap the nuclear (and conventional) arms races.

At the level of intercontinental weaponry, both the numbers and the technology were rapidly producing an unprecedented situation in which, with targeting accuracies on both sides down to a few hundred meters, the U.S. land-based Minuteman ICBM force would soon be vulnerable to the new heavy Soviet missiles. Even with the SALT agreements, 2,250 strategic systems on both sides entailed numbers of deliverable warheads that were incomprehensible. If even one warhead launched against one city was, in former National Security Advisor McGeorge Bundy's words, too much for any sane leader to contemplate, the nuclear arsenals of the early 1980s exceeded by orders of magnitude the numbers of important targets on earth and moved strategy from the perilous to the absurd.

So far as U.S. "general purpose forces", that is, army, navy, and air forces, were concerned, the negative U.S. experience with military intervention in peripheral regions did not keep the United States for long on a slimming diet. After Vietnam the U.S. defense program shrank to fit the scenario of "1.5" instead of "2.5" wars. But like so many other revolutionary effects of the 1973 Middle East War and its accompanying oil embargo and price rise, a new U.S. military requirement involving "vital interests" now exists in the Persian Gulf backed by mobile quick-reaction forces. The U.S. is now moving to what looks like a "1.75" wars strategy.

A Critique of the Postwar Experience

At a theater level, contradictions in the very notion of nuclear warfare led to a search for still newer concepts and doctrines. What emerged was in fact more of the same—renewed emphasis on a wide range of options, from war-fighting, city-avoidance strategies, to improved conventional defense through reinforcement and resupply capabilities along with the "precision guided munitions" (PGMs) that appear to give a new edge to the defense, along with longer-range "theater nuclear forces."

New Challenges to Deterrence

The intolerable nature of nuclear confrontation was brought home to leaders and people alike by the Cuban missile crisis. Many assumed that, given their deep concern about nuclear war, the Soviets would pursue a strategy of assured destruction, resulting in a situation of "mutual assured destruction" (MAD). Instead, they seem to pursue a more traditional posture of "offensive defense," which carries a worrying implication of routinizing the ability to fight a nuclear war should it break out. Few argue that any Russian wants war. (Like Bismarck, the answer of Communist leaders when asked if they want war is, in effect: "Certainly not—what I want is victory!") But some western defense experts argue that the Soviets have a built-in plan that assumes nuclear wars can be fought and won.

This apparent, if not real, asymmetry between doctrines has created a new crisis both in U.S.-Soviet relations and in the U.S. domestic dialogue about national security. The logic of MAD calls for no more force than is necessary to ride out a first-strike and retaliate lethally. Secretary McNamara levelled U.S. land-based launchers at 1,054 (where they remain), and Nixon-Kissinger accepted some larger Soviet numbers in SALT I in 1972 with the thought that it mattered little if both sides were massively deterred. But this logic, reinforced with a succession of labels for overall parity ranging from "sufficiency" to "rough equivalence," could not allay the fears of Americans like Senator Henry Jackson who worried that the U.S. had lost its "superiority." If the Soviets for their part demanded "equal security," the U.S. in SALT II (goaded by Senator Jackson) demanded equal numbers. Even that was not enough to offset the nostalgia for lost U.S. superiority, and SALT II became a divisive domestic U.S. issue.

Some would argue that mutual self-destruction deprives superiority of any real meaning. But recent arguments for vastly increased U.S. defense efforts postulated Soviet use of its superiority in a few years to blackmail the United States into letting Moscow work its will on our friends. The Committee on the Present Danger argued that U.S. ICBM vulnerability, plus Soviet civil defense preparations, would by the early-to-mid 1980s actually permit Moscow to launch a counterforce "surgical" strike against silo-emplaced missiles, killing "only a few million" Americans and then daring Washington to retaliate against either empty Soviet silos or Soviet cities—in which case U.S. cities, hitherto spared, would be destroyed, while Soviet cities, all evacuated, would minimize their casualties. This macabre scenario is argued on the ground that the Soviets do not shrink from actually fighting a nuclear war.[9]

There is no doubt that some Soviet military writers (like some in the United States) believe that, even though war may be unprecedentedly destructive, it can be "won," with significant political benefits.

This analysis of Soviet intentions is, in my opinion, convincingly undermined by new evidence and interpretation of Soviet materials. Raymond Garthoff, long-time expert on Soviet military affairs, in a thoroughly researched recent study has supplied a potent refutation.[10] Along with adducing important Soviet military writings taking the contrary argument, Garthoff points out the special Soviet need for ideological morale to be sustained through such approaches. It should also be pointed out that the argument "that the Russians are superior and coming" rarely if ever mentions China, toward which, conservatively, 20 percent of Soviet military efforts are directed. Nor does it consider the grave internal security problem the multiethnic Soviet empire would face in a general war.

To this one must add that few Americans who have actually observed at first hand the Soviet Union believe any Soviet leader would contemplate a new war with other than horror. Unlike the United States, Russia was invaded six times in the last 170 years. Its losses in World War II—and the continuous exposure of Soviet youth to that history—supply an equally compelling alternative hypothesis that they will avoid war like the plague, while arming themselves massively against any contingent treachery, betrayal, or hostile act by those they have for a half-century predicted would attack them. But the Soviet leaders perpetually baffle and often frighten the West by adventurous, risky policies and mixed doctrines, which, if taken at face value, could undermine the fragile mutual conviction that no matter what the provocation, nuclear warfare is not a thinkable policy option.

Americans believe themselves, correctly in my view, to be generally pacific and defensive in their military dispositions. But the perception of others underscores that U.S. defense also acts in fact on the Latin proverb *si vis pacem, para bellum* (if you want peace, prepare for war). The perceptions each side holds of the other are thus dangerously deformed.

Steps to Control the Process

Efforts to disarm nations precede the nuclear age. Nuclear disarmament was proposed as early as 1946 in the U.S. Acheson-Lilienthal Plan. But it is

A Critique of the Postwar Experience

only since 1955 that negotiations became serious, since 1963 that they became active, and since 1972 that they focused on the central danger to the planet.

From 1945 to 1955 the United States strove to adjust itself to the world role it had finally resolved to play. It sought ways to adapt both to the new and chilling "close encounters" with the Soviet Union and to the Promethean nuclear fire it had unleashed in the closing days of the war. For a decade, the UN listened to a sterile and often venomous argument between the West, which argued for disarmament based on verified numbers and international control of nuclear weapons, and the Soviets, who called for "banning the [U.S.] bomb," and an unverified "one-third cut" in all armed forces.

In 1955 Moscow brought to the negotiations something akin to a reversal of its previous propagandistic positions, accepting many key Western points. But the United States, by then set on its course of containment of perceived Soviet expansionism, refused the gambit. Thus occurred again one of a tragic series of lost opportunities for which both sides can take ample blame over the postwar years.

In the early 1960s, Moscow proposed a plan (grounded in early Leninesque doctrine) for what it termed "general and complete disarmament." The U.S., with much skepticism, responded with a "Western plan" calling for building up the UN's veto-free security capabilities *pari passu* with each stage of weapons-scrapping. General and complete disarmament has since become an article of faith with many governments and an object of periodic lip-service by the superpowers. It must be confessed that, given the intensity of political warfare not only between East and West, but increasingly between the newly independent countries of the south and the advanced industrial nations of the north, the likelihood of a fully disarmed world order seemed increasingly unreal.

What did become far more real than anyone had thought possible was a series of agreements, initially between Moscow and Washington, but eventually involving up to the entire family of nations, on specific issues, above all on military topics, where no nation had yet reached such an advantageous position that agreement was preempted.

Over the past 20 years a number of arms control accords have been negotiated among a shifting constellation of nations. These include the Antarctic treaty (1959), the Limited Test Ban Treaty (1963), the Hot-Line accord (1963), the Outer Space Treaty (1967), protocols regulating nuclear weapons in Latin American (1967), the Non-Proliferation Treaty (1968), the Seabed Treaty (1971), the Convention on bacteriological weapons (1972), and SALT I (1972).

A new stage of arms control was reached with agreement in Moscow, as part of the 1972 summit, to limit to two the number of antiballistic missile sites (later amended to one site); this accord aborted a portentous (and costly) new activity that threatened gravely to upset the delicate equation of mutual deterrence. In the accompanying "Interim Agreement," for the first time limits were set to further expansion of the strategic systems on both sides.

The painful and well-known history of the negotiation of SALT II, starting with the Brezhnev-Ford agreement at Vladivostok in November 1974, illustrates three important factors in the control of arms that tend to make each new step more difficult than the last. First, the Soviets have continued their steady increase in the rate of defense spending, pushing hard in the interval to develop new systems Americans find particularly threatening, notably superheavy MIRVed missiles capable of wiping out substantial elements of the U.S. land-based force, as well as active anti-satellite experiments, Warsaw Pact buildups, selective encryption of missile telemetry and a fast-growing offensive navy. Some find this malevolent; others see it as a typical Soviet characteristic of pushing as hard as they can against (but within) the limits of any agreement. The United States for its part has upgraded elements of all services, reshaped important NATO defenses, and, in FY 1980, modestly increased defense spending.

Second, linkage is inevitable between arms control and detente. The then newly elected President Carter was warned in the fall of 1976 that Moscow was worried about his antidetente campaign rhetoric. Right after the election Moscow advised visiting Americans (including this one) that Mr. Carter show his desire for continuity by sending SALT II to the Senate for ratification, then negotiating for real reductions. Instead, Mr. Carter chose to try a bold new approach that proposed deep cuts in strategic weaponry—this evidently signaled to Moscow that he was not serious. The Soviets set the process back badly in 1980 in Afghanistan.

Third, in the years that SALT II was not ratified, both sides were increasingly confronted with the accelerating output of their inventive weapons laboratories. The interval thus saw the new Soviet Backfire bomber, new generation Soviet heavy missiles, growing Soviet antisatellite capabilities, U.S. "neutron bomb" development, the superaccurate Mark 12A U.S. warhead, accelerated U.S. development of cruise missiles for every military environment, and American consideration of plans for "multiple basing" to conceal its own new generation of ICBMs. Some thoughtful critics worried that moving toward ground-based mobile missiles would entail huge costs, put into question SALT II's verifiability, and inevitably spur the Soviets to copy us in the name of "equality," thus guaranteeing a new threat in a few years. But others felt progress required equality, and also a *sense* of equality, for *both* sides.

Summary

The nuclear arms race is not based on a simple misunderstanding. Rather, it reflects profound ideological and political differences and as a result stimulates moves—political, economic, and military—that are inevitably interpreted as deeply involving the vital security interests of the United States and Soviet Union, as well as their allies. Under the circumstances genuine arms control has to be seen as an extraordinary—and promising—exception to painfully familiar patterns of age-old behavior between nations in conflict.

But given the technological dynamic, which, as President Eisenhower foresaw in his farewell address, acts more and more as an autonomous force almost independent of the will of political leadership, it can perhaps be said for the first time that there are three parties to the conflict: the Russians, the Americans, and potentially genocidal nuclear arms. We must have learned that no strategic "fix" is likely to give greater real security to either side. Nothing short of a hitherto undisplayed degree of political will is able to deflect the entrenched power of technological, industrial, and bureaucratic forces on both sides away from a permanent—and perilous—spiral.

Notes

1. Karl von Clausewitz, *War, Politics and Power* (Chicago: H. Regnery, 1962), pp. 255-256. (cf. Mao Tse-Tung: "Politics is war without bloodshed, war is politics with bloodshed.") *Selected Writings*, p. 227.

2. Friederich Nietzsche, *Twilight of the Idols, or How One Philosophizes with a Hammer* (Berlin:1889).

3. See particularly George F. Kennan, *American Diplomacy, 1900-1950* (Chicago: University of Chicago, 1951), and Hans J. Morgenthau, *In Defense of the National Interest* (New York: Knopf, 1951).

4. Earl Ravenal, "Consequences of the End Game in Vietnam," Reprinted by permission from *Foreign Affairs*, July 1975. Copyright 1975 by Council on Foreign Relations, Inc.

5. See the many citations in Raymond L. Garthoff, "Mutual Deterrence and Strategic Arms Limitation in Soviet Policy," *International Security*, Summer 1978.

6. "To Cap the Volcano," 48, no. 1 (October, 1969):1-20. Reprinted by permission from *Foreign Affairs*, October 1969. Copyright 1969 by Council on Foreign Relations, Inc.

7. "Strategy and Organization." Reprinted by permission from *Foreign Affairs*, April 1957. Copyright 1957 by Council on Foreign Relations, Inc. Some of the equally influential American writings on the new strategic picture were: William W. Kaufmann, "Limited Warfare" in *Military Policy and National Security* (Princeton: Princeton University, 1956); Albert Wohlstetter, on the meaning of deterrence, "The Delicate Balance of Terror," *Foreign Affairs* 37, no. 3 (January 1959); Herman Kahn's calibrated escalation ladder in *On Escalation: Metaphors and Scenarios*, rev. ed. (Baltimore: Penguin, 1968); and Thomas C. Schelling, on

force as coercion and communication, *The Strategy of Conflict* (Cambridge, Mass.: Harvard University, 1960) and *Arms and Influence* (New Haven, Conn.: Yale University, 1966).

8. Nevil Shute, *On the Beach* (New York: Morrow, 1957).

9. See, for instance, Richard Pipes, "Why the Soviet Union Thinks It Could Fight and Win a Nuclear War," *Commentary* 64 (July 1977).

10. Garthoff, "Mutual Deterrence."

15 The SALT I Negotiations: The Utility of a Game Theory Paradigm

Louis A. Picard

A Framework for Analysis

There has been much discussion in the international politics literature of the utility of the game theory or games of strategy model as a tool for analyzing international bargaining. A number of scholars have in particular pointed to the utility of using the prisoner's dilemma framework as the basis for the analysis of issues related to the nuclear arms race.[1] This chapter will attempt to examine the arms limitation negotiations that culminated in the SALT I negotiations (Strategic Arms Limitation Talks) to determine the utility of the prisoner's dilemma framework for the understanding of the bargaining process inherent in strategic negotiations.

The central concept of the prisoner's dilemma is that although the two players could enjoy mutual gains from the game by cooperating, the logic of the game situation forces the two players into conflict and losses for both. The prisoner's dilemma places each player in a situation in which he has very good reason to mistrust the other player, so the rational choice for each player becomes noncooperation. A player on the offense will attempt to double-cross his opponent and a player on the defense must be concerned with a preemptive double-cross from his opponent. According to Snyder, "the reward for *unilateral* noncooperation exceeds both the benefit from mutual cooperation and the cost of mutual conflict."[2]

The prisoner's dilemma model illustrates the principle of mutual suspicion clearly. The player needs to take the actions of a conscious opponent into account. The player asks what is the worst that one's opponent can do to one's self. One then defines one's own best move as one that is the best defense against the opponent's expected (best) move. The process can be summarized as follows:

1. Each side is clearly best off not to arm.
2. However, if one thinks that the other will not arm, one is tempted to arm to make gains by coercion.

The author wishes to thank David W. Tarr and Kenneth Farmer of the University of Wisconsin-Madison and William P. Avery of the University of Nebraska-Lincoln for reading and commenting on earlier drafts of this chapter.

3. The other state, fearing the first, will also behave this way, motivated to arm to protect itself.
4. The result is that the players are trapped in the double defection box of the matrix, and the two states will be trapped in costly mutual armament of an increasing scale.

Arms control negotiations can be seen in the context of the expanded game of prisoner's dilemma. The beginning of arms limitation agreements would seem to indicate that both parties are unwilling to continue indefinitely the results of mutual defection. The negotiations should be seen as an attempt to move from a mutual defection situation to one of disarmament. Since disarmament is unlikely, the goal will be some limited variant of it. Thus, the distinction is usually made between arms control and disarmament, with the former being a more modest and limited proposal. In playing the game, both sides are concerned with seeking ways of collaborating without being put into a position where the other side can blackmail the player. As Snyder puts it, "in psychological terms, the parties seek to reduce fear and suspicion, instill trust in the other party, and teach him that oneself is trustworthy."[3]

This analysis of the SALT I negotiations will attempt to determine the extent to which the Soviet Union and the United States are trapped in the mutual defection cell of the matrix and are operating within the arms race/deterrence theory paradigm.

Of major utility in the use of the prisoner's dilemma framework in the analysis of strategic bargaining is the fact that the concept can be disaggregated into a number of operational indicators of the prisoner's dilemma scheme. The focus of this chapter will be on the application of these six indicators as they apply to the SALT I negotiations. The extent to which they are operating in the SALT negotiations may have wider implications for the more general analysis of relations between the Soviet Union and the United States. The six indicators are: (1) the concern of each actor for the problem of the double cross, mutual distrust, and fear of attempts by the other side to gain a first-strike advantage; (2) attempts to build trust through negotiations by use of communication to assure the other side that a surprise attack is not intended; (3) attempts made by each side to maintain a balanced relationship throughout the negotiations to avoid an opponent's "blackmail"; (4) attempts by each side to ensure that arms reductions are limited and that emphasis is placed on regulation of weapons because each side sees the need to maintain a second-strike capability; (5) the acceptance by the players of the arms race paradigm and the use of it to justify their actions; and (6) acceptance of the principle of mutual assured destruction as an operating principal for negotiations.

SALT: The Mutual Defection Matrix

In this section I will attempt to use the six indicators to determine the extent to which the two parties are trapped in the mutual defection cell of the prisoner's dilemma. I will attempt to do this by analyzing the SALT talks in terms of these indexes and the questions they raise.

Double Cross and Mutual Distrust

To what extent are both parties in the negotiation concerned with attempts by the other side to gain a first strike advantage? It seems quite clear that mutual distrust and the fear of the double-cross play an important role in the relationship between the superpowers. According to Morton Kaplan, "One of the incentives that maintains both the qualitative and the quantitative arms race on a bilateral basis is the fear that some mistake may provide the enemy with a decisive advantage which it might attempt to seize, despite various uncertainties, during some intense crisis that threatens its regime or bloc."[4] Of concern in terms of this mutual distrust is the possibility, whether real or perceived, of the other side gaining a first strike capability.

Technological breakthroughs can be perceived as giving the possessor the potential for a first strike capability. The U.S. development of its multiple independently targeted reentry vehicles (MIRV) and anti-ballistic missile (ABM) systems was a direct result of a U.S. fear that the Soviet *Galosh* system presented the United States with a Soviet ABM threat. Soviet fears of MIRV led to the increased development of its own ABM system and the development of both MRV and MIRV capabilities.

The initiation of the SALT negotiations stems from this technological competition. The SALT talks were designed to establish an acceptance by each side of the other's ability to inflict unacceptable retribution. Although the talks were designed to reassure both parties that neither would initiate a first strike, as John Newhouse points out, each side suspected throughout the negotiations that the other might be engaged in a "hold-and-explore" gambit and was trying to buy time to catch up or jump ahead.[5]

In the negotiations themselves, a major premise was that neither side should gain an advantage over the other. James Dougherty summarized the problem clearly: "The two superpowers cannot but wonder . . . how fast and how far they could dare carry out reductions down the strategic scale before encountering the danger that mutual deterrence might give way to renascent incentives for surprise nuclear attack, based on the expectation of achieving a decisive advantage."[6] For example, throughout the negotiations, the U.S. delegation maintained what Joseph Kruzel calls "an almost paranoid fear" that the Soviet Union might be able to upgrade its air defense network into ABM capability.[7]

Soviet reactions to the U.S. forward-based systems (FBS) can be seen in a similar light. The Soviet Union's concern with FBS, although seemingly irrational from the U.S. point of view, appears clearly a case where the Soviet policy-makers were concerned about potential American capabilities being left out of the negotiations and then later being used as a threat to Soviet security. U.S. negotiators apparently recognized this later. Newhouse quotes one member of the U.S. negotiating team as saying of FBS, "We were so absorbed in our definitional problems we made no serious effort to anticipate theirs."[8]

The vulnerability of weapons has been and continues to be a major concern of the SALT negotiations. A vulnerable weapon is one that is open either to a counterforce or first-strike attack. Manned bombers, and increasingly ICBMs, are becoming vulnerable. Nuclear submarines are the only weapon system that is still invulnerable. Thus, each side is allowed to trade off a certain number of ICBMs for SLBMs. The shift institutionalized by SALT is from a vulnerable weapon to an invulnerable one; the major concern is to prevent either side's forces from becoming vulnerable and its society open to nuclear blackmail.

Debate over the treaty since its signing has also centered on the issue of nuclear blackmail. Much of the criticism argues that the United States gave too much away at SALT and that the result was a Soviet advantage. For example Lynn Etheridge Davis and Warner Schilling argue on the basis of calculated projections that the SALT agreements will result in a Soviet MIRV capability to knock out 84.6 percent of U.S. Minuteman missiles. According to Davis and Schilling the U.S. MIRV program does not pose a similar threat to the Soviet Union.[9]

More generally, there is major concern that the SALT agreements have given the Soviet Union an advantage and frozen the United States into a position of permanent inferiority in missile development and that treaty loop-holes regarding research and development and qualitative improvements have given the Soviet Union the possibility of achieving a first-strike capability. Since the SALT I agreement, there has been agitation within the defense establishment for an acceleration of nuclear programs to match the progress made by the Soviet Union, which, they argue, has "broken the spirit if not the letter of the strategic arms limitation agreement."[10] According to this line of argument, the Soviet Union has improved its nuclear position since the SALT negotiations by developing new missiles of greater power, which could be fired from existing ICBM launchers.

Many of the analyses of SALT are clearly based on the assumption that Soviet leadership does not look at arms negotiations in the same way as the United States. Whereas the United States looks on arms control as a "good

The SALT I Negotiations

cause" in itself, the Soviet Union uses the SALT talks only so long as they are to its strategic advantage. According to Dougherty, "Obviously they (the Soviet Union) would like to neutralize the great productive potential of the United States and by generating an atmosphere of "peaceful coexistence," weaken further the popular support for such new defense improvements as the Trident submarine and the B-1 bomber."[11]

The crux of the fear of the double-cross in the prisoner's dilemma is clearly demonstrated by the SALT negotiations, and its theoretical basis is clarified by the mirror-image hypothesis with its worst-case assumption. According to Snyder, the latter hypothesis argues that each side sees the other's possible aggressive intention as probable or even certain and "the adversary's *intentions* are mistakenly equated with his capabilities."[12] Thus one can envisage Soviet analysts looking at the SALT talks and arguing the strategic advantages that it gives to the United States and fearing a U.S. double-cross and return to the U.S. posture of superiority.

Building Trust through Negotiation

Much of what has been said indicates that any attempt to escape the prisoner's dilemma and the mirror image must be based on communication and the creation of an atmosphere of trust. There are a number of indications that the SALT I talks were carried out with just such a set of assumptions in mind.

The basis of such an atmosphere of trust is a series of negotiated plays in which both sides cooperate and in which players demonstrate that arguments being made are not designed to "trap" the other side. An example of such a process can be seen in the negotiations over ABM. Soviet views of the arms race changed over the period of negotiations from 1969 to 1972. Prior to 1969 Russia's defense strategy differed from that of the United States in that it was based on active (attacks on incoming weapons) and passive (preparations to absorb those weapons) defense. During the Glassboro summit the Soviet Union had opposed U.S. suggestions that both countries restrain from developing ABM systems. However, during the SALT negotiations the Soviet views toward arms control changed, and it exhibited concern for agreement on ABM. As Herbert York notes, they were given priority over offensive weapons.[13] United States and Soviet attitudes toward SALT converged during the negotiations. It seems clear that a process of signal/negotiation/signal had occurred similar to the signaling process in the expanded series of prisoner's dilemma games.

The use of the "back channel" negotiations between Henry Kissinger and Anatoly Dobrynin seemed to indicate a similar concern for establishing a pattern of trust. It was back channel contacts that led to the first major breakthrough in SALT, the agreement to leave each side free to keep most of its existing ABM program. These contacts allowed the two sides access to the other's thinking on an informal basis, and they quickly agreed on the major issues. Following the ABM breakthrough, the rest of the SALT negotiations were conducted through the back, with the front channel negotiations concerned largely with procedural and technical delays until the back channel brought the two sides together in a negotiable position near the end of the phase I negotiations.

The SALT negotiations took place in an atmosphere of what has come to be called Soviet-American détente. This process in itself is designed to lessen the 20 years of mistrust and suspicion that has built up between the Soviet Union and the United States. The progress that was made in the SALT I agreements was a result of compromises and trade offs between the two sides. Whereas one might question whether or not the final "mix" favors one side or the other, both sides made concessions.[14] The Soviet Union for example, in addition to changing its attitude toward ABMs, gave up its demand, at least for SALT I, to include FBS in the offensive weapons settlement. United States concessions included the acceptance of the concept of parity between the two superpowers after close to two decades of nuclear superiority and withdrawal of the demand for a simultaneous offensive weapons treaty. It was also led to recognize Soviet numerical superiority in some weapons systems.

It seems apparent that the political results of the SALT agreements have resulted in a number of breakthroughs in understanding between the two countries. Thus, they have created a continuing strategic dialogue between them.[15] There have been a number of mutual gains in agreements for both. Limited steps have been taken to curtail the arms race by regulating the deployment of certain types of weapons and the two sides have possibly reduced the danger of nuclear war.

Maintenance of a Balanced Relationship

To avoid an advantage for either side that might mean the beginning of a potential blackmail relationship, both sides have been concerned with the appearance and the substance of a balanced relationship. Four examples of this can be seen in the SALT negotiations: the verification issue, the question of parity, the use of gamesmanship, and the development of bargaining chips.

The issue of parity is central to the establishment of negotiations between two players. Without parity, there will be concern that any arms negotiations will solidify inequalities. We have noted some of the reasons why parity was a necessary precondition of the SALT negotiations. One as-

The SALT I Negotiations

pect of the parity question, however, continued to plague negotiations. The difference is between absolute parity and relative parity. Absolute unicameral parity, as demanded by such critics as Henry Jackson, would mean equality in all defense systems. Because of built-in differences between the two defense systems, including those of geography, this would be difficult to arrive at. Relative parity, which was used in SALT I, recognizes these differences and tries to compensate for them by balancing off inequalities to achieve an overall equality.

One of the most vexing issues of arms control discussions since World War II has been that of verification. The United States, down to the SALT negotiations, had demanded on-site inspection for fear of Soviet cheating. The latter was equally determined that verification be limited to national means, possibly to prevent the United States from gaining a psychological advantage in seeing the lack of sophistication in Soviet weaponry. However, with the development of satellite photography, national verification could be used at least to determine quantitative limitations, and this was the basis of the SALT I agreements.

A third technique that was used by each side to ensure a balanced relationship might be called "gamesmanship." The essence of this technique is to make proposals that the other side cannot possibly accept, knowing that you can gain the publicity value of the issue but also that it will not be seriously considered in the negotiations. In the SALT negotiations, proposals to ban MIRVs were of this nature. The United States called for a total ban on MIRVs and included a provision for on-site inspection, knowing beforehand that the proposal was unacceptable. The Soviets responded by calling for a ban on deployment but not on research and development, a proposal that would allow them to catch up with the United States and would thus be unacceptable to them. These proposals are in large part examples of arms control gamesmanship.

A fourth technique used in the SALT negotiations is that of the bargaining chip. Bargaining chips are weapons that are built for the express purpose of being traded off in negotiations with the other side. The two U.S. on-site ABM systems were used in part as a bargaining chip to convince the Soviets that failure to negotiate would lead to the creation of a heavy U.S. ABM system. The successful testing of MIRV by the Soviet Union might also have been used as a bargaining chip. All research and development projects also have such potential. As Joseph Coffey argues, "ongoing weapons programs are essential as bargaining chips in future negotiations on the limitation of strategic armaments."[16] They are used to ensure that bargains that are struck in arms control negotiations are equal and also that in case the negotiations break down the other side will not gain an advantage in the arms race.

Arms Control not Disarmament

The SALT participants have recognized the basic principles of deterrence, that any arms reductions that do occur should not be total in that each side has to be able to maintain a sufficient supply of weapons to reply with a second-strike after a nuclear exchange. Unfortunately, the requirements of an adequate second-strike capability to deter are not clear. Thus it seems likely that the SALT negotiations will not bring about any major reduction of weapons. Substantive arms reductions would be unstable according to deterrence theory, since with both sides in a weakened condition, one side might be tempted to preempt.

Soviet acceptance of the logic of deterrence has constituted a significant shift from its earlier posture on arms control.[17] Until the mid-1960s, Soviet emphasis was on total or substantial disarmament, and more limited arms control was dismissed as capitalist obfuscation. Beginning in the late 1950s and into the 1960s Soviet policy-makers began to approach arms control negotiations "in a manner that might promote the strategic interests of the parties concerned—by helping to economize on scarce resources, by reducing the danger of war if it should occur."[18] The SALT arrangements clearly evidence this new Soviet attitude.

*Acceptance of the Arms Race Paradigm and
Acceptance of the Theory of Mutual
Assured Destruction*

These two indicators, although analytically separate, can be treated together. The crucial question is the extent to which both sides saw these issues through the same conceptual filters. William Kintner and Robert Pfaltzgraff suggest that Soviet leaders were concerned with many of the same issues that the United States had been concerned with and suggest that U.S. bargainers had perceived a change in Soviet attitudes. Thus, the Soviet government is said to have accepted the prevailing strategic thought of the United States. Thomas Wolfe argues that the Soviet Union has come to accept the basic tenets of deterrence theory and these serve as the basis for their negotiations on nuclear arms control.[19]

The underlying assumption of the SALT negotiations is parity. As Newhouse points out, relative parity has been achieved by both sides. Each side can inflict unacceptable second-strike damage on the other. Whereas it is possible that one side or the other will attempt to reimpose superiority, it would be difficult for either to do so for any length of time. In the short run, though, parity seems clearly to have been the basis for the U.S.-Soviet arrangements in SALT I, and this seems to have been directly related to the

The SALT I Negotiations

decline in U.S. superiority in the mid- and late 1960s.[20] It was tacit recognition of this, exemplified by the Nixon doctrine of sufficiency, that allowed the negotiations to begin. The concept of parity has not been without its problems, however, and some of the thorniest ones were deliberately left out of the negotiations that culminated in SALT I. A major exclusion from SALT I was any restriction on qualitative weapons changes, and it seems clear that qualitative advantages are at the crux of any discussion of parity. The major weapons systems of concern here are MIRVs. Though the MIRVing of ICBMs was a major item on the agenda of SALT I, it was bypassed by tacit agreement.

The reasons for the absence of MIRV at the negotiating table during SALT I are related to a second assumption that was carried all the way through the negotiations. The assumption was made by both sides that verification would be by national means. With the development of sophisticated satellite equipment, the United States had dropped its demands for on-site inspection. However, MIRVing of missiles, a qualitative rather than a quantitative change, cannot be verified by national means. This means that agreements of a quantitative nature are easiest to verify and then only at the deployment and testing stage.

MIRVs are also related to the issue of parity in another way. The United States has a 2- to 3-year lead over the Soviet Union in their development. A MIRV ban in 1972 would have meant the ratification of this asymmetry. The Soviet Union does not want restrictions in an area where the United States has a technological lead, and the United States will resist allowing the Soviets to catch up because of Soviet-biased asymmetries in other areas such as missile throw-weight and conventional forces. Further, the opportunity for a complete MIRV ban is gone; to the extent that the possibilities existed, they disappeared in 1970.

Another major assumption of the SALT talks, clearly related to parity, is the acceptance, tacitly at least, by both sides, of the concept of mutual assured destruction (MAD). Whereas the long-range acceptance of this concept is in some doubt,[21] SALT I was a clear ratification of MAD. According to Andrew Pierre, this was the major significance of the ABM treaty.[22] It resulted in the rejection by both sides of any attempt at a first-strike capability, since that would require a major civil defense program. The ABM agreement means that Soviet and American cities will not be protected from enemy missiles, and this is as Thomas Schelling describes it ". . . a massive and modern version of an ancient institution: the exchange of hostages."[23]

The notion of balance seems implicit in much of the bargaining that took place during the SALT negotiations. A major goal of the two sides was the preservation of stability in time of crisis. A clearly destabilizing weapon such as ABM was thus largely eliminated and attempts were made to regulate potentially destabilizing and vulnerable weapons such as ICBMs. As Robert Wesson points out, "Implicitly, the agreements recognize the principle of mutual deterrence and both sides might accept sufficiency of assured destruction as their goal."[24] However, it seems equally clear that the SALT agreements have gone only part way toward assuring parity and mutual deterrence. Among issues not addressed were forward-based systems (FBS) of the United States, located in Western Europe and Asia. Specifically at issue are shorter range aircraft that potentially can reach the Soviet Union. The Soviet Union has suggested that the FBS be included in SALT negotiations, but has refused to discuss the inclusion of its MRBMs and IRBMs, which are aimed at Western Europe. This issue of FBS was the most difficult part of the negotiations on offensive weapons under SALT I and was one of the major reasons why there was only an interim agreement.

Other issues excluded from SALT I included any restrictions on manned bombers, restrictions on the development of mobile missiles, and limits on antisubmarine warfare. With the exception of the bomber issue all these are knotty problems that had to be faced by U.S.-Soviet negotiators in SALT II. Further, as long as these weapons are not regulated the balance becomes less steady. Research and development continue in these areas and "both sides will tend to develop their new technologies to the utmost"[25] in case the other side achieves a breakthrough or violates a part of the existing agreement.

The SALT talks were undertaken because of a mutual need to ratify the parity principle. Each side assumed that neither would initiate a first-strike if the other's retaliatory capacity was strong enough to survive a first-strike attack. Each side recognized that an unlimited arms race would undermine deterrence and that a failure to establish arms limits might mean sustaining the race indefinitely for newer and better weapons. Both sides hope to head off another major offensive weapons cycle and to stabilize arms spending.

Prior to 1974, it was assumed that the acceptance of the theory of mutual assured destruction would go hand in hand with deterrence theory. With the reestablishment of counterforce, modified though it might be, this analogy with the prisoner's dilemma seems most weak. The analogy to the prisoner's dilemma after all is that if one prisoner confesses and the other holds out, the man who confesses goes free with a reward while the other hangs. It would seem that to take the threat of mutual assured destruction away from the prisoner's dilemma takes away the threat of hanging. If both sides were to achieve counterforce capability the game might more closely resemble the game of chicken.

How likely is this to happen? It is not yet clear that a viable counterforce weapon is available that would not at the same time be counterpopulation. As Wolfgang Panofsky points out, this argument seems very similar to discussions about "clean" nuclear war, and he argues you cannot avoid killing people.[26] Further, counterforce weapons are virtually indistinguishable from weapons designed for a preemptive attack against the opponent's retaliatory forces. To the extent that this is the case, the prisoner's dilemma model seems clearly applicable. Moreover, presumably counterforce weapons of this nature could, simply, by being retargeted, pose a threat to populations, and cities would still be held hostage to enemy weapons. Counterforce weapons seem unlikely to eliminate either side's ability to massively retaliate in a second strike. Nor is either side likely to allow this to be changed.

Game Theory: Criticism and Conclusions

Up to this point I have been concerned with the use of the prisoner's dilemma as an example of the use of game theory as a tool for analysis of an arms control situation. In this section I will attempt to summarize by addressing myself to some of the criticisms that have been made of game theory in light of the attempt that has been made here to use the theory as a basis for analysis.

A major swath of criticism revolves around the question of methodology. This argument points out that game theory is best used as an analytical device. It is true that the prisoner's dilemma lacks a dynamic component and has been largely used as a conceptual arrangement or framework. Nonetheless, I would suggest that the prisoner's dilemma framework is of heuristic value in the analysis of strategic international bargaining. In this respect Eugene Meehan's fourth type of activity of formalism seems to be of most utility—the use of conceptual frameworks that are derived from formal models but are not in fact formal systems.[27] Nor do many political analysts use game theory much differently.[28] This is true not only of game theory, however, since the same criticism can be made of much of social science theory. It is true that most analysts of game theory do little more than talk about the utility of the concept and few attempt to apply it. However, as this essay has attempted to demonstrate, it is possible, by disaggregating the concept into a number of operational indicators, to use a particular game theory model as a basis for analysis.

A second criticism made of the game theory paradigms is certainly interesting if inconclusive. That involves the extent to which game theory is qualitatively different from other kinds of social science theory. Theories concerning voting behavior, attitudinal analysis, and economic behavior are based on the premise that individuals will behave in a certain way whether or not they understand the theory and how it works. A case in point is the theory of supply and demand. This is a hierarchical theory that posits certain behavior from aggregates of individuals under certain circumstances. The participants have little if any understanding of the concept. But when one turns to game theory, as Philip Green points out, the participants are not only aware of the theory, but understand it, use it, and write about it.[29] Further, it has taken Soviet decision-makers 50 years to learn the fundamentals of deterrence theory. A question that could be raised, then, of game theory analysis, and specifically the prisoner's dilemma, is the extent to which it has become a self-fulfilling prophecy. Unfortunately, the answer to this question is not clear, and in this chapter I do no more than raise the question.

Criticism that deals with the problem of application is easier to deal with. Karl Deutsch, Philip Green, and Anatol Rapoport, all question the extent to which a continual process is a game.[30] And, as Deutsch points out, if communication is possible, as we have seen in the SALT talks, is the prisoner's dilemma concept valid?[31] As has been argued here, the SALT talks can be seen as a series of interrelated subgames divided by phases and sections. Psychological experiments have shown that patterns do develop in a series of prisoner's dilemma games and that communication is possible.[32] Finally, if we are limiting our use of game theory to an analytic tool, it seems clear that a rigid requirement that we stay with the rules of the original game is largely irrelevant. We are concerned with the types of choices available to decision-makers and the kinds of constraints they find themselves in, and for this a game theory analogy performs quite well.

The question of rationality is related to a fourth set of criticisms of the game theory model. Philip Green argues that game theorists and deterrence theorists do not really expect rational behavior but merely hope for it.[33] However, all game theorists assume that it can take place. Criticism here is based on a number of related arguments. First of all, a number of students of the domestic sources of foreign policy have questioned the rational model of decision-making, pointing out that a number of other bureaucratic and political functions come first.[34] Secondly, any definition of rationality in terms of the logic of the situation can generate self-contradictions. Greene argues, "Our perception of the logic of the situation itself may be unsatisfactory."[35] Similarly, goals may be multifarious and contradictory, unlike the situation in the game where the goal is simple and clear. Again, all the comments with regard to rationality, although they are important and should be noted, are not the exclusive problem of game theory. They are rather part of the whole problem of social science analysis and are beyond solving in this essay. This set of criticisms does not weaken the utility of the concept as an analytical tool of some utility in the analysis of decision-making involving the use of force.

A set of criticisms formulated by Karl Deutsch do seem to merit some consideration, however. These involve the four interrelated concepts of motives, risks, behavior, and capabilities. Deutsch points to the fact that when one deals with a series of games, one runs up against the phenomenon of cumulative risks. These are often neglected in game theory analogies. As he puts it, "The foreign affairs of nations and states which intend to continue for long periods of time must be governed by methods that more likely than not will let them survive for generations and centuries, and hence through scores of foreign-policy encounters, fraught with some risk of war."[36]

The motives of a participant in the diplomatic game are often undifferentiated as well. There are two related problems here. The first deals with the extent to which one can assume that rational thinking can continue to occur during periods of stress. This criticism, however, becomes stranded on the same reef as the parent criticism of the assumption of rationality; that is, it is part of a greater social science analysis problem. A second criticism is more revealing. Motives, Deutsch argues, change over time. Soviet attitudes toward the ABM are an example of such a change. We thus have a problem of accurate information and evaluation. However, a response to this criticism would suggest that not only do we have a variety of changing motives but a variety of changing games. Again, an analytical use of game theory as a series of sequential confrontations would seem able to handle this criticism.

Critics of game theory also point to the fact that capabilities, both human and military/industrial, also change over time. As Green points out, this is true even if we use the extended game principle. How do we know we are in one continuous game, he argues. Not all situations are related to the game, nor do capabilities remain constant throughout it. With regard to the SALT talks, he might ask, is FBS part of the U.S./USSR game or part of a Europe/USSR game, or both? A response to the latter comment would be that these are clearly negotiable in the context of the bargaining, and with regard to the former argument, capabilities are recognized as changing within the context of the model and indeed are part of the interaction process of the negotiations of the arms control game.

In conclusion, it would seem that the major objection that critics make of the game theory paradigm is based on normative concerns. Green, for example, who is one of the most articulate of the critics, argues that game theory is both tautological and susceptible to pseudoquantification.[37] What Green is clearly saying, and perhaps should openly recognize, is that he has normative objections to the application of game theory to national security affairs. Pseudoquantification will only be accepted by those who believe that all human activities can be quantifiably analyzed, a small percentage of social scientists as a whole, and certainly very few game theorists. Major students of game theory, Hedley Bull, Thomas Schelling, and Kenneth

Boulding, all adopt the position that game theory can be used in analyzing human affairs only as an analytical device and that the quantitative aspects of the theory have very little relevance to the analysis of international relations.[38] This is not so much a reason to reject game theory as it is a cautionary note to use it carefully. As Hedley Bull points out, the basic point of Green's analysis is that the technique and rigor that game theory has brought to the analysis of international bargaining should not be allowed to prevent the researcher from looking at the political choices that are made in such negotiations. Nor should analysts ignore the fact that game theory and strategic arguments can be used as a political weapon to build support for selected policies. The point he makes, however, is that "this . . . is an argument for recognizing the limits of rigor and precision and for being on guard against their misuse, not for abandoning rigor and precision in favor of something else."[39] With these caveats in mind it seems clear that the game theory analogy is of some utility in the study of two-sided bargaining such as that which occurred at SALT.

Notes

1. Among others, Anatol Rapoport and Albert M. Chammah, *Prisoner's Dilemma: A Study in Conflict and Cooperation* (Ann Arbor, Mich.: University of Michigan Press, 1965); Anatol Rapoport, "Prisoner's Dilemma-Recollections and Observations," in Anatol Rapoport, ed., *Game Theory as a Theory of Conflict Resolution*, (Dordrecht, Netherlands: D. Reidel Publishing Co., 1974); and Anatol Rapoport, *The Big Two: Soviet American Perceptions of Foreign Policy* (New York: Pegasus, 1971). See also Jerry I. Shaw and Christer Thorslund, "Varying Patterns of Reward Cooperation: The Effects in a Prisoner's Dilemma Case, *Journal of Conflict Resolution* 19, no. 1 (March 1975):108-122. See also Daniel Ellsberg, "The Crude Analysis of Strategic Choices," *American Economic Review* 51, no. 2 (Mary 1961):472-478; Nigel Forward, *The Field of Nations* (Boston: Little, Brown, 1971); and Warner Schilling et al., *American Arms and a Changing Europe: Dilemmas of Deterrence and Disarmament* (New York: Columbia University Press, 1973).

2. Glenn Snyder, "'Prisoner's Dilemma' and 'Chicken' Models in International Politics," *International Studies Quarterly* 15, no. 1 (March 1971):68.

3. Snyder, "'Prisoner's Dilemma,'" p. 101.

4. Morton A. Kaplan, in Morton Kaplan, ed., *SALT: Problems and Prospects*, (Morristown, N.J.: General Learning Press, 1973), p. 9.

5. John Newhouse, *Cold Dawn: The Story of SALT* (New York: Holt Rinehart, 1973), p. 3.

6. James Dougherty, "Arms Control in the 1970s," *Orbis* 15, no. 1 (Spring 1971):196.

7. Joseph Kruzel, "SALT II, The Search for a Follow-on Agreement," *Orbis* 17, no. 2 (Summer 1973):357.

8. Newhouse, *Cold Dawn*, p. 176.

9. Lynn Etheridge Davis and Warner Schilling, "All You Ever Wanted to Know about MIRV and ICBM Calculations But Were Not Cleared to Ask," *Journal of Conflict Resolution* 17, no. 2 (June 1973):231-239.

10. Drew Middleton, "U.S. Is Stressing Accuracy over Size in Developing Latest Nuclear Weapons," *New York Times*, 26 May 1974, p. 1.

11. James E. Dougherty, "The Soviet Union and Arms Control," *Orbis* 17, no. 3 (Fall 1973):770.

12. Snyder, "Prisoner's Dilemma,'" p. 77.

13. Herbert York, *Arms Control* (San Francisco: W.H. Freeman, 1973), p. 262.

14. As does Dougherty, who argues that the Soviet Union got the best of the deal. Dougherty, "Arms Control in the 1970's."

15. Kruzel, "SALT II," p. 363.

16. Coffey, "The Savour of SALT," p. 14.

17. See Walter C. Clemens, "Nicholas II to SALT II: Continuity and Change in East-West Diplomacy," *International Affairs* 49, no. 3 (October 1973):398-399, and Dougherty, "Soviet Union and Arms Control," pp. 753-760 for discussions of this change in Soviet attitudes.

18. Clemens, "Nicholas II to SALT II," p. 398.

19. Thomas W. Wolfe, "Soviet Approaches to SALT," *Problems of Communism* 19, no. 5 (September 1970):1-10. This argument ignores the separate question of whether or not the Soviet Union should have to accept U.S. strategic tenets, a question that is outside the concern of this study. For a discussion of the difficulties inherent in any analysis of the policy-making process in the Soviet Union either from the unitary command paradigm or from the bureaucratic politics model see William R. Kintner and Robert L. Pfaltzgraff, *SALT: Implications for Arms Control in the 1970's* (Pittsburgh: University of Pittsburgh, 1973), pp. 29-30. Lawrence Caldwell argues a modernist view for Soviet policy-makers as predominant. He says they place great weight on the need for arms control to shift the Soviet economy toward consumer goods. See Caldwell, "Soviet Attitudes to SALT," Adelphi Papers no. 75 (1971).

20. Robert L. Lawrence, *Arms Control and Disarmament* (Minneapolis, Minn.: Burgess, 1973).

21. Colin S. Gray, "Rethinking Nuclear Strategy," *Orbis* 17, no. 4 (Winter 1974):1145-1160.

22. Andrew J. Pierre, "The SALT Agreement and Europe," *World Today* 28, no. 7 (June 1972):282.

23. Thomas C. Schelling, *Arms and Influence* (New Haven, Conn.: Yale University Press, 1966), p. 239.

24. Robert G. Wesson, "The Soviet-American Arms Limitation Agreement," *Russian Review* 31, no. 4 (October 1972):337.

25. Francois Duchene, "SALT, the Ostpolitik and the post-Cold War Context," *World Today* 16, no. 2 (December 1970):501.

26. Wolfgang Panofsky, "The Mutual Hostage Relationship between America and Russia," *Foreign Affairs* 52, no. 1 (October 1973):111.

27. Eugene Meehan, *Contemporary Political Thought: A Critical Study* (Homewood, Ill.: Dorsey Press, 1967), p. 296.

28. For example, Karl W. Deutsch, "Game Theory and Politics: Some Problems of Application," *Canadian Journal of Economics and Political Science* 20, no. 1 (February 1954):76-83; Snyder, "'Prisoner's Dilemma,'" and Richard Snyder, "Game Theory and the Analysis of Political Behavior," in James N. Rosenau, ed., *International Politics and Foreign Policy* (New York: Free Press, 1961), pp. 381-390. None of these writers makes any more expansive claims for game theory.

29. Philip Green, *Deadly Logic: The Theory of Nuclear Deterrence* (Columbus, Ohio: Ohio State University, 1966).

30. Karl W. Deutsch, *The Analysis of International Relations* (Englewood Cliffs, N.J.: Prentice-Hall, 1968), Green, *Deadly Logic*; and Anatol Rapoport, *Fights, Games and Debates* (Ann Arbor, Mich.: University of Michigan Press, 1960).

31. Deutsch, *Analysis of International Relations*, pp. 120-123.

32. Stuart Oskamp and Daniel Perlman, "Factors Affecting Cooperation in a Prisoner's Dilemma Game," *Journal of Conflict Resolution* 9, no. 3 (September 1965):359-374.

33. Green, *Deadly Logic*, p. 161.

34. Graham Allison, *Essence of Decision* (Boston: Little, Brown, 1971).

35. Green, *Deadly Logic*, p. 172.

36. Deutsch, *Analysis of International Relations*, p. 129.

37. Green, *Deadly Logic*, pp. 109-110.

38. Hedley Bull, "Strategic Studies and Its Critics," *World Politics* 20 no. 4 (July 1968):593-605; Thomas C. Schelling, *The Strategy of Conflict* (New York: Oxford University Press, 1960); and Kenneth Boulding, *Conflict and Defense* (New York: Harper, 1962).

39. Hedley Bull, "Strategic Studies," p. 601.

Index of Names

Abt, Clark C., 126
Acheson, Dean, 28
Adams, Henry, 13
Adrien, Pierre-Marie, 127
Allison, Graham, 224, 225
Amman, Ronald, 178
Ansberry, William, 223
Aron, Raymond, 18
Aspin, Les, 163
Astor, David, 126
Attlee, Prime Minister Clement, 228
Augenstein, Bruno, 178
Avery, William P., 239

Bacon, Francis, 12
Bacon, Kenneth H., 179
Ball, Desmond, 83
Barnaby, Dr. Frank, 62
Baumgardner, Marion F., 129
Bechhoefer, Bernard G., 146
Beecher, William, 147
Ben-Zvi, Abraham, 126
Bertram, Christoph, 179
Betts, Richard K., 126
Bismarck, 8, 233
Bloomfield, Lincoln Palmer, xi, 225
Bobrow, Davis B., x, 115, 126
Boffey, Philip M., 163
Bolingbroke, Lord, 12
Boulding, Kenneth, 251
Brams, Steven J., 127
Brennan, Donald G., 104-113
Brewer, Garry D., 126
Brezhnev, Leonid, 81, 229
Brodie, Bernard, 224
Brown, Secretary of Defense Harold, 191, 202
Brown, Neville, 207
Brown, Seyom, 42
Bull, Hedley, 213, 223, 251
Bundy, McGeorge, 108, 229, 232
Bupp, Irwin C., 178
Burt, Richard, 146
Butterworth, Robert Lyle, x, 149, 163, 179

Caldwell, Lawrence, 253
Callahan, M., 128
Canby, Steven L., x, 85
Carter, President James, 37, 40, 81, 185, 187
Chammah, Albert M., 252
Chan, Morgan, 226
Chayes, Abram, 11, 114, 146
Churchill, Winston, 9, 126, 226
Clarke, Duncan, 195
von Clausewitz, Karl, 99, 225, 237
Clemens, Walter C., Jr., 146, 253
Cleveland, Harlan, 146
Coffey, Joseph I., ix, 69, 147, 245, 253
Cohen, Raymond, 126
Cohen, Samuel T., 147
Columbus, Chistopher, 6
Conant, Melvin A., 65
Critchley, Julian, 127
Critchley, W. Harriet, xi, 45
Crittenden, Ann, 191

Da Gama, Vasco, 6
Davis, Jacquelyn K., 71
Davis, Lynn Etheridge, 241, 253
Davis, Morton D., 127
Davis, Vincent, 179
Dobrynin, Anatoly, 243
De Gaulle, Charles, 232
Deutsch, Karl W., 250-254
DeWeerd, Harvey A., 127
Dougherty, James, 241, 243
Douhet, Giulio, 98, 99
Duchêne, François, 254
Dulles, Secretary of State John Foster, 228
Dunn, Lewis A., 147
Dupuy, Trevor N., 146, 147

Edwards, David V., 146
Ehrman, John, 18
Eisenhower, President Dwight D., 206, 228
Ellsberg, Daniel, 252
Endicott, John, 223

Epstein, William, 145, 213, 223
Etzioni, Amitai, 128

Farmer, Kenneth, 239
Flax, Alexander H., 178
Ford, President Gerald, 187
Forward, Nigel, 252
Foster, James L., 126, 223
Fourquet, General d'Armeé Adrienne M., 99
Freedman, Lawrence, 126
Frye, Alton, 113
Fulbright, J. William, 103

Garthoff, Raymond L., 113, 237, 238
Garwin, Richard, 114, 147
Geiger, Theodore, 14
Gellner, Charles, 163
George, Alexander, 41
Gilpin, Robert, 42
Goering, Hermann, 204
Gold, Fern Racine, 65
Goldman, S.C., 127
Gompert, David C., 19, 147
Goodpaster, General, 89
Gray, Colin S., 127, 145, 198, 253
Greb, G. Allen, 127, 224
Green, Philip, 250, 252, 254
Greenwood, David, 99
Greenwood, Ted, 127
Graebner, Norman A., 43
Guderian, Heinz, 98, 99

Halberstam, David, 42
Hall, Samuel L., 179
Halperin, Morton, 223
Hamilton, Alexander, 12
Hammerman, Gay M., 146
Handel, Michael, I., 126
Hardin, Russell, 126
Harkavy, Robert E., x, 129, 146, 147
Hartz, Louis, 43
Hay, John, 9
Hayes, John H., 126
Hazlewood, Leo A., 126
Heuer, Richard J., 126
Hilsman, Roger, 43

Hobbes, Thomas, 43
Hoeber, Francis P., 179
Holloway, David, 178
Holst, Johan J., 113
Horelick, Arnold L., 126
Hughes, G. Philip, 83
Hume, David, 12
Humphrey, Senator Hubert, 150, 163
Huntington, Samuel P., 42
Husbands, Jo, 147

Iklé, Fred C., 107, 114, 128

Jackson, Henry, 233, 245
Jervis, Robert, 126
Johnson, President Lyndon, 42, 191
Jones, Charles O., 157, 164
Jones, T.K., 207

Kahan, Jerome, 113, 114
Kahn, Herman, 104, 128, 147, 237
Kaplan, Morton A., 241, 252
Kaufmann, William W., 41
Kelman, Herbert C., 127
Kemp, Geoffrey, 147
Kende, I., 62
Kennan, George, x, 28, 42, 43, 237, 266
Kennedy, President John F., 30, 41, 187
Kennedy, Robert, 83
Keohane, Robert S., xi, 43, 62
Khrushchev, Premier Nikita, 219, 229
Kindleberger, Charles, 18
Kintner, William R., 113, 246, 253
Kissinger, Henry A., 23, 41, 218, 229, 233, 243
Knorr, Klaus, 62
Kolko, Gabriel, 42
Kolko, Joyce, 42
Kolodziej, Edward A., xi, 21
Korb, Lawrence J., x, 179, 181
Kosygin, Aleksei, 104
Kruzel, Joseph 241, 253
Kupperman, R.H., 126

Laird, Secretary of Defense Melvin, 165, 202
Lapp, David, 112

Index

Larson, Thomas, 223
Lash, Joseph P., 18
Lawrence, Robert L., 253
Lee, Kai, 3
Leebaert, Derek, 145
Lehman, John F., 147
Levin, N. Gordon, 42
Levine, Richard, 191
Lewis, Davis K., 127
Liddell-Hart, Basil H., 18
Lindbergh, Charles, 204
Link, Arthur, 42
Lippmann, Walter, 28, 41, 42
Liska, George, 18
Lodge, Henry Cabot, 13
Long, Franklin A., 126, 129, 146, 163
Lord, Carnes, 13, 127
Lowenthal, Mark M., 127
Luttwak, Edward N., 14, 143, 146, 147, 197, 207

McNamara, Secretary of Defense Robert S., 102, 106, 112, 230, 233
Magdoff, Harry, 42
Mahan, Admiral Alfred Thayer, 7, 12, 18, 126
Makins, Christopher, 84
Malenkov, G.M., 229
Mao Tse-Tung, 229, 237
Marshall, Gen. George C., 29
Martin, Laurence W., 18, 199, 207
Medalia, Jonathan E., 83
Meehan, Eugene, 249
Menaul, Steward W.B., 114
Middleton, Drew, 147, 253
Millis, Walter, 191
Modelski, George, xi, 3, 18
von Moltke, Helmuth, 225
Morgan, Patrick M., xi, 209
Morgenthau, Hans J., 213
Morris, Frederic, 224
Murdock, Clark, 113
Murphy, Robert D., 163
Myrdal, A., 128

Nader, Ralph, 201
Napoleon, Bonaparte, 8

Natchez, Peter B., 178
Nietzsche, Friederich, 225, 237
Nixon, President Richard, 40, 187, 218
Neuman, Stephanie, 147
Newhouse, John, 113, 147, 241, 252, 253
Nye, Joseph S., xi, 43, 62

O'Donnell, Kenneth, 187
Ohlert, Lt. Cmdr. Edward J., 83
Osgood, Robert E., 41, 42
Oskamp, Stuart, 254

Panofsky, Wolfgang, 246, 248
Parmentola, John, 114
Pell, Senator Claiborne, 150
Pelton, Joseph N., 127
Peres, Shimon, 116
Pericles, 13, 119
Perkins, Dwight, 223
Perlman, Daniel, 254
Perroux, Françoise, 4
Perry, William J., 83, 84
Pfaltzgraff, Robert L., 147, 253
Pfeiffer, John, 223
Philip II of Spain, 6
Picard, Louis A., xi, 239

Quester, George H., xi, 195
Quinlan, Mary Kay, 192

Ramberg, Bennett, 146
von Ranke, Leopold, 6, 18
Rapoport, Anatol, 250, 252, 254
Rathjens, George, 111, 114, 146, 163, 224
Ravenal, Earl, 225, 237
Reppy, Judith, x, 165
Rhinelander, J.B., 147
Rosecrance, Richard, 18
Rosenau, James N., 254
Roberts, Chalmers M., 146
Roosevelt, Franklin D., 9, 10, 13, 18, 226
Roosevelt, Theodore, 9, 13
Root, Elihu, 13
Ross, Dennis, 224

Ruhle, Hans, 84
Rumsfeld, Donald, 191

Sandys, Duncan, 228
Schelling, Thomas C., 127, 209, 251, 252, 254
Schilling, Warner, 241, 252, 253
Schlesinger, James, 202, 230
Schmidt, Helmut, 81
Schneider, William Jr., 113, 179
Schreiber, Jean-Jacques Servan, 42
Scott-Stokes, Henry, 147
Seiberling, John, 164
Sforza, Ascanio, 6
Shapley, Deborah, 178
Shaw, Jerry I., 252
Shlaim, Avi, 126
Shute, Nevil, 237
Slater, Jerome, x, 42, 101, 147
Smart, Ian, 147, 200, 207
Smith, Gerard C., 113
Smoke, Richard, 41
Snyder, Glenn H., 62, 239, 240, 252, 253
Stafford, Roy, 223
Steinbruner, John D., 129
Stockfish, J.A., 224
Straffin, Phillip D., Jr., 127

Talleyrand, 106
Tarr, David W., 239
Taylor, Maxwell, 41
Thompson, Murray, 62
Thorslund, Christer, 252

Thucydides, 13, 18
Tinajero, A.A., 83
de Tocqueville, Alexis, 41
Trager, Frank N., 62
Truman, President Harry, 9, 187, 226, 228
Tsipis, Kosta, 74, 114, 128
Tucker, Robert W., 42

Warnke, Paul, 213, 223
Warrington, Robert D., 115
Weiler, Lawrence D., 113, 146
Weinraub, Bernard, 164, 191
Wesson, Robert G., 248, 254
Wiesner, Jerome B., 111, 114
Wilcox, R.H., 126
William III of Dutch Republic, 7
Williams, William A., 42
Willrich, Mason, 147
Wilson, Charles E., 206
Wilson, George, 191
Wilson, Woodrow, 9, 42, 206
Wohlstetter, Albert, 224, 237
Wohlstetter, Roberta, 127
Wolfe, Thomas W., 246, 253
Wolfers, Arnold, 18
Woolsey, R. James, 179

York, Herbert, 127, 128, 179, 219, 224, 243, 253
Yorke, Valerie, 126
Young, Elizabeth, 112

Zumwalt, Elmo, Jr., 178

Index of Subjects

ABM (Anti-ballistic missile(s)), 23, 135, 138, 220, 241, 251; abolition of, 101-105; arms race and, 105-112; city defense by, 102-104, 110; Congress and, 104; failure of, 105; MAD and, 105-112; population defense, 101-112; SALT I and abolition of, 101-105; stability of, 102-112; treaty, 105-112
ACDA (Arms Control and Disarmament Agency) 129, 136, 143, 153-158, 218
ACIS (Arms Control Impact Statement), 149-162; ambiguity of, 154-155; analytic assessment, 155-157; Congress and, 158-159; decision-making process, 156; defense versus arms control, 155-157; formulation of, 155-157; implementation of, 157-158; issue area of, 155-157; national defense security policy, 157
Access: change, worth and, 61; changes in as strategic threat, 60; definition of, 49-55; dimension, 55; effect on strategic value, 59; impact of, on security relations, 59-62; independence of worth in strategic value assessment, 49; international strategic environment and, 49; key element of strategic value, 49; security, importance of, 59-62; strategic value, 49-55; types of, 50; worth, effect on, 59
AD-70 (Alliance Defense-70), 86
Adequacy of, American military means, 24-28
Advanced Research Projects Agency. See ARPA
Air-launched ballistic missile(s). See ALBM
Air-launched cruise missile(s). See ALCM

Alliance, joint c^3/I and, 121
Alliance defense 70. See AD-70
Alliance relationships, cruise missile and, 69
American security: adversaries of, 31-34; divisibility by economic and political regimes, 36-38; favorable conditions for, 31-36; globalization of, 36-38; international security and, 28-29; secrecy and consensus and, 40; threats, allies and adversaries, 31-34; world division and, 22-23
American security policy: absolute military and, 34; arms control and, 21-41; assumptions, 21-22; consensus effect on, 38-40; elements of, 21; evaluation of, 31-40; global strategy and, 28-29; guide for use of military force, 21-31; interior and internal influences on, 26; international security and, 28-29; key assumptions for, 31-40; new rationale for, 21-31; postwar, 22-30; public support for, 29
American security policies, public support for, 30
American third world guarantee, dependability of, 23
Angola, 37
Anti-ballistic missile(s). See ABM
Anti-submarine warfare. See ASW
Argentina, 137
Arms: arms control and, 69-82; cruise missile and, 69-82; impact statement and, 149-162
Arms control: ACIS and, 155-157; accords and, 35; agenda, 131-134; American ascendancy and, 24; American security policy, 21-41; bipolarity and, 221; bureaucratic politics, 143-144; communications and, 214; cruise missile and, 69-82;

259

Arms control (cont.)
domains, 129-145; domestic politics and, 217-218; game theory analysis of, 249; goals of ACIS, 150-154; governmental support, 215-217; impact of program, 149-162; international politics and, 213; interrelations and typology, 131-133; military R&D, 165-178; missile accuracy and, 198-202; negotiations, policy of mutual suspicion, 239; non-proliferation, 145; nuclear, Soviet-American alignment, 31; paradox of, 223; parity, nuclear and, 34; prisoner's dilemma and, 118; RDT&E program, 175-178; regimes, 131-134; SALT ban on cruise missile, 78; strategic, and nuclear deterrence, 17; strategic deterrence and, 210-211; strategy for security, 209; technology development and, 211-212; types of, 221; typology of, 131-133; United States and, 143-145

Arms control and disarmament policy. See ACDA

Arms control impact statement. See ACIS

Arms race: ABM treaty and, 105-112; action-reaction cycle theory, 106; deterrence and, 195-207; escalation of superpowers, 101-105; mutual technical advantage of, 232-233; nuclear, prisoner's dilemma, 239-252; nuclear, U.S. security interests, 237; security dilemma, 106; strategic, antidotes to, 196-197; strategic, issues of, 195-207; western conception of, 204

ARPA (Advanced Research Projects Agency), 172

Assumptions for effective American security policy, 21-41

ASW (Anti-submarine warfare), 140, 203

Atlantic alliance: American nuclear guarantee and, 26; economic competition in, 32; Warsaw Pact, effect on, 32

Ballistic-missile submarine nuclear. See SSBN

Belgium, 196

BGM-109 (Navy cruise missile(s)), 70

Biological warfare. See BW

Bipolar structure in world politics, 16

Bipolarity and arms control, 221

BMD (Ballistic missile defense), 111

Brazil, 32, 136, 137

Bureau of Oceans, Environmental and Scientific Affairs. See OES

Bureau of Politico-Military Affairs. See PM

BW (Biological warfare), 130, 133, 212

C^1 (Communication system), 91, 151, 153, 157, 162

C^3/I (Communication, command and control, and intelligence), 115, 118, 120; criteria for bargaining, 117-118; deterrence value, 118; perspectives for, 125-126; regimes, source of official information, 120; systems, alliance deterrence, 121; systems, doctrine of flexible response, 121; third parties and, 119

Cambodia, 33, 34

Capability of cruise missile, 73-76

CAT (Conventional Arms Talks), 130, 131, 134, 136, 140, 144

CCD (Conference on the Committee for Disarmament) 140

CENTO (Central Treaty Organization), 22

CEP (Circular error probable), 70, 74, 195-203; missile accuracy and, 201-202

CG (Consolidated Guidance), 183

Change in strategic value. See CSV

Chemical warfare. See CW

Chile, 134

China, 4, 31, 33, 34, 46, 53, 55, 130, 185

Circular error probable. See CEP

Cold War: American world expansion and, 26; bipolar threat system of, 33-34; economic effects of, 26-27; multipolar structure and, 33-34
Communication, Command and Control, and Intelligence. See C^3/I
Communications, arms control and, 214-215
Communist Party of the Soviet Union. See CPSU
Comprehensive Test Ban. See CTB
Congress, ACIS and, 158-159
Congressional Research Service. See CRS
Consensus: danger to, from external influences, 39-40; divided, effect on security policy, 38-40; effect of global politics on, 40; effects on security policy, 38-40; external influences on American, 39; secrecy and, 40
Consolidated Guidance. See CG
Conventional Arms Talks. See CAT
Counterforce: alternatives to MAD, 109; strategic arms race and, 196-197
CRS (Congressional Research Service), 151, 153
Cruise missile: accuracy of, 73; alliance relationships, 76-78; arms control and, 69-82; capabilities of, 70-72; case of, 69-82; cost effectiveness and, 72-76; European role, 71-72; military balance, effect on, 79
CTB (Comprehensive Test Ban), 130, 134, 136, 142
CTBT (Comprehensive Test Ban Treaty), 137, 142
Cuba, 34, 138
CW (Chemical warfare), 130, 132, 140
Czechoslovakia, 213

Defense: abolition, and offensive system, 105; reasonable, 111-112
Defense budget: flexible funding level of, 186; force structure and, 181-190; GNP and, 186; political realities and, 189; policy structure of, 181-190; problem of size, 188
Defense expenditure, 25-26
Defense System Acquisition Review Council. See DSARC
Democratic states, international security and, 29
Department of Defense. See DOD
Department of Energy. See DOE
Deployment: arms control and cruise missile, 70; cruise missile and, 70; in Europe, 78
Deterrence: adequacy for, 24-26; alternate strategies for, 231; alternatives to MAD, 109; American military means for, 24-26; ASW and, 195-207; Atlantic Alliance and, 26; balance of terror, 108; change, by superpowers, 110; conventional force and, 87; cruise missile deployment and, 78; danger of accident, 109; definition of, 87; escalation of nuclear weapons, 105-112; European freedom of action and, 78; light attacks and, 110-112; MAD as defense, 101-105; missile accuracy and, 198-202; mutual, and security, 11; nuclear: arms control, 211; counterforce, 23-24; forces in Europe, 77; strategic balance and, 211; role of tactical nuclear forces, 77; strategic arms control, 210-211; tactical nuclear force and, 87; theory of necessity, 214; types of arms control and, 221
Disarmament, U.S. approach, 225-237
DOD (Department of Defense), 151, 161, 167-173, 181-191, 218
DOE (Department of Energy), 151, 154, 155, 161, 167
DSARC (Defense System Acquisition Review Council), 172, 173
Dutch Republic, 6, 7, 85

EDIP (European Defense Improvement Program), 86
Egypt, 32, 136, 139, 140

Energy Research and Development Administration. *See* ERDA
ENMOD (Environmental Modification), 130
ERDA (Energy Research and Development Administration), 144-188
Escalation of nuclear weapons: Soviet Union, 106; United States, 105
Ethiopia, 37
European Defense Improvement Program. *See* EDIP
European role, cruise missile and, 71-72
Experimental missile(s). *See* M-X

FBM (Fleet ballistic missile(s)), 190
FBS (Forward-based systems), 242, 248
Federal Republic of Germany. *See* FRG
Finland, 85, 196
"First strike", possibilities of, 195-202
Fleet ballistics missile(s). *See* FBM
Force: military, use and control of, 21-41; structure: linkage problems, 181-190; national security policy and, 184-189
Forward-based systems. *See* FBS
France, 7, 11, 69, 76, 196
FRG (Federal Republic of Germany),[9, 11] 86

Game theory: criticism of, 249-252; paradigm, SALT I and, 239-252
GAO (Government Accounting Office), 15, 152
General and Complete Disarmament. *See* GCD
GLCM (Ground-launched cruise missile(s)), 141
Global political system: bipolar structure, 16; unipolar structure, 4; world powers, 4
Government Accounting Office. *See* GAO
Great Britain, 7, 8, 16, 76
Greece, 26-29
Ground-launched cruise missile(s). *See* GLCM

Gross National Product. *See* GNP

Health, Education and Welfare. *See* HEW

ICBM (Intercontinental ballistic missile(s)), China and, 102
Iceland, 140
India, 34, 136, 137
Indonesia, 140
Information regimes, arms control and, 115-116
Intercontinental ballistic missile(s). *See* ICBM
Intermediate-range ballistic missile(s). *See* IRBM
International relations and states-system model, 14
International security, American interests and, 28-29
International strategic environment, description of, 49-55
Iran, 29, 36, 53, 55, 134
IRBM (Intermediate-range ballistic missile(s)), 78, 165, 198, 219, 232, 233, 236, 242, 247
Israel, 122, 134, 136, 140, 142
Italy, 5, 16, 26

Japan, 29, 38, 117
JCS (Joint Chiefs of Staff), 181, 182, 218
Joint Strategic Planning Document. *See* JSPD
JSAM (Joint Strategic Assessment Memoranda), 183
JSPD (Joint Strategic Planning Document), 181

Kenya, 142
Korea, 29, 117, 122

Laser beams, 111
Liberia, 140
Libya, 133
Limited Test Ban. *See* LTB
LIRR (Long Island R.R.) 201

Index

Long cycle, living with, 21-41
Long cycles: strategic policy and, 3-17; theory: antecedents of, 12-13; circular sequence of events, 3-19; empirical basis, 5-9; propositions of, 4; social science theory, 13
Long-term defense program (NATO). See LTDP
LTB (Limited Test Ban), 130
LTDP (Long Term Defense Program), 86, 87, 98

MAD (Mutual Assured Destruction), 233, 247; ABM treaty and, 105-112; alternatives to, 109; causes of failure, 107-109; defense of, 106-107; deterrence and, 233-234; deterrent defense, 101-105; immorality of, 107; SALT I negotiations, 246-247; Soviet Union and, 101-105
Maneuverable re-entry vehicle(s). See MARV
Marshall Plan, 26, 29
MARV (Maneuverable re-entry vehicle(s), 201
MBFR (Mutual and Balanced Force Reduction), 130, 133, 138, 141, 142
MDFR/MFR (Mutual and Balanced Force Reduction and Mutual Force Reduction), 115
Medium-range ballistic missile(s). See MRBM
Medium-range cruise missile(s). See MRCM
MEL (Military Expenditure Limitation), 130, 132
Military force: absolute military power and 34-36; dilemmas of American and international security with, 41; domestic opinion and, 21; European reenforcement and, 31; guide for use and control, 21-41; impotence of, 34-37; nuclear parity and, 34; strategic value and, 47
Military means, American, adequacy of, 24-28

Military power, world power and, 11
MIRV (Multiple Independently-targetable Re-entry Vehicle(s), 201-205, 212, 218, 220, 236, 241, 242, 245, 247
Missile accuracy: CEP and, 199; deterrence and, 198, 202; problems of, 200-202; Soviet military power and, 206
MLF (Multilateral force), 23
MR/IRBM, 74, 81, 82
MRBM (Medium-range ballistic missile(s)), 77, 248
MRCM (Medium-range cruise missile(s)), 74, 76, 79
MRV (Multiple re-entry vehicle(s)), 241
Multiple Independently-targetable re-entry vehicle(s). See MIRV
Multilateral Nuclear Forces. See MLF
Multiple re-entry vehicle(s). See MRV
Multipolar structure of long cycles theory, 4
Mutual and Balanced Force Reduction. See MBFR
Mutual Assured Destruction. See MAD
M-X (Experimental missile(s)), 142, 218

National power, international security and, 35
National Science Foundation. See NSF
National Security Council. See NSC
NATO (North Atlantic Treaty Organization), 31, 32, 47, 69, 76-82, 85-98, 121, 129, 139, 141, 170, 185, 223, 230-236; doctrine of flexible response, 69; financial status of, 85-86; function of, 85-98; joint c^3/I and, 121; military defense problem of, 89-92; RIM and, 94-98; Soviet-American alignment and, 31; strategy, nuclear weapons and, 87
NATO Guidelines Area. See NGA
Navy cruise missile, Tomahawk. See BGM-109
NEPA (National Environmental Protection Act), 157
NGA (NATO Guidelines Area,) 85

Nonproliferation policy, 145
Nonproliferation treaty. See NPT
North Atlantic Treaty Organization. See NATO
North Korea, 26, 34, 138
Norway, 35, 72, 140
NPT (Nonproliferation Treaty), 137, 138, 139, 141, 142
NSC (National Security Council), 143, 144, 151, 157, 181
Nuclear disarmament, 234-236
Nuclear and nonnuclear roles, cruise missile, 73-76
Nuclear forces: deterrent role and, 77; maintenance of, 196; warheads for cruise missiles and, 74
Nuclear level, counterforce deterrent posture and, 23
Nuclear particle beams, 111
Nuclear weapons: NATO strategy and, 87; strategic arms race, 195-207; suicidal aspect of, 230
NWFZ (Nuclear weapons free zones), 130, 132, 135, 139

Oceanic theories and long-cycle theory, 12-13
OES (Bureau of Oceans, Environmental and Scientific Affairs), 144
Office of Management and Budget. See OMB
Office of Secretary of Defense. See OSD
OMB (Office of Management and Budget), 181
OPEC (Organization of Petroleum Exporting Countries), 37, 47
OSD (Office of Secretary of Defense), 172, 183

Pakistan, 23, 33, 136, 142
Parity, SALT I negotiations and, 246
PD (Presidential Decision), 181, 184
Peoples Republic of China. See PRC
PGM (Precision-Guided Munitions), 233
Planning, Programming and Budgeting System. See PPBS
PM (Politico-Military Affairs), 144

POM (Program Objective Memoranda), 183
POMCUS (Prepositioned Equipment), 91
Population, defense of, 101-112
Portugal, 5, 6
PPBS (Planning, Programming and Budgeting System), 181, 184, 187
PRC (Peoples Republic of China), 144
Precision-Guided Munitions. See PGM
Presidential Decision. See PD
Prisoner's dilemma, 240, 252; arms control negotiations and, 240-241 C^3/I and, 118
Program Objective Memoranda. See POM

Radiological Warfare. See RW
R&D (Research and Development), 92, 165-178; military program, 165-178; United States and, 167-170
RDT&E (Research, Development, Test and Engineering), 167-178; arms control program, 175-178
Rechstreeks Instromerd Mobilosbel. See RIM
Regimes, c^3/I use of, 115
Remotely Piloted Vehicles(s). See RPV
Research and Development. See R&D
RIM (Rechstreeks Instromerd Mobilosbel, 92-97; NATO forces and, 94-98
RPV (Remotely Piloted Vehicle(s), 73
RW (Radiological warfare), 130, 132

"Safeguard" system, 103
SALT I (Strategic Arms Limitations Talks), 78-82, 130, 144, 175, 205-220, 232, 239-252; ABM abolition, 101-105; arms control, 246; arms race and, 246-247; game theory paradigm and, 239-252; mutual defection matrix, 241-249; negotiations communication, 243-244; offensive systems, 105-106; technical competition, 241; verification issue, 244
SAM (Surface-to-air missile(s)), 72

Index

Saudi Arabia, 32, 36, 53, 55
Sea power and world power, 12-13
SEATO (South-East Asia Treaty Organization), 22
Security: consensus effect on, 38-40; international: American economic interests and, 28-29; global strategies and, 36; nation-state alignment and, 35; national power and, 35; political interests and, 28-29; Soviet-American alignment and, 31; policy effectiveness and, 38-40; relations: aspects of, and strategic value, 62; strategic value and, 59-62
SHAPE (Supreme Headquarters, Allied Powers), 98
Short-range ballistic missile(s). *See* SRBM
SIOP (Single Integrated Operations Plan), 200
SIPRI (Stockholm International Peace Research Institute), 199, 200
SLBM (Submarine-launched ballistic missile(s)), 242
SLCM (Submarine-launched cruise missile(s)), 76, 78
South Africa, 133, 136, 138
South-East Asia Treaty Organization. *See* SEATO
South Korea, 24, 34, 134, 136, 139
Soviet Union, 4, 27, 30, 33, 36, 46, 55, 141: ABM system and, 101-105; information regimes and, 124; military potential, 202-207; nuclear arms escalation, 106; nuclear parity, 34
Spain, 6, 11, 134, 140
Special Session on Disarmament. *See* SSOD
SRBM (Short-range ballistic missile(s)), 72
SRCM (Short-range cruise missile(s)), 73, 78, 82
SSBN (Ballistic-missile submarine nuclear), 140
SSOD (Special Session on Disarmament), 129

Stockholm International Peace Research Institute. *See* SIPRI
Strategic Arms Limitations Talks. *See* SALT
Strategic policy: American security, 30; long cycles, 3-17; United States, 3-17
Strategic threat, nature of, 47-55
Strategic threats, 60-62
Strategic value: aspects of security relations, 62; changing, effects of, 55-59; definition of, 45-64; geographical location and, 48-55; key elements of, 47-64; problems of, 45-64; role with military force, 47; threat assessment problems, 45-64
Strategy: American military, 225-237; arms control, 209-223; deterrence of NATO, 86-89; European concept of, 86; NATO flexible response, 86
Submarine-launched ballistic missile(s). *See* SLBM
Submarine-launched cruise missile(s). *See* SLCM
Supreme Allied Commander, Europe. *See* SACEUR
Supreme Headquarters, Allied Powers, Europe. *See* SHAPE
Surface-to-air missile(s). *See* SAM
Sweden, 12, 85
Switzerland, 12

Taiwan, 134, 137, 185
TERCOM (Terrain Contour Matching System), 70, 76
Territory: access in strategic value, 49; definition of, 49; international strategic environment, 49; key element of strategic value, 48-55
Threat assessment and strategic value, 47-55
Truman Doctrine, 22, 28
Turkey, 29

Unipolar structure of long-cycles theory, 4
UN (United Nations), 124, 235

United States: absolute military power and, 34; analysis of strategic policy, 17; approach to disarmament, 225-237; arms control, policy making, 143-144; balance of terror, 108; Cold War and, 23, 25, 29; decline of relative power, 35; deterrence concepts, 78; doctrine of flexible response, 121; global security and, 29; MAD as deterrent defense, 101-105; military R&D program, 167-170; non-proliferation policy, 145; nuclear force escalation, 106; Soviet civil defense program and, 86; strategic models for, 12-13; strategic policy and, 3-17: ambiguity of, 226-228; deterrence in, 230-233; global context of, 226-227; nuclear weapons and, 227; Soviet adversary state, 226; world order responsibility of, 30

Vietnam, 22, 29, 34, 36, 168

Warsaw Treaty Organization. *See* WTO

West Germany, 38

World division, American security policy, 22

World War III, prospects of, 197

Worth: component of strategic value, 56; degree of dependence and, 52; degree of scarcity and, 52; definition of, 49; dimensions of, 50; high strategic value and degree of access 60; international strategic environment and, 49; key element of strategic value, 48

WTO (Warsaw Treaty Organization), 71, 72, 81

Yugoslavia, 134, 137

ZBB (Zero-Based Budget), 181, 184, 187

About the Contributors

Lincoln Palmer Bloomfield is professor of political science at the Massachusetts Institute of Technology. He has served for four years in the U.S. Navy and for twelve in the Department of State. He is the author of several books and monographs in international politics and organization and a frequent contributor to foreign policy journals. At this writing he is on leave to the staff of the National Security Council.

Davis B. Bobrow is professor of government and politics at the University of Maryland. He has served as a consultant to the Office of the Secretary of Defense and the Arms Control and Disarmament Agency. He is the coauthor of *Understanding Foreign Policy Decisions: The Chinese Case*.

Robert Lyle Butterworth is an associate professor of political science at The Pennsylvania State University. His extensive analysis of the arms control impact statement, "Gauging the Effects," is forthcoming from the Center for International Security Studies, University of Pittsburgh. His books include *Moderation from Management*, an analysis of the developmental impacts of conflict management by international organizations, and *Managing Interstate Conflict*, a compendium of data on interstate security disputes since 1945.

Steven L. Canby is president of a defense policy consulting firm in Washington, D.C. He was formerly a Rand Corporation economist and a research associate of London's International Institute for Strategic Studies. Mr. Canby is a graduate of the United States Military Academy and Harvard University.

Joseph I. Coffey is director of the Center for International Security Studies and professor of public and international affairs at the University of Pittsburgh. His previous positions were chief of the Office of National Security Studies, Bendix Systems Division; research analyst at the Institute for Defense Analyses; staff member of the President's Committee on Information Activities Abroad; executive assistant to the special assistant to the president for security operations coordination; and assistant director for programs, Special Studies Project, Rockefeller Brothers Fund.

W. Harriet Critchley is at the Institute of International Relations, University of British Columbia, where she is completing a major study on the Arctic and future Canadian security policy.

Lawrence Korb is professor of management at the U.S. Naval War College and adjunct scholar at the American Enterprise Institute. He has been a consultant to the Office of the Secretary of Defense and the National Security Council.

George Modelski is professor of political science at the University of Washington. He is author of *A Theory of Foreign Policy* (1962) and *Principles of World Politics* (1972) and editor of *SEATO: Six Studies* (1962).

Patrick Morgan is professor of political science at Washington State University. He is the author of *Deterrence: A Conceptual Analysis* (1977), *Theories and Approaches to International Politics* (1975), and coeditor of *Participatory Democracy* (1971).

Louis A. Picard is assistant professor of political science at the University of Nebraska. His research interests include international bargaining and arms transfers, African politics, and development administration.

George H. Quester is a professor of government at Cornell University and has served as director of its Peace Studies Program. He is the author of *The Politics of Nuclear Diplomacy* (1973) and his most recent book is *Offense and Defense in the International System* (1977).

Judith Reppy is an economist with degrees from Mount Holyoke College, Yale University, and Cornell University. In 1973 she joined the Peace Studies Program at Cornell University as a research associate, where she has concentrated on the study of the U.S. program of military research and development.

Jerome Slater is professor of political science at the State University of New York at Buffalo. He is the author of two books and numerous articles on various aspects of American foreign policy and national security policy.

About the Editors

Robert E. Harkavy is an associate professor of political science at The Pennsylvania State University, specializing in national security policy, arms control, and U.S. foreign policy. He earlier served with the Atomic Energy Commission and the Arms Control and Disarmament Agency, and was recently a senior research fellow with the Peace Studies Program at Cornell University. Professor Harkavy is the author of *The Arms Trade and International Systems* (1975) and *Spectre of a Middle Eastern Holocaust: The Strategic and Diplomatic Implications of the Israeli Nuclear Weapons Program* (1978) and coeditor of *Arms Transfers in the Modern World* (1979).

Edward A. Kolodziej is professor of political science and former head of the Department of Political Science at the University of Illinois. He is the author of the *Uncommon Defense and Congress: 1945-1963* (1966) and *French International Policy under De Gaulle and Pompidou: The Politics of Grandeur* (1974). Professor Kolodziej is a specialist in American and European foreign and security policy and policy-making and is a frequent contributor to professional journals in his areas of interest.